THE COMPLETE GUIDE TO EMAIL MARKETING

8 Steps to Success: From Getting Started to Sending Your Emails

by Gini Graham Scott, Ph.D.

**Author of 50+ Business and Self-Help Books
Email Marketing Company Director for
13+Years**

THE COMPLETE GUIDE TO EMAIL MARKETING

TABLE OF CONTENTS

FOREWORD

Email marketing is a powerful tool for promoting and selling any kind of product – from books, classes, and coaching to selling a service or physical product. THE COMPLETE GUIDE TO EMAIL MARKETING features the techniques you need to gain visibility and credibility and build your business for more sales and profits.

It includes eight steps based on combining the eight books in the series, which cover: these key topics:

Book I: Getting Started: Deciding on Your Goals and Products
Book II: Creating Your Products from Books to Blogs
Book III: Creating Your Products from Videos to PowerPoint Training
Book IV: Finding Emails to Build Your Business
Book V: Buying and Validating Email Lists for Large Mailings
Book VI: Using Emails to Increase Local and Online Sales
Book VII: What to Say in Your Emails
Book VIII: Sending Emails

All of these books are available separately, but here they are combined together for the first time.

BOOK I: GETTING STARTED
DECIDING ON YOUR GOALS AND PRODUCTS

12

CHAPTER 1: INTRODUCTION

In the last decade, email and Internet marketing has exploded, as more and more companies have experienced booming sales growth through online marketing. Increasingly, too, individuals are sending and responding to emails on their smart phones.

I'll first cite some stats which show the growing power of email marketing, and then focus on the importance of using this approach, along with the social media, for any individual or company with all types of products or services to increase visibility and sales.

The Growing Power of Email Marketing

Email marketing has become so powerful because of many factors, including the growing number of people online and the development of all kind of online platforms to make email marketing more targeted and personalized. Also, email marketing can be used to link to the social media, video platforms, live streaming events, and more.

Just consider the reports from the Statistical Portal, which obtains statistics and studies from more than 18,000 sources.[1] There are 2.5 billion email users in the world as of 2015, about 233 million of them in the U.S.

---

[1] http://www.statista.com/topics/1446/e-mail-marketing

alone. According to estimates, by 2019, there will be 2.9 billion email users worldwide, 255 million in the U.S. To reach this market, advertisers have spent $2.7 billion in 2016, and are expected to spend over $3 billion in 2019.

The stats also show that 64% of consumers trust the emails which they signed up to receive. Other Statistical Portal research found an average open rate of about 17%, while 20% of 2015 survey respondents said they were influenced by advertising emails to make online purchases. Another study with the email marketing platforms Get Response and MailChimp, found that the average open rate was about 20% for individuals, with the highest rates for those in the financial services industries and consumers. The average click-through rate for those clicking an email link for further information was about 3%.

This response rate is vastly higher for triggered emails, which are personalized and sent to those requesting these emails – about 94% to 98%, with the responses highest in the business publishing, media, consumer services, and financial services.

The growth of email marketing has also been stimulated by the increasing number of mobile users, since people can check their email while on the go and can easily seek out various sources of information.

Then, too, there are an increasing number of platforms to better target and interact with email recipients. For example, triggered emails based on a prospect's behavior can be focused so they are more relevant, timely, and provide more value to the individual recipients. Emails can also be designed to be transactional emails, where a person confirms a download or request, and then is asked to take some kind of action. Each transactional email might occur when an individual is invited to download a PDF ebook after being invited to enter their email to learn more information about a webinar or event, and then is invited to sign up at a discounted rate for responding now. As another example, once a prospect expresses interest in something, this can result in a personal follow-up email or phone call to discuss their interest in different programs. Some marketers even set up multiple trigger points, such as when someone hasn't clicked on an email in a month, two, three, six, or 12 months, after which the marketer sends different offers to re-motivate the prospect.

These email campaigns have become increasingly linked with social media and other points of engagement based on the prospect's expressed interests. For example, an email can invite a person to see an embedded video, visit a website, take a survey, or enter their email in a box to get a free report as a gift, along with gaining access to a series of discounted offers which will not be repeated. Also, certain platforms can be used to filter who gets what emails based on the buyer's behavior, previous purchases, and expressed interests. Many marketers also use tests with alternate email subject lines – 47% of them, according to a MarketingProfs.com report "The State of Email Marketing by Industry." and many marketers try out different layouts and templates to see what is most effective.[2]

Over the next few years, email marketing is likely to become even more sophisticated, according to several dozen marketing experts who described the likely trends in "The Future of Email Marketing 2016 Edition."[3]

Among some of the predictions:

[2] http://www.marketingprofs.com/charts/2016/29374/the-state-of-email-marketing-by-industry
[3] http://www.emailmonday.com/the-future-of-email-marketing

- Increased or "hyper-personalization" will occur, whereby third party services will help with increased deliverability, testing, live content, analytics, and better information on customers and the effects of different emails on them.

- More triggers will be developed to further target emails to customers.

- Marketing automation will be used in designing, sending out and targeting emails.

- Email marketing will continue to be one of the channels with the highest return on investment.

- More automation will be used to send out targeted campaigns, instead of doing email broadcasts.

- Improvements will occur in the look and feel of emails, since anyone can now create very professional email campaigns with drag-and-drop technology, based on using already created templates, photos, graphics, and logos, to easily insert content to attract consumers.

- Animations will be increasingly used to liven up videos and interactive capabilities, so the consumer can find emails more entertaining and actively engage with the message.

- More and more people will use their smart phones and other mobile devices to receive and open their emails.

- Email will become more personalized and interactive, whereby a person responding to an email can reach a real live person for a more individualized response.

- Email communication will be increasingly connected with the Internet of Things.

- There will be an increase in the number and sophistication of triggered emails, which will draw on the use of external data sources to become even more targeted and helpful for recipients.

- A growing number of emails will incorporate designs and color, such as emojis, colorful animations, and video demonstrations.

- More emails will use countdown clocks with changing prices for offers.

- Emails will increasingly feature hashtags, social share buttons and links to foster the connection between email marketing and social media content.

- There will be a growing link between the email experience and the marketer's website or app.

- These emails will become increasingly intelligent by not only incorporating information about the consumer or business recipient to personalize the email, but these emails will take into consideration the environment, trends in the news, and the interests of a targeted community. For instance, when it starts raining, a "smart" email could send out an announcement about umbrellas or a book about the weather.

- Better tracking and measuring devices will be used to better assess how well an email campaign is working, as well as assessing the effectiveness of different elements of the campaign.

- An increasing number of email messages will be sent out.

All of this automation and research on what works isn't enough though. There is a continued need for email messages to be clear and compelling to get people to open and read them and click through for further information or interactive opportunities. Then, too, marketers using emails have to make their messages full of useful content or persuasive orders to get through the increasing volume of emails from other marketers.

Another challenge is that a growing number of email authentication and other security measures can counter the efforts to make the email better targeted and automated. So email marketers have to be more careful in what they send and how they send it, so it isn't blocked by spam filters.

These trends may seem daunting to the individual or small company seeking to do email marketing. Yet, more and more, platforms can automate many of these features, including targeting and personalizing the campaign, so it is possible to do very sophisticated campaigns on a limited budget with plug and play technology.

Thus, email marketing can be very effective, especially with these new platforms. They make it very possible to conduct a marketing campaign with a limited budget and limited time commitment, given the power of automation and the relatively low cost of the software and services available for anyone setting up an email campaign.

Why this Book

I was inspired to write this book after I began researching different email marketing and social media approaches in order to recommend a program for developing blogs and other marketing materials for a man with two books on criminal justice issues. Now he wanted to expand his reach by developing more blogs to turn into books and then sell those. But while it might be a simple matter to create a series of blogs and turn them into another book for his collection, he still had to get people to know about these books and promote them.

Unfortunately, some of the traditional marketing channels are closed to most authors who are publishing their own books or are published by small publishers, since there are now many millions of self-published books. So pitches to the traditional media are not enough at a time when the media is focused on celebrities, other high-profile individuals, and companies, and advertising budgets for mainstream newspapers, magazines, radio, and TV are astronomical. However, emails, the social media, websites, blogs, and videos have emerged as an alternate source of publicity, and going viral can be a way for a book, product, or service to take off with a limited budget if it captures the public's imagination. Then the traditional media comes calling. But how does that transformation from just another product to a big seller happen? How can someone use email marketing, along with the social media, websites, blogs, and videos, to sell and promote whatever they want to sell?

To answer these questions, I began researching the various approaches and platforms available in order to recommend a platform for this client. In the process, I discovered a whole community of internet and email marketing professionals who have created new methods of marketing, along with new software platforms, systems, and trainings for using these different approaches.

I have also drawn on my experience of over 13 years as the founder and director of an email marketing business, Publishers, Agents and Films, based on connecting writers, filmmakers, and others by email to publishers, agents, the film industry, and linking professionals to other professionals. As of November 1, 2016, I sold the company to new owners, though I am still involved in helping them market and promote the business, and in developing books and training materials, including this one, to help them expand the business.

This company involves creating a database for selected industries (such as publishers, agents, film producers, film distributors, book reviewers and bloggers), and using special software to send out a personalized letter from an individual's own email to contacts with certain characteristics. For example, contacts might be targeted by filters, such as the type of book published or the contact's city or county, to determine if they should get a particular mailing or not. The company's main challenge was collecting information on the correct contact and that person's email and interests in order to update the databases and getting rid of returned emails and changes in contact information to keep the databases continually updated. And from time to time, I bought new directories and lists for different industries. Then, too, the company had had the continuing challenge of finding clients, which I did by creating a company website, making presentations about the service at local business group meetings, and sending out press releases to get media stories. Over the years, the service was very successful, resulting in about 1500 clients.

So this use of emails to link individuals to targeted contacts in a selected industry was one proven method which was very successful and still is. Then, I discovered all of these other methods to get clients and publicity, as I researched other ways to promote my client's books and to recommend which platforms he should use.

This book represents the results of this research, along with some sample programs you can use. It is written primarily for those who have their own books, digital products, physical products, and services, or those who want to create a program to market themselves and build their brand as speakers and workshop leaders. It is also designed for those who want to seek out affiliates to market their materials. Additionally, affiliate marketers may find much of this material helpful in deciding what products and services to promote and how.

This focus on those with their own product or service includes several million independent authors and independent entrepreneurs, as well as the owners and managers in large companies seeking alternate ways to market their products and services. In addition, company owners, managers, professionals, and sales agents interested in using email marketing to contact local buyers will find this information helpful in finding emails, creating lists, and writing effective email letters.

The Many Different Email Marketing Approaches

This book will cover the many different ways of using email marketing and related promotional platforms to promote books, informational products, physical products, or services. These include:

- Developing your own products and services or marketing those of others with various materials, including blogs, PowerPoints, videos, newsletters, books, PDFs, and training programs.
- Using social media platforms to promote your products and services, including on Facebook, Twitter, LinkedIn, and Pinterest;
- Creating a website, landing pages, sales pages, squeeze pages, thank you pages.
- Building lists to capture emails.
- Obtaining endorsements and testimonials.
- Setting up a sales platform to take orders and fulfill orders, such as through Clickbank, ClickFunnels, JVZoo, and WarriorPlus.
- Using emailing platforms, especially for newsletters, including Constant Contact and MailChimp.
- Creating a system for sending out personalized emails using GroupMail Plus and an SMTP mailing service, such as SendGrid, Turbo-SMTP, SMTP.com, AuthSMTP, and SMTP2Go.
- Advertising on major ad platforms, including Facebook, Google, YouTube, and Udemy, targeting those ads to your market.
- Posting your announcements on multiple platforms through automated scheduling, such as by using Buffer, Pindrill, and IFTTT.
- Joining an Internet and email marketing community to get insights on marketing and find joint venture partners to market your products and services, such as through ClickBank, and the Warrior Forum.
- Buying and creating targeted lists through list brokers, such as Emarketing Solutions and Emaillist.
- Cleaning up your purchased and old lists through email clean-up services, such as Mailbox Validator and DataValidator.
- Building traffic to your website or blog.
- Using services to build your list or build traffic to your website, such as Fiverr.
- Creating workshops, seminars, teleseminars, and webinars, such as through Meetup and local organizations, based on your book, product, or service.

- Obtaining traditional PR through press releases and press services, such as PRWire, BusinessWire, PRWeb, PRBuzz, and ExpertClick.

- Working with a publicist to develop a PR or social media campaign.

- Using a query service, such as Publishers, Agents and Films, to send out queries for you to selected industries and targets, such as to publishers, agents, the film industry, professionals, and the media.

- Deciding on the best strategies for you and developing your plan of action.

- Learning about and selecting the various software and cloud-based programs for creating content, sales material, order processing, and other materials that help to automate building lists and traffic in order to increase your earnings.

- Working with a consultant to help you decide what to do.

This series of books will help you learn about the different approaches you might use, so you can decide on the best approach for you, whether you want to do it yourself or work with a marketing specialist to help you create and implement an action plan.

CHAPTER 2: GETTING STARTED

Setting Your Goals

As you embark on using email marketing for your products (which includes any books, services, and affiliate products, since I will be using this term to encompass all of them), it is important to set goals for yourself and then set up and implement some action steps to achieve them.

I have been to many programs and read many books that use the term "goals" interchangeably with "mission" and "vision," though usually these latter terms are more general in characterizing your larger purpose in life or your overall view of how your see yourself or your company. For example, your mission might be helping others overcome health obstacles to achieve success, while your vision is seeing yourself as a person dedicated to contributing to others through your commitment to healing for success.

By contrast, your goals are the more specific objectives you want to achieve, along with the time frame and steps you need to achieve these goals. Those goals are specific and strategic, and they should be realistic so you are likely to achieve them by following the steps you have laid out in the time you plan to accomplish them.

You can set goals in different areas of your life. You might have life goals for achieving more happiness through closer relationships with family members and friends. You might have business goals to increase sales by seeking out more referrals online through email marketing and offline through increased participation in business networking and referral groups.

I have also been to programs that advise participants to set desired and realistic money goals for the next year, or the next few months. The workshop is designed to help participants decide what to do to achieve those goals. After determining an income goal, participants lay out their proposed activities with a timeline for what they expect to accomplish when, along with their financial returns at each stage on the timeline.

For the purposes of setting up an email market success program, I recommend establishing your goals in terms of what you want to create, sell, and distribute. This book is designed to help you set up and implement your goals. An accompanying goal might be to achieve a certain level of income through this method. But put creating, selling, and distributing content as your first priority, which will be both profitable and satisfying. You want to commit yourself to things which inspire and motivate you, because you truly like or feel a passion for them, and so want to share and sell them to others. As they say, "Do what you love and the money will follow." That is true as long as you choose something realistic, where there is a market or a market can be developed.

In other words, you want to do both – set goals which really inspire you, goals for which you feel a passion, as well as goals which are realistically achievable because they are based on what a market out there really wants – or can be educated to recognize the value in that product.

Deciding On Your Current Goals

If you haven't already done this, choose a niche or specialty, along with an identity or brand. You may have multiple interests, but unless they fit together under one rubric, create a separate identity or brand for each one. Then, separate your goals for each identity or brand. If you are just getting started with email marketing, it's best to choose a single identity, and establish this, before you try to develop goals and implement them for a separate brand. This way you gain success in one arena and then replicate it in others, rather than spreading yourself too thin in the beginning.

If you already have a particular focus or identity, great, choose that and develop your goals and the steps to implement them for that arena, though be open to other possibilities if your initial choice is a hard sell with a limited audience.

If you don't already have a particular focus or identity, select among your interests to find what you want to focus on initially. Whatever you select, develop products which can include books, articles, blogs, videos, physical products, and services in that area to sell, to help you promote and sell other items, or both.

How to Choose Your Identity or Focus and Your Goals

If you aren't sure of your identity or focus, you can use a number of techniques to help you decide, and you can also meet with life, business, and career coaches to help you with your decision. Skip over this section if you are already clear on what you want to do.

Here are some ways to decide what your focus should be.

1) Take into consideration your main interests and passions. Ideally, choose something that you really like, since this will keep you motivated and interested in developing books and other products in this area. You are also more likely to have more knowledge and expertise in the subject, so you can better establish your credentials as an authority, which will help you promote your product through email marketing, attract media interest, and gain buyers. However, this should also be an area with a good-sized market of likely buyers. Or you might be able to create this market by educating prospects on the value of what you are selling. You also need to create and sell something that is new and different, or if it is similar, it should be something you can offer at a lower price.

SMART Goals
S Specific
M Measurable
A Achievable
R Realistic
T Timely

    If there is no current market or not one that can be developed, select a different niche or brand and focus your efforts on building that.

    For example, suppose you have developed a great interest in creating art objects from found materials you collected on the beach. Besides selling these as one-of-a-kind items, you hope to create books of photos or videos of these art objects and conduct workshops on how to make your own found artworks. However, after you do a few online and in-person pitches, you find that only a small number of buyers want to purchase these art pieces, books, and training programs, and affiliate marketers aren't interested in marketing these artworks either. Under the circumstances, since you find that your passion project can't be marketed successfully, you need to select something else to market.

    2) <u>Consider the major audiences and markets for your book, product, or service</u>. If you are still selecting your area of focus, think about the audience or market you want to reach. Ideally, the niche is one where you already have some interest, knowledge, or both, though you can first choose your market and then develop an interest that could, in time, become a passion. There are certain markets that are especially receptive to email marketing, such as health and fitness, weight loss and diet, making money, self-help, personal development, and relationships, so you have an already receptive audience you can more readily reach. But you can find other niches and look at their relative size with some research, such as putting the names of the markets you are considering in Google Search along with the words "number" or "size", and you will get information on the size of the market in the U.S. and internationally. For example, some other potentially

profitable niches might be safety and security, home improvement, spiritual development, and inspiration and motivation.

Ideally, select a niche or identity that combines what you love with market potential. If in doubt or if you really want to make money, choose the market option and try to become more passionate about that.

Selecting Among Alternatives

What if you come up with a number of alternatives and are still deciding what's right for you? There are two methods to help you choose among different possibilities. One is using a more rational approach, where you create a chart and use rankings; the other is the more intuitive method, where you visualize the different possibilities and see what works best for you. Or try both approaches, so you get double validation if you have made the right choice. If you are still unsure, try the process again with another option.

1) <u>Using Your Reason to Make a Choice</u>. If you like making charts and ranking alternatives, choose this approach. In this approach, you make a chart featuring the different possibilities, list any pros and cons that come to mind, and rate each option from 1 to 5, based on how much you like that choice. Then, pick the option with the highest score. If there's a tie, review those items again and re-rate them to break the tie. If you still can't make a choice, you might pursue both options. Or turn your decision over to chance by putting the highest scoring options on the back of business cards, index cards, or small slips of paper. Then draw one, and voilá, you have your choice.

2) <u>Using Your Intuition to Make a Choice</u>. Here you use your powers of visualization to guide your selection process. To do so, first find a comfortable place where you can be alone and turn down the lights or turn them off. Then, get very relaxed, using any method to get in a meditative state. For example, with your eyes closed, give yourself a countdown from 1…2…3…4…5, and tell yourself that you are gradually feeling more and more relaxed. Or put on some calming music, such as the sound of waves at the ocean, to put you in this state.

Once you feel very relaxed, imagine the different options before you and see yourself applying that choice. Do this for each option, and observe your experience. If necessary, put each option on a card, draw that card, briefly open your eyes, and read that option. Then, back in your meditative state, visualize yourself applying that option, and do that for each choice.

After you have experienced each possibility, ask yourself: "Which choice do I want to make now?" and see an image or phrase for that option come to mind. Then, that is the focus or brand identity you will pursue.

Deciding on Your Products

Once you have chosen your brand identity and niche, the next step is choosing the different products you are going to sell or use in promoting the products you sell. A good way to start is with a primary product or line of related products, whether these are books, digital products, physical products, services, or programs. Later you can consider the supporting products you might add to build your visibility, authority, and sales.

First, list the products you want to sell, which might include books, training videos, workshops and seminars, webinars, and physical products.

Next, list two products to use for promotional purposes, such as articles, blogs, PowerPoints, videos, press releases, announcements, posts, and other materials.

You can use the charts on the following page to enter this information. You can always add to these charts when you have additional products for sales or promotion. You will probably get more ideas for different types of products as you read the books in this series.

Later, you can use another chart for any new brands or focus for your marketing arsenal.

PRODUCTS TO SELL OR USE IN PROMOTIONS			
Products to Sell	**Stage of Development (Avail or TBA)**	**Cost to Develop or Promote**	**Sales Price (On or After Launch)**

PRODUCTS TO USE IN PROMOTIONS			
Products for Promotions	Stage of Development (Avail or TBA)	Cost to Develop or Promote	Special Offers or Discounts

Developing Your Products for Sales and Promotion

Once you decide on the types of products to sell, which might include products you have already developed, the next step is developing those products so they are ready to sell or be used for promotional purposes. The charts can help you keep track of where you are in the development process. Once something is completed and is ready for sale or for a promotion, indicate that it is available (A) so you can now sell it through various platforms and use various promotional tools to promote it.

Following are some general guidelines for developing different products and services, to be covered in more depth in future books.

Books: These can be sold in various formats, including regular-sized published books of 150-350 pages; short books (35-100 pages); mini-books (25-35 pages); and PDF books of any size, but typically 20-50 pages.

Blogs/Articles: Blogs are posts on websites; articles can be posted, but are typically published in newspapers, magazines, and e-zines, as well as on websites. They typically range from 400-1000 words, and are used to promote books and other products for sale, though they can be combined into books. The copy can also be converted into the text for PowerPoints and videos.

PowerPoints: These can be used for training programs, in which the subject covered is expanded into individual videos or a series of videos from 5 minutes to an hour. Or these can be introductory promotions of to 10 minutes to introduce viewers to the product, so they will want to buy it.

Videos: Like PowerPoints, these can be used for training programs, where the subject covered is expanded into individual videos or a series of videos. Or these can be introductory promotions to introduce viewers to the product, so they will want to buy it.

Press Releases: These can be developed to promote the introduction of a particular product, feature a news story related to the product or company, or highlight ongoing developments and offers. They can be featured on various platforms and provide links to the company website or to product opportunities.

Query Letters: These can be used to reach out to individuals on a list of potential buyers, partners, media contacts, and others. They can be written in various ways, and, like press releases, they can include links to the company website or to product opportunities.

Social Media Posts: These can be featured on the major social media platforms, including Facebook, Twitter, LinkedIn, Instagram, and Pinterest. They can also be posted through special software, such as Pindrill and Buffer, so you can write a series of posts and schedule them to be posted over the next few days.

Advertising Copy: This can be developed to post ads and links to your products, trainings, or other informational pitches. You can post these ads on a variety of portals, such as Facebook and Google, or submit them through various platforms, such as on websites targeted to a particular audience, like Warrior Plus, which is a platform directed towards email and Internet marketers.

Photos and Graphics: Besides being used in books, PowerPoints, training programs, and product catalog sheets, photos and graphics are increasingly used in blogs, press releases, query letters, social media posts, and ad copy. Besides taking these images with cameras and smartphones, you can obtain royalty free stock images from a variety of sources, including stock photo houses like Adobe Photos and 123RF. There are also software programs for creating digital products which have their own collection of images, such as Animoto and Maggazzine.

Music: Aside from creating your own music or hiring someone to provide the music, stock houses, such as Pond5, can provide you with low-cost music clips, and many platforms for creating digital products have their own music library, such as Animoto.

Physical Products and Services: While these digital platforms and email marketing techniques are ideal for selling digital products in the form of PDFs, and mp3 audio, and mp4 video files, these techniques can be used for selling any kind of physical product or service. You can also combine selling physical products or services with selling information products. For example, you might combine selling diet supplements with a book about dieting and a video training program on weight control. You can include opportunities for consulting services, too.

Putting It All Together

Once you learn about all of the possibilities for using email marketing for sales, the next step is choosing among these alternatives to decide on the best approach for you. While this book can help familiarize you with the many options and help you choose on your own, you might get further help from an email marketing consultant.

Some of the major considerations in selecting what approach to use include the following:
- What products and services will most appeal to the audience or market for these products or services?
- What major platforms are likely to get the most response from this audience or market?

- What budget do I have for marketing and promotion, and what marketing approaches and platforms are likely to be the most productive for this market given my budget?

- How can I test out which marketing and promotional approaches and platforms are most cost effective?

- How much time do I have to devote to selling, marketing, and promoting my products and services?

- Do I want to use email marketing to obtain leads for local contacts, since I already have the products and marketing materials to present to them through follow-up via email, phone, or one-on-one contacts?

The following chapters and books will describe these different alternatives, as well as suggest different ways of determine what is best for your particular situation. I have divided these different approaches and platforms into a series of short books, which is a recommended way for publishing content today, along with supplementing these books with videos, PowerPoints, and training programs. Eventually, I may combine these together into a single book.

Now get started in thinking about what you can do, and in future books I'll describe the different approaches and programs to help you decide what to do, create a specific action plan, and implement it to your continued success.

BOOK II: CREATING YOUR PRODUCTS
FROM BOOKS TO BLOGS

CHAPTER 1: GETTING SET TO MARKET YOUR PRODUCTS: CREATING YOUR BOOKS

In getting set to market your products – which encompass everything you are selling including books, services, training programs, consulting and affiliate products – you need to have a hub, or a series of hubs, where you direct your customers. One approach is to have one central hub for all your sales, another is to create a series of hubs – sometimes called linking or sales pages - for different products. Or you might link different hubs together for different purposes, such as if you use one hub for branding you, your company, or your line of products, and link from this to other hubs for sales and training.

Commonly, this hub will be your website or a series of websites for different brands, such as one hub for yourself and your company and other hubs for different brands you have created. For example, I have one website that focuses on me and my books – www.ginigrahamscott.com; another website features writing and publishing for clients at Changemakers Publishing and Writing (www.changemakerspublishingandriting.com) another is devoted to film projects at Changemakers Productions (www.changemakersproductions.com);and another features my literary agency at Media Arts Literary (www.mediartsliterary.com). I have other websites for other projects and services, such as one for a company I used to own and now help with marketing and promotion: Publishers, Agents, and Films (www.publishersagentsandfilms.com), which links writers to publishers, agents and the film industry. And now I am creating another website for this line of books: Changemakers Publishing and Marketing.

Importantly, each of these websites represents a different type of product or service with its own brand, so it makes sense to separate them. It's like the distinction between having different retail stores with different products with different names and identities – such as Best Buy for electronics and computer products.

While the website has traditionally been the online hub, today other possibilities include landing and sales pages which are part of a sales funnel, and Facebook accounts, which can be used to set up multiple company pages and groups. And today, marketers us all sorts of sales packages and approaches to get buyers to not just buy one product, but to get other products which will make the first one even more powerful and useful so usually once you buy one thing, you will get even more offers to buy something more.

Following are the major categories of products you might develop yourself or obtain from an affiliate:
- books in print, digital, or audio formats
- blogs and articles
- videos
- PowerPoint trainings and informational presentations
- physical products and services

While I discuss how to develop different types of products separately, these categories are often combined in the sales process. For example, you might get access to certain articles or training modules in return for purchasing another product or service. You might get a book or software as part of a class with video modules. Such combinations are all part of a product and sales mix and match that has become common in the email and Internet marketing world, as sellers come up with a variety of offers for prospective buyers, and buyers often are sellers of still other products and services.

So now, enter this world, and choose what you want to develop and market. The emphasis will be on marketing your own products, though you may additionally be an affiliate or sales representative who is selling products created or marketed by others.

CHAPTER 2: CREATING AND PUBLISHING BOOKS

Email marketing can be a good way to promote your book or series of books for a number of reasons. Your book or books can also help you promote other products and services because of the extra authority, credibility and visibility a book gives you. Moreover, once you have one book, additional books, written materials, and programs on that topic can help you not only sell that book, but enable you to sell other materials, products, and services. That's because there is an incremental effect as you add additional materials, and thereby gain even more authority, credibility, and visibility, which translates into more promotion and sales.

For instance, a book with real estate tips for getting more money when you sell a house, or techniques for buying a house for less money can help a broker attract clients who want to sell or buy a house. A book with photos of previous projects showing before and after results can help a landscape designer, architect, or contractor show off his or her skills.

While a good website can provide examples of previous work, references, and sales information, not everyone can view a website right away, such as if you are at a presentation in a coffee shop or at a meeting. So a short book can provide this information on the spot, or you can use it as promotional material you can leave out at meetings and events or hand to a prospective client in a one-on-one presentation. Then, too, if you want to do workshops and seminars, a book can provide you with authority and credibility for attracting attendees to your presentation, as well as getting speaking bureaus or meeting planners to schedule your program. Thus, you can make money through back of the room sales, which are often more profitable than selling the book to a publisher and getting a royalty.

In other words, there are multiple reasons for having a book, and it goes without saying that any book you write has to be good. It has to be well-written, informative, and provide good valuable information, presented in an attractive, appealing way.

Writing Your Book

You can create your book in various ways. You can write it yourself, and as needed, use your notes, research, interview transcripts, recordings of workshops and seminars, and other materials to create it. You can incorporate photos, and if it's a digital book, you can use links to videos that play when the reader clicks. You can narrate or work with a narrator, as a work-for-hire or a shared royalty deal, to create an audio book. You can also combine previously written blogs into a book or capture pages from your website to create part or all of your book, using a program such as Designrr.

If you don't have the time or inclination to write your blogs or book, you can work on all or part of your material with a ghostwriter. You can also draw on and adapt material from already written article, blogs, and PLR books, which are already written royalty free materials on thousands of subjects, available from various PLR providers.

You can see details on how to turn your blogs into books or work with a ghostwriter in my books: *Turn Your Blogs into Books* and *How to*

Find and Work with a Good Ghostwriter, available on Amazon, Kindle, and Audible.

If you want to illustrate your book, you can do this inexpensively and quickly in numerous ways. One way is to take photos with a digital camera or your smartphone, transfer them onto your computer as JPEGs, and insert them as pictures into your manuscript. Preferably take and save these photos at a 300 dpi resolution or higher, since that will give you the best print quality. Or hire a professional photographer to take photos and give you the photos – or a selection of the best photos – as JPEGs. As necessary, use different types of software programs to crop and edit the photos, such as Photoshop or Camtasia. You can also create composite images or add text and graphics to your photos using these editing programs.

Another way to illustrate a book is by using a screen capture program, such as SnagIt, Screencaster, or Screencast-o-matic, to create still photos from a PowerPoint or video, such as if you have done a talk on your topic, created a demonstration of the subject of your book, or collected photos or graphic images that seem appropriate for your topic.

Finally, you can use a stock images house, such as AdobeStock or iStock, to buy images for a few dollars. You simply put in key words to find those images that best match your topic. There are some more expensive sources, such as Getty Images, but this can become pricey, especially if you are using multiple stock images. While it is possible to acquire images for free from the Internet, such as by going to Google images, you have to be careful, since many of these images are copyrighted, and you could end up with problems by using such images.

In any event, however you write your book, with illustrations or not, you want to end up with a Word file, or a Pages file on a Mac, which you can save as a Word file. Some writers use Google Docs to create their manuscript and save it on Google Drive, although I like having the file on my computer rather than up in the cloud. But increasingly writers are turning to cloud-based programs.

Once you have completed your manuscript, turn the final product into a PDF. For some e-book use, you may additionally want to create e-pub or e-mobi files that are used by some services to create ebooks for mobile devices. Today, many of these procedures are automated, so you can easily create these files with a few clicks from your original manuscript in Word or Pages.

Finding a Publisher or Agent for Your Book

If you have a traditional publisher for your book, you can still use the email marketing techniques described in this book series, and your publisher will love you for it, since most publishers rely on writers to promote their own books. Publishers typically send up to a few dozen print copies to book reviewers and trade publications, and hope for the best. But beyond that publishers expect you to do most of the legwork. Unless you are already famous or well-known on the speaker circuit, publishers don't pay much upfront – perhaps $1000-5000 for most books these days. They invest little in PR or they ask you to contribute to the PR budget, such as by paying 40% to the full cost of ads about your book in trade publications or publications for book lovers.

Traditional publishers can also be difficult because many, especially the larger ones, won't be interested in publishing your book in any of the fields that are very competitive – notably the self-help, popular business, health, and motivation/inspiration categories – since there are too many books on these subjects, so they are generally only looking for high-profile authors. Another problem with traditional publishers is that it will usually take a year to 18 months before most books come out, and even a little longer if you are working through an agent, since it can take a couple of months before an agent offers to represent you and another few weeks while the agent gets ready to start pitching your book.

By contrast, once you have your manuscript completed, your book can be published in a matter of days, even hours, and go on sale within a day or two for a print or ebook and in a week or two for an audiobook. Even better, as long as you are able to successfully distribute and promote your book, you will make much more, since you will keep most of the proceeds from the sale. The amount depends on the format of your book (print, ebook, or audiobook), which platform you use (such as CreateSpace, Kindle, or ACX), and if you are selling a PDF directly through a platform (such as ClickBank, JVZoo, or Warrior Plus) or are selling it through an affiliate, who typically gets about 50-80% of the income, while the cost of the PDF is minimal. I'll discuss these different platforms in a subsequent book on selling your products. Here the focus is on creating or obtaining the products to sell.

Include a copyright page with the title, copyright date, and name of the copyright holder, which could be an individual author or authors or the name of a company, along with some language about your reserving all rights, unless you provide written permission to use your material. For example, a copyright notice might be something like this.

TITLE OF YOUR BOOK
Copyright © 20__ by Author's or Authors' Name(s)

All rights reserved. No part of this book may be used or reproduced by any means, graphic, electronic, or mechanical, including photocopying, recording, taping or by any information storage retrieval system without the written permission of the author except in the case of brief quotations embodied in critical articles and reviews.

Include your contact information on the title page or at the end of the book. Optionally include a page or two with information on the author or authors in the beginning or end of the book. For the contact information, include the company name, address, email, website, and ideally a phone number, to make it easy for buyers to contact you for more information.

Producing Your Book

Once you have a completed Word document, you can use that to sell your book through a number of platforms, such as on CreateSpace, Kindle, and Draft2Digital. These have the software needed to convert a Word document into the e-pub or e-mobi formats needed for their platform. However, for other platforms, as well as for direct sales from your website, you need a PDF, since that's what you will provide to the customer, either by a direct download or a link to a location where the customer can access and download the PDF.

<ins>Formatting Your Book for Publication</ins>

If you are selling your book as a PDF, which the customer obtains through a direct download or link, you don't need to format the Word document in any special way. It can be in the standard 8 ½ x 11 letter size with standard 1" or 1.25" margins, or perhaps slightly smaller .75" margins. You can use any line spacing you choose, though normally the manuscript will be single or double spaced, though sometimes you might set it to 1.5 lines or some other spacing you prefer. You can insert photos or graphics wherever you want, as long as they are no larger than the margins, though you can make them smaller.

Then, you simply save and voilá, you have your ready-to-go PDF. The one feature to add might be creating an attractive cover to promote the book wherever you advertise it, as well as a cover for the document. You can easily create this by inserting a picture, along with some text above, below, or in a text box inside the picture which features the book's title, author's name, and optionally a line or two of additional information, such as your previous publications, the date of publication, a short testimonial or two, and the like. You can also obtain already designed covers where you just change the text through an online service, such as Maggazzine (www.maggazzine.com)

Using a Word document will also work with an e-book platform like Kindle or Draft2Digital, which can format your original document into the format needed for its platform.

However, if you are publishing your book as a paperback with a platform like CreateSpace, take into consideration the size of the book, the font size, and other factors, so your book is ready to go. This formatting process can take an hour or two, depending on the length of your book and the number and size of your photos or graphics. You can do it yourself, or have others do it for you. For example, Changemakers Publishing has a service which includes formatting and publishing your book on

CreateSpace, or you can hire the CreateSpace design team or other self-publishing book companies, such as Lulu and BookBaby, to set up your formatting and publishing, though their pricing is substantially more expensive.

Generally, the most popular book format is 6"x9" with .75 left and right margins for books up to 399 pages, and 1" top and bottom margins are common. It's best to use single spacing with no spaces between paragraphs and adjust any photos, graphics, and tables to fit on a page or put them on the following page. You should normally have a Table of Contents, and update it after you change any formatting, so it has the new page numbers and is formatted to the new size of the manuscript. Preferably put the page numbers on the bottom of the page, since otherwise the number will appear on the outside margin of the odd number pages, which are on the right when you open the book, and the inside margins of even number pages, which are on the left, unless you can adjust the page numbers to always be on the outside margin.

Turning Word Documents into PDFs

Turning your Word document into a PDF is easy. In either Windows or Mac, you can simply save a Word document as a PDF, or in Windows you can click "Print" and then save it as an Adobe PDF document. The advantage of printing rather than saving the entire document as a PDF is that you have the option of saving it as a file that is higher quality than a standard PDF. In this case, click properties and change the default setting in the dialog box from "Standard" to "PDF/X-1a200".

Should you use any footnotes, it is best to turn these into end notes at the end of each chapter or at the end of the book. To put the end notes at the end of each chapter, you have to put each chapter into a separate file, save that as a PDF, and combine the separate PDFs into the complete book, by inserting each PDF one after the other until they are all in a single book.

Using the Designrr Platform to Create Your PDFs

Another way to create PDFs is with a special software program, such as from Designrr, which enables you to import copy from a website into their software. This includes a number of different templates that provide an attractive cover design, which you can modify with your own photos and different text fonts and sizes. This platform is most suited to importing large blocks of text, although it can import other website copy. After posting, you have to adjust some of the spacing and formatting, which can take a few minutes to a few hours, depending on the length of the PDF and the amount of formatting required. Once you create the PDF, you can publish it like you would any other PDF on a platform like CreateSpace.

One advantage of a program like Designrr is that it can create a more professional looking PDF, if you are providing a file or printout directly or if you are uploading the file to a publishing platform. It has a sleek, professional look since each page will have its own attractive border, and you can easily create an attractive PDF cover or interior title page if you later use the PDF on a publishing platform.

To illustrate, here are a few pages from some books I created with Designrr.

How to Write, Publish, and Promote Your Website, Blogs, and Books

Gini Graham Scott

Changemakers Publishing and Writing helps writers, publishers, and others write, publish and promote their books.

We also write, ghostwrite, and edit:

- Articles & blogs
- Website and marketing copy
- PR releases
- Instructional materials
- Research reports
- Original scripts and adaptations from books
- Query letters to publishers, agents, producers, and others

All writing is by Gini Graham Scott, Ph.D., J.D., who has published over 50 books with major publishers, including Random House, Prentice Hall, Simon & Schuster and AMACOM. She has written hundreds of articles and blogs and thousands of query letters.

She has launched her own publishing company – Changemakers Publishing – which offers over 50 titles, primarily in the areas of self-help, popular business, work relationships, popular culture, and social trends. Recent books help writers find publishers, agents, film producers, and distributors.

We help writers publish their own books in print-on-demand and e-book formats or find mainstream publishers, and film producers through our affiliated companies, including Publishers, Agents & Films.

Examples of different types of books by Gini Graham Scott are below. She conducts workshops and seminars on the topics of selected books as well as on how to write, publish, and promote your own book. Samples from different books are available, and her books are available through AMAZON, many bookstores, and Smashwords, Kindle, and other e-book formats.

You can now see video portfolios of the various services we offer at www.changemakerspublishingandwriting.com/videos-of-books.

WRITING AND GHOSTWRITING

Gini Graham Scott can help you with different types of writing, working from your rough draft, notes, transcripts of talks or workshops, or interviews with you by phone or in person.

The types of writing and ghostwriting include:

- Books and proposals
- Articles and columns
- Web and marketing copy
- Film and TV writing
- Other material

You'll see some guidelines for getting started on the website.

How to Make Professional Connections
in Any Industry

How to Connect with Professionals

Here's a new way to easily connect with professionals in key industries

For example, you might contact them if:

* You have a product, service, video, website, or other materials to appeal to them.
* You want to be power partners.
* You want to tell them about a business opportunity where you might work together.

We help you write effective queries, ads, or press releases, as well as articles, blogs, books, marketing materials, and video scripts. We are a division of:
Publishers, Agents and Films,
which has successfully connected writers and others with publishers, agents, and film industry contacts for over 12 years.

How to Make Professional Connections in Any Industry

A Testimonial to How Well It Works

"I used the Professional Connection to send out queries about my book to seek endorsements, press coverage, book readers. My queries went to thousands of contacts including book reviewers and bloggers, attorneys, court and city government employees, seniors, retires, including about 200,000 book readers. I found the service very helpful in developing my letters and sending them out. I also found it helpful the way the service was able to target my query to selected states, and if I wanted to do so, I could have targeted selected cities and counties. I even got one reviewer who wrote a very detailed and thoughtful review about my book on Amazon. I recommend this service highly." **Paul Brakke"**

Author of American Justice?americanjustice@hishook.com

How to Make Professional Connections in Any Industry

How We Can Help

For more information, check out who we are, see tips on approaching professionals for different types of offers and opportunities, and visit our media section, which features press releases and clips about us.

There's also a FAQ section and a list and description of our main affiliates, who can help you make contacts with other industries,

Want help designing a website for your business? Our web designers offer discounted rates for our clients.

SUCCEEDING
IN BUSINESS
IS ALL ABOUT
MAKING
CONNECTIONS

How to Make Professional Connections in Any Industry

As you can see from the above examples, such a PDF creation program can provide a more polished designer look than converting a Word file with text and image inserts. This platform is especially ideal for a promotional booklet, though for most books, starting with a Word file is fine, since you will separately be creating a cover, while the Word document or PDF will be an interior file to go inside that cover.

Publishing Your Book

Once you have your completed manuscript, you are ready to publish your book. Today, self-publishing is easier and less expensive than ever. No wonder nearly a million or more of these books are published each year.

The stats show the growing success of self-publishing over the last few years. According to the Bowker Self-Publishing Report for 2010-2015, over 727,125 indie ISBNs were issued in 2015 for print and digital books, an increase of over 21% from the previous year, and the 2016 numbers are likely to be even greater. The vast number of print books were published on Amazon's CreateSpace, which issued 423,718 ISBN's in 2015, while the largest number of ebooks were published through Smashwords, which issued 97,198 ISBNs in 2015. Kindle is the other big ebook platform, though it doesn't require ISBN registration.

Meanwhile, a growing number of ebooks are published by independent publishers – 45% of them as of January 2016, according to the Author Earnings Report.[4] On Kindle alone, non-traditionally published books make up nearly 60% of all purchases in the U.S. and about 40% of all consumer dollars spent on e-books.[5] A growing number of independently published books have even become Amazon best sellers – about half of Amazon's top 10, top 20, and top 100 best-selling e-books. Slightly over half (51%) of all print books are published by indie publishers, and another 7% from single-author publishers.

Audiobooks have become another major market for self-publishers, primarily through digital downloading or streaming, since audiobooks no longer have to be sold on cassette tapes or CDs. They are the fastest growing segment in publishing, up to $1.77 billion in sales in the United States alone, according to the Audio Publishers Association.[6] Approximately 3.9 million audiobooks were downloaded in 2015 compared to 2.5 ebooks read in various formats.[7] The growth of self-published audiobooks has also zoomed, up to 30,000 in 2016, compared to 20,000 in 2015. A key reason for audiobook's rapid growth is Audible's ACX

---

[4] http://authorearnings.com/report/february-2016-author-earnings-report
[5] http://authorearnings.com/report/september-2015-author-earnings-report
[6] Porter Anderson, "Golden Headsets: Audiobooks' Growth Is Music to Publishers Ears," *Publishing Perspectives*, November 28, 2016.
http://publishingperspectibves.com/category/features
[7] http://goodereader.com/blog/interviews/global-audiobook-trends-and-statistics-for-2016

platform, which brings together independent authors and narrators. Another reason is that people can easily access audiobooks on a smartphone wherever they are.

In other good news for self-publishers, online sales are increasing, and indie authors have a huge advantage online in being able to market their books more quickly and at lower prices than traditional publishers.

Thus, there is a growing opportunity for selling independent books, and email marketing can play a major part in drawing attention to them. Making this kind of publishing even easier is that once your manuscript is ready to go, much of the publishing platforms are free if you do it yourself, although plenty of help is available from book designers, packagers, and editors who can consult with you or publish your book for you. Still, you have to take further steps through marketing and promotion to generate interest in your book and sales, which is where email marketing comes in. Using one of the email platforms or services, you can quickly send information through personalized bulk emails about your book to bookstores, book reviewers, bloggers, the traditional and social media, and individuals in your field and others who might be interested in your book. A subsequent book will deal with how to do this promotion.

Following are guidelines for how to publish your book in print, e-book, and audiobook formats so you can do it yourself or know what's involved in seeking outside help. While you can publish each type of books separately, an easy and seamless way to do so is by publishing a print-on-demand book first; then use that cover and interior file for your e-book. Finally, produce your audiobook with the help of a narrator or make the recording yourself, if you can follow the guidelines for audio production.

CHAPTER 3: CREATING AND PUBLISHING POD BOOKS

There are dozens of printers and print-on-demand publishers that are turning manuscripts into books. Among some of the best known ones are Lulu, BookBaby, Outskirt Press, Trafford Publishing, iUniverse, AuthorHouse, and Xlibris. A number of publishers, such as Wiley and Hay House, have set up self-publishing arms, which are separate from the company's royalty published books. Additionally, book packaging companies such as the Jenkins Group, and local book designers and publishers help with self-publishing, too. Many of these options can be fairly expensive, starting at around $1500 for designing and producing your book, plus an additional charge for more than 5 or 10 book copies. You can readily find these publishing companies online for more details and comparison shopping.

Using the CreateSpace Platform

My favorite publishing platform is CreateSpace, which is part of Amazon. The platform itself is free, and it offers about 30 cover templates which you can use to design your front and back cover, although you can design your own cover or hire a graphics designer, as long as you follow the company's specs. Once you set up your account and choose your ISBN – provided by CreateSpace, under your name with a CreateSpace ISBN, or you bring your own ISBN, you enter details about your book. These include the title and any subtitle, author's name, book size, background color, text, paper stock, and a publisher logo if you have one. Additionally you add a book description, back cover copy, and include an optional author's photo and bio. After you upload your interior file, which can be in a Word document or a PDF file, you are done with the basics.

Then, you have to set the pricing for the U.S. and other countries, which has to be at least a minimum amount, based on the number of pages, whether in color or black and white. Additionally, you have to set up the distribution, which initially includes the CreateSpace bookstore, Amazon, and Amazon affiliates worldwide. You can set up expanded distribution through bookstores, libraries, and academic institutions.

You can easily make changes in almost everything except the ISBN number for a title. Even after the book is published, you can withdraw it to make further changes, such as changing the title if potential customers don't like it. You can submit a different cover photo or back cover. if you come up with a better design or want to make back-cover copy changes to better describe the book or have changes in your work or life.

A big advantage of the CreateSpace platform is that it is free. Also much of the process of submitting your interior file or submitting all your files for review is automated, so it can take just a minute to submit the manuscript and less than a day for the staff to review and approve it. If it isn't approved, the staff will explain what's wrong and suggest guidelines for you to review to fix the problem.

How to Publish Your Book on CreateSpace

Although CreateSpace provides detailed guidelines for what to do, these sometimes can be confusing, so you might want a professional's help to navigate this, which is something my company, Changemakers Publishing, does. Contact us at www.changemakerspublishing.com for details.

To illustrate how to publish your book, I have included screen shots of the basic steps involved in publishing it. To begin, set up an account, which includes providing your name, email, password, bank, credit card, and tax information. Then, open up your Member Dashboard, where you click "Add New Title" for each book you want to publish. Initially, no titles are listed, though once you start publishing books, they will be listed under their title name, status, title number, and a link to click to place your orders.

Since I'm using my account to illustrate, the dashboard includes other titles, along with the royalty balance from the US, UK, and countries in Europe.

createspace

Books | Music | Film | Free Publishing Resources | Member Spotlight | My Account

Community Help Cart

an Amazon company

Hi, Gini Graham! [Log out]   Site ▾ Search Site

My Account
Member Dashboard
Add New Title

Get Feedback
Manage Previews
Community

My Account
Message Center
View Reports
View Purchases
Edit Account Settings

Contact Support

NEW! Matte finish is available for book covers. Select your Title below and then under Distribute, click Cover Finish.

NEW! Reach readers for free with Expanded Distribution options. Select your title below and click Channels on the Project Homepage.

Member Dashboard
Gini Graham Scott, Member ID 538383

Message Center   ⚠ 173 alerts ✉ 310 messages

Royalty Balance Details   Show: Total December

$123.46   £6.06   €16.18
USD   GBP   EUR

My Projects   [Add New Title]

Sort By: Recently Updated ▾
☑ Show subtitles and volume numbers

Title Name	Status	Des Unda		ID
The Complete Guide to Using Book 1: Getting Started...	Incomplete			6035222
The Massage Wash Experience	Available		Order Copies	6753677
The Massage Wash Experience In Full Color	Available		Order Copies	6753305
Turn Your Video or PowerPoint...	Available		Order Copies	6752477
Turn Your Video or PowerPoint... With Black and White Photos	Available		Order Copies	6759207
How to Write, Publish...	Available		Order Copies	6745174
How to Write, Publish... Pocket Edition	Available		Order Copies	6749145
The Price of Justice in America Commentaries on the...	Available		Order Copies	6746631
20 Rhymes for Your Success Tips on How to Be the Best	Available		Order Copies	6736452
How to Find Publishers, Agents... And How to Publish and...	Available		Order Copies	6731097
All other titles			17	

Once you have your account set up and click "Add and New Project," you will be asked to put in basic information about it, including its name and type of project. I'll use the name of the book which will include this chapter: "The Complete Guide to Using Email Marketing to Promote Your Book or Business." Since this will be a paperback, I'll check that. You have to put in your initial title to get started, but you can change it later if you come up with a better name.

createspace

Books | Music | Film | Free Publishing Resources | Member Spotlight | My Account

Community Help Cart

an Amazon company

Hi, Gini Graham! [Log out]   Site ▾ Search Site

Start Your New Project

Refine Your Work
Ask the Community
Create a Preview
Get Instant Resources
Book Editorial Services
Book Illustration Services
CreateSpace PDF Submission
Spot Printing

Required

① Tell us the name of your project

The Complete Guide to Using Email Marketing to Promote Your Book or Bu

You can change your title at any time before you submit your project for review.

② Choose which type of project you want to start

☑ Paperback   Audio CD   DVD
                                    Video Download

💡 Learn More About the Process
→ Setup Instructions can give you an overview of the setup process.

③ Choose a setup process

| Guided | A step-by-step process with help along the way. | [Get Started] |
| Expert | A streamlined single-page experience for those familiar with the process. | [Get Started] |

About Us   Contact Us   Twitter   Facebook   Press Room

Then, click "Get Started" for the "Guided" option, since you want help in going through the process. This will take you to the "Title Screen," where you can add a subtitle if you have one, along with the name of the author or authors. If more than one author, click "Add Contributors" and provide the additional information. If you want to include an illustrator, list him or her here. You can leave the other screens about whether this is a series, the language, and the publication's date blank. Here's a filled out example of this screen below.

Hit "Save and Continue" to go on, which will take you to the ISBN screen. I recommend getting the free CreateSpace ISBN, which you can use in all sales venues. It will show up as a CreateSpace book, though you can put your own logo on the back cover. It is much more expesive to get another type of ISBN. It costs $99 to get your own ISBN through CreateSpace, and it costs $125 to get one ISBN or $250 for 10 ISBNs from Bowker, the official ISBN provider, to get your ISBN there. If you sell PDFs direct to customers through other sales channels, you don't need an ISBN. So in getting started, it makes sense to take the free option. Once you choose this option, you'll see an explanation about what it means to choose a free ISBN, so you can still choose another option. Otherwise, click "Assign Free ISBN," which is then locked in for this book.

You can always republish this book with another ISBN, if you want to make any updates or variations on the book – such as having one book with color photos and another with black and white photos.

Here's the notice you get after you select a CreateSpace ISBN. It shows the number of the ISBN and the lock symbol indicating that the ISBN number is forever tied to this book.

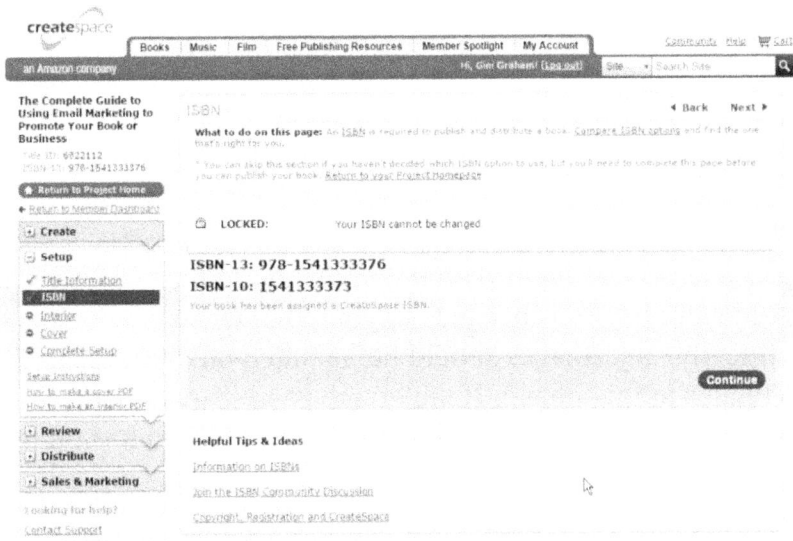

Creating Your Interior

After you hit continue, you next have choices to make about the interior. The default setting is a 6" x 9" book with a black and white interior on white paper, although you can change the size, color, and paper stock. Unless you have a good reason, it's best to stick with the defaults, since these are the most popular book formats. However, if you will be using color photos or illustrations, choose color, and then you might want to choose a larger size to show off the photos. That's what I did in this book series, since I want to use a number of color photos to better illustrate the points I am making. So in this case, the books will all be 7" x 10," and the images will be in full color.

As you can see, I had plenty of options to choose from. I could even create my custom size. But it is better to stick to a more common standard for more distribution options, since distribution is more limited for books in unusual sizes.

Although not required, it is a good idea to begin each chapter on an odd number page, so it shows up on the right side of the book after it is printed. Add extra pages as needed, so your chapter will be on the right hand side. Ideally, any images should be included on the same page as the text which relates to this image. If the image is on its own page, I recommend putting the image on an odd number page, so it is on the right side, which is more readily viewed by the reader.

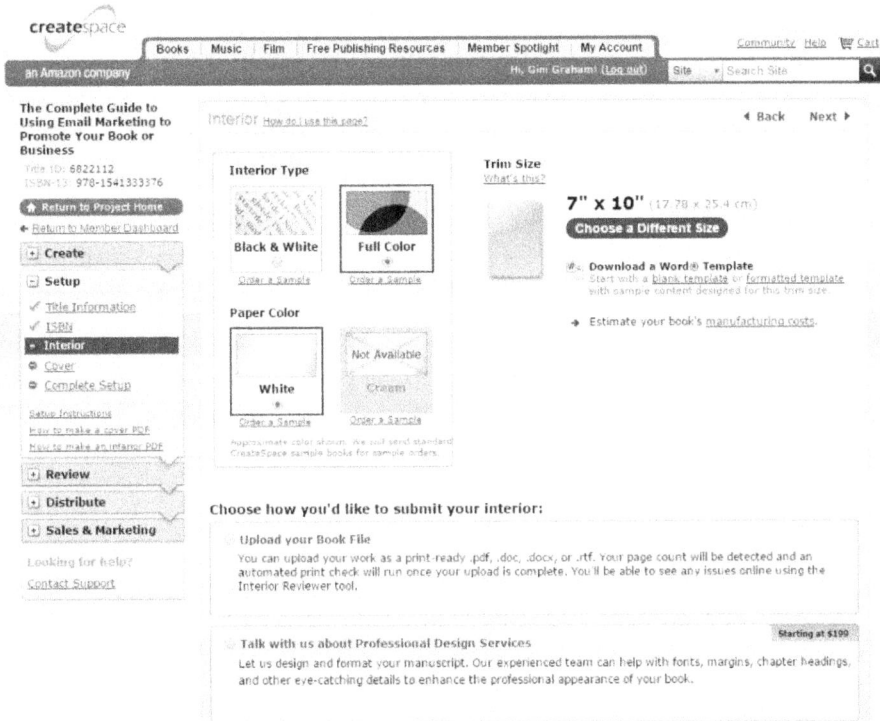

Once the interior file is ready with your completed manuscript in a Word or PDF file, you can upload it. Your manuscript should be formatted in the correct size and margins for it to be accepted. If not, the manuscript review process will identify if there are any errors, so you can correct any serious errors or let them go if less important. For example, a common caution occurs when you have less than 300 dpi images, which is the usual standard for printing, where "dpi" stands for "dots per inch." The more dots or pixels per inch, the higher the resolution, and images may become blurry if the resolution is too low and the image size too large. However, today, many individuals use cameras on cell phones with a lower resolution, and commonly images on the web are at 72 dpi, so the book can be printed with lower resolution images, though you will get a warning that these images are less than the full 300 dpi standard.

Should you forget to change the letter-sized Word or PDF document to a smaller size to match your choice, you will get a warning that the text or images in the manuscript are not the correct size so they overlap the margins. In this case, one fix is to go back to the original Word document and format the manuscript to the correct size there, including reducing the size of any photos as necessary. The other fix, if you have a PDF document, which can't be reduced in size, is to save the PDF as a JPEG, which will turn each page into a JPEG image, which is numbered in sequence. Then, you can insert each JPEG as a picture in the same order in the original document (and you will have the page number on each page to guide you, although you can crop this out of the JPEG and put the page number in the Word document). Once you have a Word document with all of the needed images, you can save or print it as a PDF in this new size and upload that.

To illustrate, I've uploaded a 7" x 10" document with color photos using the "Browse" button, since this is the format I have chosen for this book. After I hit "Save", CreateSpace uploads the file, processes it, and does an automated print check, which takes a few minutes. If you wish, you can start working on your cover, and CreateSpace will notify you when the print check is done.

Once the print check is complete, you will get a notice if CreateSpace found any issues with your file, so you can see what they are and correct them. Or, if you have that option, you can decide to ignore any of these issues and publish despite that interior problem. For example, here I have been notified that the print check found one issue with my file.

When you launch the interior reviewer, you will see what this issue was when you flip through the pages. If you have to make a correction, you can always upload a different file, such as if you make changes in this file or use another file.

For example, after I clicked the sliders to flip from page to page, any problem on that page is indicated by a small red and yellow marker. Then I can decide if this is not a serious issue, so I can ignore it, or if I have to fix the file or upload another. In this case, the issue was the lower dpi images, which I ignored in publishing the book. Though I used the interior file from another book to demonstrate the process, since I'm still writing this book, this example illustrates the review process that all books go through.

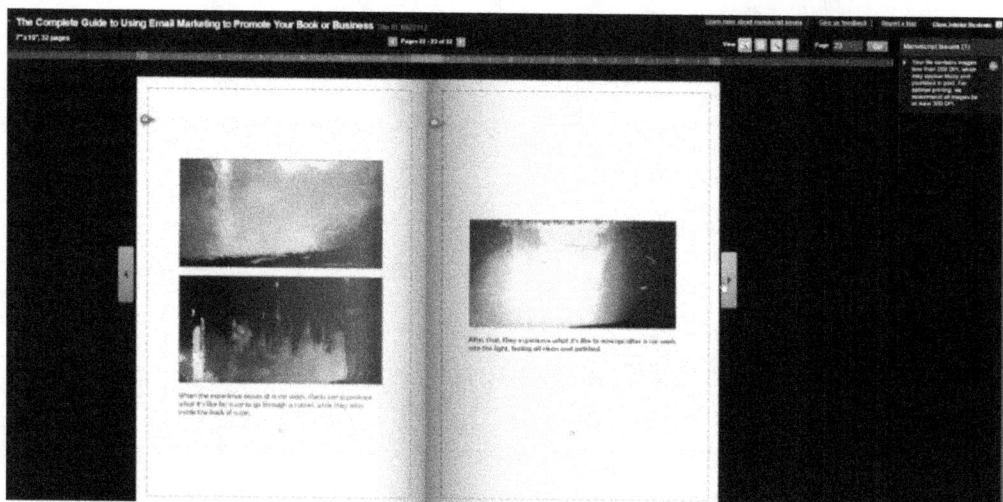

After reviewing for any issues indicated by CreateSpace – or any problem, I noticed, I hit "Save and Continue," which allows me to ignore the issues and continue or upload another file, in which case I would go through the review process again. Once I hit "Save and Continue," I'm back at the "Create a Cover" screen.

Creating Your Cover

In building your cover, you have three options:
- build your cover online, which involves using the template and adding or changing information to create a book cover,
- choose a professional design service starting at $399 to create the cover,
- upload a completed PDF file, usually one done by a graphics designer, which exactly meets the specifications.

Normally, you want to build your cover online, because using a template is the less expensive and easiest way to go, since you just need a cover photo or illustration which costs from nothing if you have the picture, to a few bucks from a stock photo house. The alternatives of having a CreateSpace designer or outside designer will be much more expensive. Figure on about $500-1000 for a designer to create an original cover.

Once you choose "Build Your Cover Online," you choose a design template and can modify it. You have 30 templates to choose from.

The Ash 7 x 10 Spineless   The Aspen 7 x 10 Spineless   The Birch 7 x 10 Spineless

The Bonsai 7 x 10 Spineless   The Boxelder 7 x 10 Spineless   The Cedar 7 x 10 Spineless

◀ Previous Page   Page 1 of 5   Next Page ▶

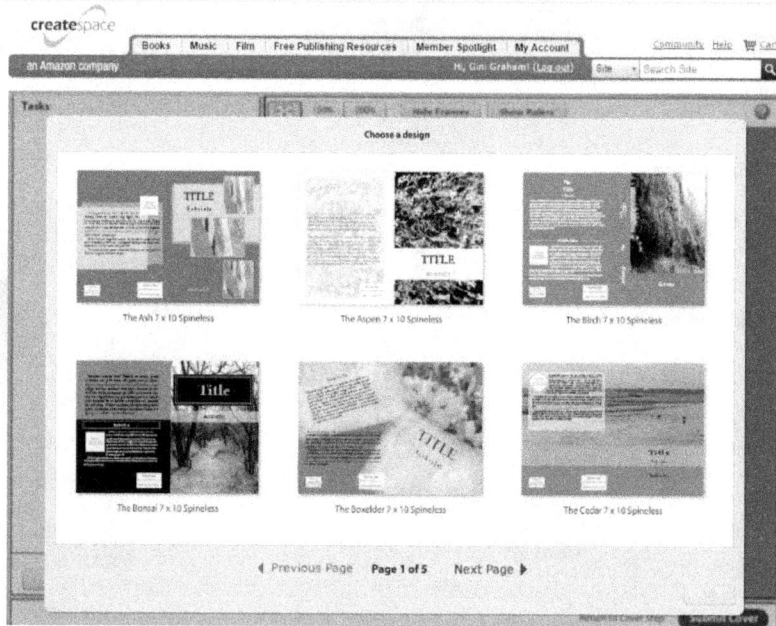

I'll choose the Oak, since I have a line of books using this template. For consistency, it's a good idea to use the same style for a series of books or for all of your books to build your brand.

The Mulberry 7 x 10 Spineless   The Oak 7 x 10 Spineless   The Pagoda 7 x 10 Spineless

The Palm 7 x 10 Spineless   The Pine 7 x 10 Spineless   The Poplar 7 x 10 Spineless

◀ Previous Page   Page 4 of 5   Next Page ▶

Next, you have a number of choices to modify the template. These include changing the color of the background and fonts, adding an author bio and photo, and uploading a publisher logo or not. You also have to write your back cover copy, and sometimes you can modify the overall theme. With most templates, you can also add a front cover photo, which is a very important choice, since it is a major factor in sales. Normally, the photo will feature one strong image, but you can create a composite image, using a program like PhotoShop. Here's what my cover looks like after I made all these adjustments, except for adding the back cover copy.

If you are creating your own cover or working with an outside designer, you will submit your cover – in this case as a PDF – following detailed specs on the cover size and layout, based on the size of the book and the number of pages. As the above design indicates, the back cover is on the left; then there is a spine with its exact width determined by the thickness of the paper and the number of pages; and the front cover is on the right. You will get the precise specs from the publisher and have to follow them exactly, or you have to do your cover again. For instance, I had one client who didn't do this and ended up with the front cover on the left and back cover on the right, which might be fine for a poster, but not for a cover for a published book. So, of course, the review team sent back the cover and she had to redo it.

Then, you set up your distribution channels, which not only include Amazon in the U.S. and Europe and the CreateSpace store, but can also include bookstores, online retailers, libraries, and academic institutions. The CreateSpace platform makes it easy to set up these distribution arrangements with the click of a few buttons. Plus you can add in information about your book, including a description, your author's bio, and keywords.

Finally, determine pricing. You have to at least price the book at the minimum for that book, which is based on the size of the book, number of pages, and whether it is in black and white or color. Plus CreateSpace adds a mark-up from the price of the book to you as the author. Using color will substantially increase the price, but choose color if you have color photos and illustrations, which are an important part of the book. The mark-up for sales will typically be about 2 ½ times the cost to you.

For example, a small book of up to about 75 pages will be about $2.15 when you order it, but the minimum price will be about $5.50. If you publish the book in color, the minimum price will be about $3.50 with a minimum price of $9.00. You can mark-up the price however you want, though think strategically. If you plan to primarily use the book for promotional purposes, keep the price low; but if you want to combine online sales with turning the material in the book into an introductory course at a reduced price, price the book higher, so your price for the course will be lower than the book in order to encourage more sign-ups. Whatever price you set, CreateSpace will convert this into other currencies for sales in other markets.

For example, since I am mainly planning to use these email marketing books for promotional purposes, I have set a low price of $9.95, since the minimum price is $9.15. I have used the common pricing for books which ends in $.95. Once I set the price, the platform fills in the royalty for the different sales platforms, as well as sets the sales price in the currencies for other countries

` The final step after filling in all of the required information is to submit your files for review. Once you submit your files, you will usually hear back within 24 hours, and if your book is accepted, you review the proof. After you approve it, your book will be published immediately on CreateSpace, and it will be available on Amazon within a few hours.

Should there be any problems with your manuscript, such as a mismatch between your title on the cover and your title page, the review will catch this and advise you, so you can make the correction. Then, you have to submit your files again. If you still want to make changes, you can do so now and resubmit your files. In fact, even after your book is published, you can make changes, where you unpublish your original version, resubmit your interior and cover files again, and go through the same approval process.

      Should you decide to self-publish with another print-on-demand publishers, you will go through much the same steps, though the particular platform for entering information will differ.

      Since you have a non-exclusive publishing agreement with CreateSpace, you can always publish this material anywhere else, as well as remove it from the CreateSpace platform at any time.

CHAPTER 4: CREATING AND PUBLISHING EBOOKS

The two main ways of publishing e-books are as PDFs and as e-books available from e-book platforms, such as Kindle and Smashwords, the two most popular platforms.

While PDFs might be used to create the interiors for traditional and self-published books, they also might be considered e-books, in that they are used by e-mail marketers in several ways:

- providing gifts as lead magnets to build lists and sell other books and courses,

- providing additional information for courses and trainings,

- being sold as a digital product available online.

As e-books, they are generally provided to customers as email attachments or are available for downloading from a website or online delivery service, such as Dropbox or Hightail. Or often in online sales, they are delivered automatically by an autoresponder, such as AWeber or GetResponse, or they may be provided to purchasers through an online sales portal, which offers products and services from multiple vendors, such as ClickBank, JVZoo, WarriorPlus, and Zaxaa. Many PDFs are also sold as PLR (private label rights) books, which customers can use for their own purposes by relabeling or freely adapting the material in these books, which are supposed to be copyright free. Sometimes, though, these articles have the authors' names and copyright notices. Since online filters for plagiarism can identify duplicate copies of a copied work, it is best to revise and adapt any material you want to use to make it your own.

Using PDF or Word Documents

However they are created, PDFs can be used for stand-alone sales, and they are ideal for this purpose if you are using them to offer unique targeted copy for a particular market, such as sales materials for the online marketing community or new equipment for furniture makers. Also the PDFs are ideal ways of featuring or summarizing information from a training program or boot camp.

Alternatively, PDFs, along with Word and text documents, can be used to create e-books which can be read on the Kindle and other mobile devices or tablets with an e-reader app. One advantage of using more popular e-book publishing platforms, like Kindle, Smashwords, or Draft2Digital, is they also provide distribution. For example, Smashwords has distribution arrangements with about two dozen online book sellers, including iBooks, Baker & Taylor, Kobo, Scribd, while Draft2Digital has partnerships with Apple, Baker & Taylor, Kobo, and Scribd, while Draft2Digital has partnerships with Apple, Barnes & Noble, Kobo, Inktera, Scribd, Baker & Taylor, and several others. Kindle books automatically get distributed through Amazon, as well as through other international distributors.

One advantage of publishing with any of these platforms is they are non-exclusive, so you can publish the same books on other platforms, though some distributors, such as Apple, will restrict sales to only one of these platforms. You can see these three main platforms below.

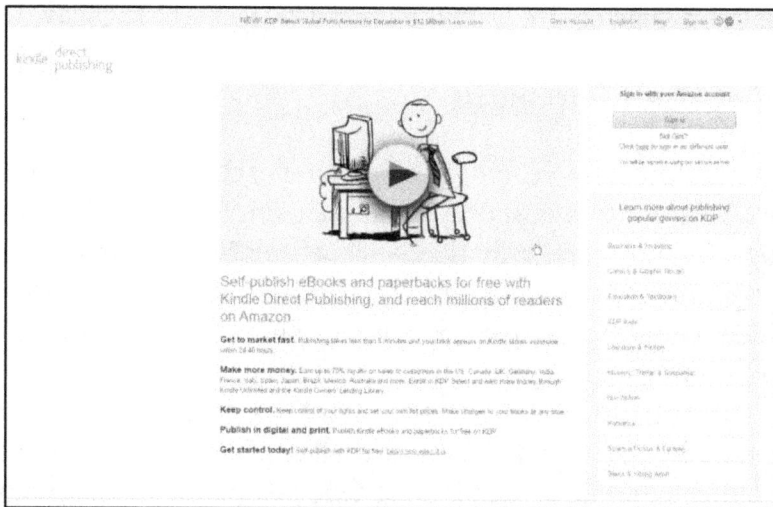

Global eBook Distribution to Major Retailers and Thousands of Public Libraries

Earn 60% of list price from major ebook retailers and up to 80% list at the Smashwords Store

Many of the self-publishing companies distribute through these platforms, such as Lulu and BookBaby, which will set up your print book and format your e-book for sale on Kindle. You can variously pay for design and production work and earn money back through varying royalty deals, while the platforms are free when you set up book publishing with them directly.

However, while you can publish on multiple platforms, different companies have different formatting requirements for submitting your material. For example, Smashwords has very specific requirements for formatting your Word document, so you have to set the size of the fonts, spacing, use of tabs, lines between chapters, and other requirements according to specs, which can take a long time for formatting. For example, it took about 5 or 6 hours for one of my assistants to format a 200 to 300 page manuscript. By contrast, Draft2Digital has software that can do all of the necessary set up from a Word document, and Kindle can convert a Word file or PDF into its own format.

While you can set up a Kindle account directly, if you publish your book on CreateSpace, which I recommend, you can easily convert your published book there to Kindle. In fact, all you have to do after your CreateSpace book is approved is to click the "Publish on Kindle" button and create an account there, with your name, contact information, credit card, and tax information, just as on CreateSpace. After that, you can import your already created CreateSpace cover, and you can have Kindle convert your already CreateSpace PDF or upload another interior file as a Word or PDF document. Usually, I have found that the CreateSpace interior files convert to Kindle's platform just fine, including closing up spaces between chapters and eliminating extra pages. But if you want even more control of the process, create a separate Word document without any blank pages and spaces between chapters.

Publishing Your Book on Kindle

Following is an example of what the Kindle interface looks like after you click the "Publish on Kindle" button. Once you provide the necessary account information and transfer your files from CreateSpace or upload your own files, you have to set up distribution and pricing.

As indicated below, the cover for one of my books *Turn Your Video or PowerPoint into a PDF or Book* is already set up to be transferred to Kindle if I want. I can also download the cover and interior file onto my computer for future use. This process is especially useful if you have previously uploaded a Word file, since now you have a PDF, too.

Thus, you can opt to transfer your CreateSpace file to Kindle or upload a file from your computer. You can also download the cover file created in CreateSpace onto your computer to use yourself for other purposes. If you are uploading a file from your computer, Kindle prefers using a doc, docx, HTML, MOBI, ePub, RTF, Plain Text, and KPF (Kindle Package File), but it will accept PDF files.

Then you indicate if this is a public domain work or not (it isn't), and if you want to select digital rights management (DRM), or not.

76

Choosing DRM means you won't permit the unauthorized transfer of your Kindle book to others. If you are mainly using your book for promotion, you don't want this limitation. But if primarily hope to earn money from your book, you would designate that you want the DRM rights.

Once you submit your files to Kindle (or KDP, short for Kindle Direct Publishing), you sign in with your account if you have already set this up. Or you can sign up for an account now.

After you sign in or sign up, your book will be added to your KDP bookshelf, and you can make changes or add to the information about your book. You can see a preview of how it will look on a smartphone.

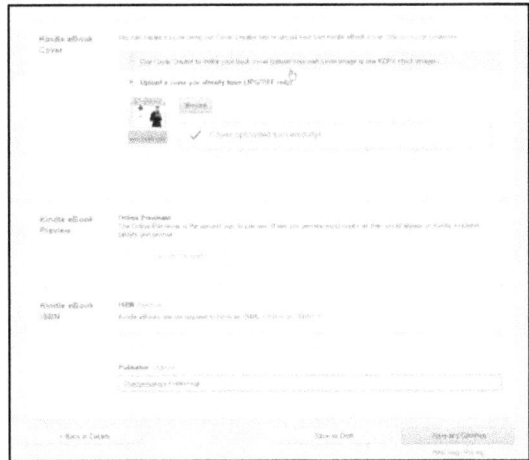

Finally, you set up your distribution and pricing arrangements. If you want, you can enroll in KDP select, which is an exclusive arrangement in which Kindle promotes your book for three months, in return for your sharing the royalty fund with other books in the program. The royalty amount is based on how many pages people read of your book, and during this time, your book is only on Kindle. To end your book in KDP Select, you have to cancel, or the 90 day period automatically renews. Since you want to make your e-book available through other distribution sources, don't enroll in KDP select.

Normally you want to select all territories. You can choose between receiving a royalty of 35-70%. If you are mainly using the book for promotion, a 35% royalty is fine, since you can price it between $0-$200, though generally it's best to make it free or sell it for $.99 or $1.99. To get a higher royalty with a higher profit return, you can get a 70% royalty by pricing your book between $2.99 and $9.99. To help you decide, you can see the amount of royalty you would get at each price point and royalty rate for each sale in the countries where Kindle books are distributed.

Another option is whether you want to include your book in Kindle's Matchbook program, whereby anyone who buys a print book from Amazon can buy the Kindle edition for a reduced price. This ranges from free to $2.99, with the available price points depending on your how you have set your Kindle price. For example, since I set the price at $2.99, my only options were $.99 or free. You additionally can include your book in Kindle's lending program or not, though you have to do this if you choose the 70% royalty. This lending program means that buyers can lend a book they have purchased on Amazon to friends and family members for up to 14 days. If your book is designed for promotional purposes, set it to free.

Then, you are done and ready to publish. Just click the "Publish Your Kindle Book" button and you're ready to go.

Matchbook	**Enroll in Kindle MatchBook** (Optional)
	Give customers who purchase your print book from Amazon the option to purchase your Kindle eBook for $2.99 or less. Learn more about Matchbook
	☑ This title is enrolled in Kindle Matchbook. Uncheck to opt out of the program
	Free ‡ Estimated royalty: $0.00
Book Lending	**Allow Kindle Book Lending** (Optional)
	Allow your customers to lend your Kindle eBook after purchasing it to their friends and family for a duration of 14 days. Learn more about Kindle Book Lending
	☑ Allow lending for this book Why is this locked? ▾
Terms & Conditions	It can take up to 72 hours for your title to be available for purchase on Amazon.
	By clicking Publish below, I confirm that I have all rights necessary to make the content I am uploading available for marketing, distribution and sale in each territory I have indicated above, and that I am in compliance with the KDP Terms and Conditions.

| < Back to Content | Save as Draft | Publish Your Kindle eBook |

You will get an acknowledgment that your book will be available on Kindle within 72 hours. If you have not already published your book on CreateSpace, you can use the same information and manuscript to readily publish it there.

For example, here's the announcement I got to let me know my book would be up for sale on Amazon in the next 3 days.

CHAPTER 5: CREATING AND PRODUCING AUDIO BOOKS

Given the popularity of audiobooks, these are produced by numerous publishers, including large traditional publishers who are producing audio versions of hardcover and paperback books. A growing number of publishers and online retailers are selling these books directly to consumers too. Some of the most well-known ones include Kindle Unlimited, Scribd, Barnes and Noble, iTunes, Audiobooks.com, Apple iBooks, and Audible.

The royalty rates are very favorable to audiobook authors. On most platforms, including Audible, iTunes, and Amazon, authors receive an average of 25% to 35% of the retail price.

Recording Standards

While authors can create their own audiobooks by recording their books or manuscripts, they have to meet minimum standards to produce a recording that is acceptable to audiobook distributors and retailers. You can't just connect a mic to a mixing board, because you have to control for all sorts of things for a professional quality recording. Among other things, you have to have consistency in your audio levels, room tone, noise level, spacing, and pronunciation. Keeping a consistent sound level is especially important, because if there are extreme highs and lows in volume, the listener has to keep adjusting the volume or the receiver, which detracts from the listening experience and may result in poor reviews and reduced sales, as Michael Kozlowski notes in "Global Audiobook Trends and Statistics for 2016."[8]

Some other requirements include these:
- You need to include opening and closing credits which state the title of the book, the name of the author, or authors, and the publisher.
- You need to state that this is "the end" at the conclusion.
- You must have a 1 to 5 minute sample, so the prospective listener can get an idea of the rest of the book in order to make a purchase decision.
- You must record your book in separate chapter by chapter segments for many distributors, such as Audible, Apple, and Amazon. You can't just record a single file that is several hours long.
- You have to include .5 to 1 second of room tone at the beginning and end of the recording.

---

[8]Michael Kozlowski, "Global Audiobook Trends and Statistics for 2016." http://goodreader.com/blog/interviews/global-audiobook-trends-and-statistics-for-2016

- You can't have any extraneous sounds, such as mic pops, mouse clicks, bursts of air, and street noises.

- You have to set the volume level to stay within a certain range.

- The uploaded file size can't be larger than a certain amount -- 170MB, and you have to record at a certain kilohertz (kHz) bandwidth – 44.1.

To achieve these requirements, you need professional quality recording equipment and a well-insulated, quiet area to make the recording. If you can't meet these standards, seek out a professional who is familiar with these requirements and has the necessary recording facilities.

Recording and Marketing Your Audiobook

One way to market your audiobook once you have a completed recording is through the Author's Republic (www.authorsrepublic.com). This distribution service was developed by Audiobooks.com, which provides a way to distribute independently published audiobooks to over a dozen audiobook retailers, including Audiobooks.com, Audible, iTunes, Amazon, Barnes & Noble, Scribd, Downpour, and Tunein. The company also distributes to libraries, such as through Findaway and Overdrive. Since the Author's Republic is an aggregate distributor, you have to already have a completed audiobook.

After you indicate which retailer and distributor partners you want to sell your audiobook, which could be all of them, you have to submit your book for a review. It has to meet the minimum standards. If not, the company will advise you accordingly so you can fix your files or metadata. Once your book passes muster, it can go on sale anywhere from 5 to 60 days after acceptance. After that, you will receive 70% of what your audiobook earns across over 30 channels, including all major distributors.

Should you need help in creating the audiobook, Author's Republic has a half-dozen recommendations for services that will create the book to professional standards, including Deyan Audio (www.deyanaudio.com), Spoke Media (www.spokemedia.com), Pro Audio Voices (www.proaudiovoices.com), VoicesforBooks.com (www.voicesforbooks.ccom), BeeAudio (www.beeaudio.com), e-AudioProductions (www.e-audioproductions.com), and Common Mode, Inc. (www.common-mode.com).

These services have all have worked closely with voice artists who can do your narration, though you can hire a union or non-union voice actor, such as through Voices.com (www.voices.com); Voice123 (www.voice123.com), or VoiceBunny (www.voicebunny.com). To find an actor, you post your job on their marketplace or review their talent pool to find the perfect narrator, based on a variety of options, including age, gender, and years of experience. These services can provide you with a pool of thousands of voice actors to choose from. A good way to choose among them is to provide a few paragraphs to a page of text from your manuscript for each actor to read from, along with some guidelines on what you are looking for in a narrator. Then, you can listen to a sample audition recording to help you decide.

In selecting a narrator, it is important to learn if they will take care of proofing, editing, and mastering the narration. While many narrators include these services, in order to provide you with a final recording that is ready to submit to distributors, some don't. This mastering involves preparing and transferring the recorded audio from the final mix to a data storage device. It is best if the narrator can handle this procedure rather than you having to find an audio engineer and editor. While there are experts in this area, such as SoundBetter (https://soundbetter.com) and e-AudioProductions (http://www.e-audioproductions.com), finding an outside editor and engineer can add another layer of complexity to getting a ready-to-market audiobook.

There are two major arrangements for paying for the narrator.

- Pay-for-Production, where you pay the narrator a set fee per finished hour of the recorded or fully-mastered produced audio. In this case, you own the recording, and can use it for as long and for whatever purpose you want.

- Royalty Share, where you split the revenue with the narrator, so the narrator receives a certain percentage of future sales. Usually this is a 50-50 split, but the narrator's percentage can vary depending on his or her experience and visibility in the industry.

If you are paying the narrator, the cost of a finished audiobook can vary based on your book's length and the narrator's charge per finished hour of audio. Generally, each hour of recorded audio takes double that amount of time in the studio, so 5 recorded hours takes around 10 hours in the studio. Editing and other post-production work can be even longer, depending on the narrator's audio engineering skills.

To figure out the length of a narrated book, use the typical rate of speech of about 9400 words per hour and divide this into the number of words in your book. So if your book has 30,000 words, this will be a little over 3 hours to narrate. Then, factor in the cost per hour of the narrator. If a narrator is a SAG or AFTRA union member, the minimum fee per finished hour is $225; while non-union professions are free to charge whatever they want, which is commonly $100 to $250 per hour. So for a 3 hour narrated book, the cost would be about $300 to $750.

Alternatively, if you can find a narrator who likes your book and would like to narrate it for a royalty split, that can be more cost effective. This royalty split is ideal if you have many books to turn into audiobooks, since you won't know how well the books are doing until they are in distribution and you launch a marketing campaign to boost sales. That's what I've done with my audiobooks – 40 so far with sales of about 525 units in five months. While one book has sold nearly 200 copies, most have sold around 10 to 30 copies at an average price of $4 for the shorter books up to $8 for the longer books. If you do the math, you'll find that it was much more cost effective to share the royalties than to pay a narrator.

For example, the book that sold 200 copies earned about $1600, with $800 to me. But if I hired a narrator for this book of about 90,000 words, I would have paid about $1000 to $2500 for 10 hours of recording. And my costs relative to earnings would have been much more in the case of my other books, which sold 10 to 30 copies. Plus since I had 40 books, my costs would have been astronomical. So definitely, if you can set up a shared royalty deal, do so, unless you are certain you can sell a ton of books and earn over $1000, so you net more than you would with a royalty share arrangement.

Certainly, you can narrate your book yourself, though then you need the appropriate equipment, including a computer or tablet with recording software, a good microphone, and headphones for self-monitoring, as well as a quiet location. Additionally, you need a good voice for the narration, and you have to follow the appropriate procedures for making the recording, editing it, and handling the post-production. Whew!

Using the ACX-Audible Platform to Record and Sell Your Book

If these arrangements to find a narrator or narrate your book yourself sound complicated, that's because they are. The easy solution, which I have done, is using the ACX platform that connects book authors to narrators and distributes the books through Audible, which has been the dominant audiobook self-publishing company for a number of years. ACX is a division of Audible.com, which is an Amazon subsidiary.

This platform provides an easy-to-use format, which enables you to select your printed book on Amazon and offer it, within minutes, to hundreds if not thousands of narrators on a royalty share arrangement – or you can offer to pay the narrator if you prefer.

If a narrator is interested in narrating your book, he or she submits a short audition, and you can choose among those auditioning who will be the best fit. If the narrator accepts your offer, you are on. You send the full manuscript; then the narrator sends you the first 15 minutes. If you approve this, the narrator completes the book. If you approve this final narration, the ACX team reviews the files to make sure they are up to standards. If they are, your audiobook will be up for sale on Audible in about two weeks. Or the ACX team will tell you and the narrator if there are any problems, and what to do to fix them. Once the narrator makes the fix, you submit the files for approval once again. Meanwhile, you have to provide the artwork for the cover, using either original art, or you can adapt the original book cover to fit. After that, Audible seeks to market and sell your book, including on Amazon, and iTunes, as well as on Audible. You can supplement these efforts with your own promotional campaign, along with an email outreach to your mailing list and leads.

How You Can Use ACX

To show how the ACX platform works, here are step-by-step guidelines so you know what to expect and can prepare your materials to use this system.

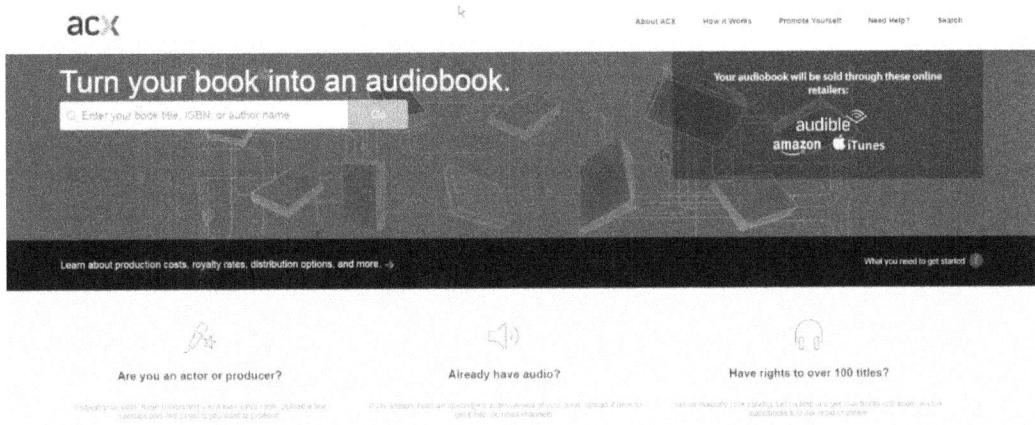

As with any platform, the first step is to set up an account.

Then, you add a title that is already on Amazon, confirm that you have the audio rights for your book so you are the rights holder. Next, you create a profile for your title by describing your book and the type of narrator best suited for it, such as a speaker who is authoritative, inspirational, motivational, warm, or has other characteristics, and is male, female, or either. Then post a 1-2 page excerpt from your book as an audition script for potential narrators.

Next, you offer your book to narrators to produce your book. Those who are interested in being considered will send you auditions, and you listen to them. After that you make your choice. In all but two postings for narrators, I found I got at least one, and sometimes two, three or four interested narrators.

Once you choose the narrator you like most, you make an offer for a royalty share or payment deal based on the narrator/producer completing the first 15 minutes by a certain date, and completing the whole audiobook by a future date. I have only used the royalty share arrangement, and each time my offer has been accepted, with one exception, the narrator/producer has completed the book, though sometimes a little later than originally agreed. In the one case that the narrator didn't come through, I offered up the project again and found another narrator who completed the book.

After you approve the first 15 minutes, the narrator will record he full project. If you want the narrator to make any corrections, you can do so and you can ask for up to two rounds of corrections, though I have only made a few minor corrections, such as asking the narrator to shorten the copyright notice or move the author's bio to the end.

Once the book is done, you submit it to ACX to review. If you have agreed to pay the producer, you pay the producer directly once you approve it, and you now have a non-exclusive arrangement with ACX and Audible, so you can distribute the book through other channels. Alternatively, ACX treats any shared royalty agreement as an exclusive arrangement. Once your book passes the review process, it goes up for sale.

Now you can promote the book in various ways, and ACX offers a variety of suggestions, including using email marketing and the social media. As the book sells, you will earn royalties, payable each month, paid directly into your bank, and you can see how your book is doing on your sales dashboard.

So that's a brief overview of how the recording-sales process works. Now I'll illustrate this with some examples, showing how I posted and worked out arrangements with a narrator for one of my books.

An Example of Using the ACX Platform

As the following illustrates, ACX offers three options when you sign up and want to turn your book into an audiobook to be sold on Audible. One is the royalty share arrangement where you split the 40% royalty with the narrator. Another is where you pay the narrator a flat fee for production and agree to an exclusive option with Audible in return for receiving the full 40% yourself. Finally you have the option of paying for production and having a non-exclusive arrangement with Audible, so you can arrange for distribution with other parties in return for a 25% royalty with Audible.

Three Options For You

Here's a summary comparison of the three basic payment and distribution options currently available for audio production deals on ACX. Note that this is a summary only. See the ACX Book Posting Agreement and Production Standard Terms for actual terms that apply:

	OPTION 1 **Royalty Share** with Exclusive Distribution to Audible	OPTION 2 * **Pay For Production (Flat Fee)** with Exclusive Distribution to Audible	OPTION 3 * **Pay For Production (Flat Fee)** with Non-Exclusive Distribution Rights to Audible
Payment to Producer Choose a Royalty Share deal or a one-time Pay for Production fee.	Royalty payments from Audible are shared equally between Rights Holder and Producer	Rights Holder pays Producer a one-time fee for production	
Distribution Grant Audible exclusive or non-exclusive distribution rights. Either way is powerful— our third party distributors get audiobooks in front of buyers. **The difference is this:** Royalty rates are higher when distribution is left exclusively to ACX.	ACX exclusive distribution— through Audible, Amazon, and iTunes** via ACX, as well as wherever else Audible chooses. Under this model, Audible has the exclusive right to distribute the audiobook. If you choose this option, the audiobook cannot be distributed by any entity except ACX **in any market or format.**	ACX exclusive distribution— through Audible, Amazon, and iTunes** via ACX, as well as wherever else Audible chooses. Under this model, Audible has the exclusive right to distribute the audiobook.If you choose this option, the audiobook cannot be distributed by any entity except ACX **in any market or format.**	Non-exclusive distribution— through Audible, Amazon, and iTunes** via ACX, as well as wherever else Rights Holder chooses. Under this model, Rights Holder can grant distribution rights to parties other than Audible **in any market or any format**.
Royalty Rate	40% of retail sales split equally between Rights Holder and Producer. In other words, each gets 20% of total retail sales.	40% of retail sales paid to Rights Holder.	25% of retail sales paid to Rights Holder.
Bounty Payment Earnings can increase with these extra payments.	ACX pays Rights Holder and Producer $50 every time the audiobook is the first audiobook purchased by an AudibleListener™ member on Audible. The $50 payment is split 50-50 between Rights Holder and Producer, amounting to $25 each. See terms.	ACX pays Rights Holder $50 every time the audiobook is among the first audiobook purchased by an AudibleListener™ member on Audible. See terms.	
Royalty Payment Frequency ACX sends a monthly statement and a check or electronic payment to US users(when there's at least $50 to be paid). Users in the UK receive electronic payments and statements monthly.	Separate payments sent to Rights Holder and to Producer (when there's at least $50 to be paid).	Payments to Rights Holder (when there's at least $50 to be paid).	

To turn your book into an audiobook, click "Add Your Title" and enter the name of your book which has already been published on Amazon in the search bar, and it will turn up. If other books have the same or a very similar title, they will show up, too. Once you find your book, click the "This is My Book" button. If you have multiple versions, such as one book in color, another with black and white photos, or books in different sizes, select one of them, since the narration will be the same.

Since this is an audiobook, the illustrations normally won't matter, unless they are an essential part of the book. In that case, once the final audiobook is approved, you will send the ACX staff a PDF with the illustrations, along with instructions so the reader can follow along. Or the narrator may need to add in some instructions in the text to refer to a particular illustration. Otherwise, figure that the illustrations won't be included in the audiobook.

Where there are multiple versions, pick the book with the best cover. For example, choose the cover that doesn't include any special language about which edition this is, such if a cover indicates this is the pocket edition or has full color or black and white photos.

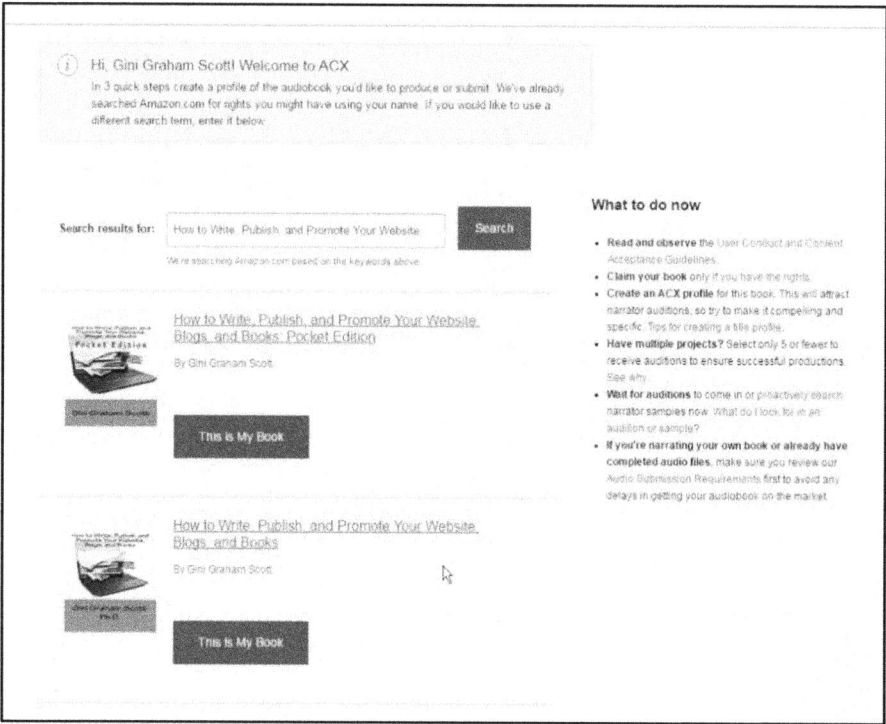

Next, unless you plan to provide the audio files yourself, indicate that you are looking for a narrator and producer. Choose this option, unless you know what you are doing in creating an audio recording or want to work with your own experienced narrator, because the specs for creating an audiobook are really demanding and you can't readily do this without the right equipment and knowledge.

You are claiming How to Write, Publish, and Promote Your Website, Blogs, and Books, by Gini Graham Scott

How can ACX work for you:

Whether you want to find a Producer to help you create your audiobook, or if you already have the audio, ACX is here for you.

Simply choose the path to the right that best fits your needs and get started.

I'm looking for someone to narrate and produce my audiobook.

I already have audio files for this book, and I want to sell it.

I want to find out how to narrate this book and upload files later.

The next step is agreeing to ACX's terms, indicating that you understand this will be a binding agreement with the narrator/producer. You also agree that you have full audio rights and that you have the option to make this an exclusive or nonexclusive deal.

These are our terms. Please read and agree to continue...

Print

Legal Contracts

ACX Book Posting Agreement

Last revised 04/06/2014

Version 2.0

This **ACX Book Posting Agreement** ("Agreement") is a binding agreement between you, or the company or entity you represent, if you are entering into this Agreement on behalf of a company or entity ("you"), and Audible, Inc. ("Audible", "we" or "us"). It sets forth the terms you agree to when you make a book available for production as an audiobook on the audiobook production service and rights marketplace available at www.acx.com ("ACX") (any book you make available on ACX for production as an audiobook, a "Book"). You enter into this Agreement each time you make a Book available on ACX. That means that there is a separate Agreement between you and us for each Book you make available on ACX.

Clicking "Agree & Continue" will mean that:

- You have the audio rights to the book.
- You want to add your book to ACX to get it produced as an audiobook.
- You will be able to meet potential narrators and producers for your book on ACX, and also may be contacted by audiobook publishers who may want to purchase the audio right to your book (and then produce it off of the ACX system).
- You will distribute the completed audiobook, at minimum, through ACX's distribution channel (Amazon, Audible and iTunes).
- You will have the choice to distribute it on an exclusive or non-exclusive basis.
- Any information you put into your book's ACX title profile is accurate.

I have read the above ACX Book Posting Agreement and agree to its terms

Agree & Continue

The next step is to describe your book, indicate copyright details, the book's best category, the narrator's voice, and other characteristics. For example, I indicated below that I am the copyright holder for both the print and audio book, that the print version was copyrighted in 2016, and that this is a non-fiction business book.

Next, I entered some details about the ideal narrator's voice, such as indicating that either gender is fine, that this is in English, that I'd like someone with a general American accent and an adult with an authoritative voice. After that, I can add more details about what I'm looking for in a narrator. Generally, I indicated that I'm looking for someone who can speak as if they are having a conversation with the listener. Finally, I added an audition script. This should be a few pages from the full manuscript, put into its own PDF, Word, or text file, and uploaded using the Browse button. I usually upload the PDF file, which I used to upload the book on Amazon.

Additional comments:

Just speak as if you are having a conversation with the listener.

(1935 characters remaining)

Here's your chance to provide directions or advice to Producers who may audition for this book. It is also a good place to make your book as appealing as possible to ACX Producers. For example, you can include marketing information, selling points, best-seller status, awards, foreign language translations and reviews. Additionally, please include information about the Author's reach and fan-base (i.e. 5,000 followers on Twitter, 8,000 fans on Facebook).

Audition script:

Provide an audition script, so Producers will be able to submit their best performances for your work. You may upload your audition script, or click the link to type it in the box below.

How to Select A Strong Audition Script:

- Your audition script should total no more than 2-3 pages.
- Your Producer will voice all characters and scenes in your book. If your book has multiple lead characters and/or accents, make sure to feature them in your audition script.
- We recommend selecting multiple relevant scenes featuring these characters to make up your audition script.
- Include additional detail on characters/scenes in the in the Audition Script Notes section below.
- Read more about selecting a strong audition script on our blog.

Audition Script Notes:

(2000 characters remaining)

Choose audition script file from your computer:
[Browse]

You can upload Word, PDF or TXT files.

If you have trouble uploading your file, you can input your audition script as text.

[Save & Continue]

Next indicate the number of pages and your payment arrangements, which in this case was about 5000 words and a royalty share, which has to be an exclusive agreement with a 40% royalty, through Amazon, ACX, and iTunes. So far, I have found a royalty share has been a good arrangement, since I've sold 525 copies in 5 months, with almost no promotion by me, though if I began doing this with the techniques described in this book, I'm sure the sales would be much more.

After listing this information about the pages and payment arrangements, I can review the offer and make any changes. If it's fine, I can now post it and request auditions.

How to Write, Publish, and Promote
Your Website, Blogs, and Books
By Gini Graham Scott

Estimated Length: 0.0 hours
Project Budget: Royalty Share
Word Count: 5,000
Language: English
Distribution: Exclusive
Territories: World

1
2
3 Review & Post

ABOUT THIS TITLE   AUDITION   PRODUCE AUDIOBOOK   AUDIOBOOK SALES

HOW TO WRITE, PUBLISH, AND PROMOTE YOUR WEBSITE, BLOGS, AND BOOKS introduces a company that can help you with all types of writing and publishing – from books and scripts to blogs and website copy. The book features these topics. - Writing, ghostwriting, and editing - Guidelines for getting started - Self-publishing your book - Finding publishers and agents -
Show more

Requires a narrator who can perform

		Title information	
Genre	Business	Date posted to ACX	Dec. 31 2016
Fiction/Nonfiction	Nonfiction	Original publication date	2016-11-27
Language	English	Published by	
Gender	Male or Female		CreateSpace Independent Publishing Platform
Character Age	Adult	Amazon sales rank	0
Accent	American-General American	Amazon rating	☆☆☆☆☆ 0.0 (0 ratings)
Vocal Style	Authoritative	View this title on Amazon »	

Comments from the Rights Holder:

Just read it like you are talking to the listener

Post this title to ACX so narrators can audition for your book, or save and continue later.

[Post to ACX]   [Save & Continue Later]

Once you click "Post to ACX," your book is available for auditions, along with any other books you have previously submitted. For instance, here's my book ready to go. The screen indicates any previous sales of other books as of that date, such as 509 sales in my own case.

Welcome, Gini Graham Scott

from Changemakers Publishing | Today is 31 December 2016

Total Units Sold: 509

OPEN FOR AUDITIONS (2)   OFFERS (40)   IN PRODUCTION (1)   RIGHTS NOT POSTED (6)   COMPLETED PROJECTS (35)

Filter & Sort

Before the Modern Russian Revolution: A Memoir About Traveling in the U.S.S.R. in a Time of Transformation
by Gini Scott

POSTED ON 30 December 2016

0 auditions received
Share your progress with your fans

How to Write, Publish, and Promote Your Website, Blogs, and Books
by Gini Graham Scott

POSTED ON 31 December 2016

0 auditions received
Share your progress with your fans

That whole process took about 10 minutes, so it is very quick to post a book and look for a narrator. Then, you wait for any auditions. If prospective narrators like your book, you will get a request, usually within a day or two of posting.   In fact, within a day, I already got one audition, as indicated on the audition page below.

You then hear a short audio clip of a minute or two from each prospect, and you listen and decide who you prefer as a narrator. Once you decide, you make your royalty share offer and provide a date when you expect the first 15 minutes (I usually allow a week) and a date for the finished project (I usually allow 1 or 2 weeks, depending on the length of the book; a little longer if it's a longer book).

For example, here's my offer to one narrator below. After previewing my offer, if all looks okay, the offer goes to the narrator for his acceptance.

Should the prospective narrator need more time, he or she can write asking for an extension, though that has only happened to me twice out of 40 books.

After accepting the offer, the narrator will submit a 15 minute sample for your comments and any requested changes for your approval. If you ask for changes, the narrator will make them. Once you send your approval, the narrator will submit all of the files—one for the introduction with a title, author, and narrator; others for each chapter; an author's bio if you want one; and closing credits.

For example, the submission process looks something like this. After I have sent in my offer and the narrator has accepted it, I have to send the manuscript. Once I do, the narrator sends me the first 15 minutes. After I approve that, I wait for the finish audio, as in the case with my second manuscript *The Empowered Mind*.

Welcome, Gini Graham Scott

from **Changemakers Publishing** | Today is 1 January 2017

Total Units Sold *

As of 01/01/17

512

View Sales Dashboard

OPEN FOR AUDITIONS (1)	OFFERS (46)	IN PRODUCTION (2)	RIGHTS NOT POSTED (6)	COMPLETED PROJECTS (38)

Filter & Sort

Send Manuscript >

How to Write, Publish, and Promote Your Website, Blogs, and Books
by Gini Graham Scott

First 15 minutes is due 7 January 2017 | Finished audiobook is due 21 January 2017

Review the contract that was accepted 01/01/17

Send Message to Producer

Share your progress with your fans

Wait for Finished Audio >

The Empowered Mind: How to Harness the Creative Force Within You
by Gini Graham Scott PhD

First 15 minutes was due 26 December 2016 | Finished audiobook is due 13 January 2017

Review the contract that was accepted 12/22/16

Send Message to Producer

Share your progress with your fans

Along the way, the narrator will post files as they are completed, until they are finished, while I have to post a copy of the cover in at least a 2400 x 2400 pixel format. These steps are indicated below.

How to Write, Publish, and Promote Your Website, Blogs, and Books
By Gini Graham Scott

This title is IN PRODUCTION

Jan 07 2017 — First 15 minutes due

Jan 21 2017 — Finished audiobook due

Estimated Length: 0.5 hours	Project Budget: Royalty Share	Word Count: 5,000
Language: English	Distribution: Exclusive	Territories: World

Cover art requirements

Request Changes   Approve Audiobook

Let your fans know about your progress: Tweet #ACX_com   Share

ABOUT THIS TITLE	AUDITION	PRODUCE AUDIOBOOK	AUDIOBOOK SALES	Edit Retail Information >

Full Production - 0 hrs 2 mins 45 secs*

Click on the titles of each section below to listen to the audio. There you can also rename each chapter.

▶ Opening Credits (00:00:12)	how to write open.mp3
▶ Guidelines For Getting Started (00:02:09)	how to write guidelines chapter.mp3
▶ Closing Credits (00:00:24)	how to write close.mp3
Retail Audio Sample (5 minutes or less)	

* Current running time, which does not include the retail audio sample

At each stage, you get to review and ask for any changes, and once you feel satisfied, you approve it. For example, here are the final files in my book project, along with my revised art, since my first artwork had large white borders on the sides rather than being a true square.

Once I approve the final recording with all the files, the ACX staff reviews it to see if the recording meets its audio standards. If any further changes are required, the ACX staff will advise the narrator and the author what to correct. My experience is that the narrators usually get it right the first time, and if necessary, quickly make any corrections.

Meanwhile, if you haven't already done so, you have to upload your cover art, which you can adapt from your CreateSpace or Kindle Cover, so it's in a square format of at least 2400 x 2400 pixels. You can't just slap on a border, unless the border fits in with the color and look of your original art, so you may have to do some PhotoShopping to crop or otherwise adjust your cover to ACX's specs.

Once both your cover and audiobook are approved, you are done. The book goes up on sale, generally within 2 weeks, and you will even get some complimentary download coupons you can pass on to friends, associates, and the media to help stimulate sales.

So as you can see, this is a fairly simple, easy to navigate way to quickly get your audiobook published, once you have a published POD or ebook on Amazon. If you don't find an outside narrator for a royalty share, you can always try to do it yourself or find a narrator and producer to create the finished files for your audiobook.

CHAPTER 6: CREATING AND PUBLISHING YOUR BLOGS AND ARTICLES

Your blogs and articles can also be a product you can sell or use to promote other products and services.

One approach is to turn your blogs or articles, along with any talks you do, into a book which you can sell. This is a process I describe in more depth in *Turn Your Blogs Into Books*, available on Amazon, Kindle, or as an audiobook. The other approach is to use your blogs or articles as a free gift to introduce others to what you are selling. Some online marketers call this a lead magnate, since this gift is used to get leads for future mailings.

Turning Your Blogs and Articles into Books

You can turn any blogs or articles into a book. The key to success is to have some organizing theme for the book. If you already have a series of blogs or articles on a topic, just put them together to create your book. Alternatively, create an outline and use that to write a series of blogs or articles on that topic. Then, these can readily be turned into chapters or sections of chapters in your book.

Figure on about 700-1500 words for each blog or chapter, though some bloggers write shorter blogs – 300-350 words. In that case, combine a few shorter blogs together by topic or theme into a chapter. If you have a more complicated topic, such as providing support for a political position, a longer blog of 1500-2500 words is fine. Once you have 3 to 7 blogs or chapters, that's enough for a short book of about 5000-10,000 words.

While you can post your blog using a number of blogging platforms, ideally include your blogs on your website. You can feature them there as www.yourdomain.com/blog, or create a page based on the subject of your blogs. For instance, if you have written the blogs as marketing tips for your field, you might call the page www.yourdomain.com/marketing-tips.

The advantage of posting the blogs on your website is that they serve double or triple duty. They can attract people to your website, since people just have to click a line to go to your main site or backtrack from your blog page to your site's home page. The blogs can later be put in your book, or they can be used as free gifts or lead magnets to invite people to give you their email or purchase other products or services from you. You can also post a link to your latest or a selected blog on Facebook, Twitter, or other social media platforms to attract visitors to your website. Regularly posting blogs also helps to increase your SEO rankings.

If you need help in creating these blogs, you can work with a ghostwriter to write them for you from your ideas, discussed in my book *How to Find and Work with a Good Ghostwriter*, which is on Amazon, Kindle, and on Audible as an audio book.

Once you have all of the blogs for your book, the next step is to collect them together into a single manuscript in Word, select a title, and turn all of the headings into headers and subheaders to create a Table of Contents. Additionally, add a copyright notice, your author bio, and contact information, as described in the discussion of publishing your book. Then, you can upload your book as a Word document, or create a PDF and upload that into the publishing platform. You can create your cover either by working with a designer or from a template.

Besides selling your published book through Amazon, Kindle, and Audible, you can sell it as a PDF or use the PDF as a free gift, much like you might use an individual blog or article.

Use Your Blogs or Articles as a Free Gift

The goal of using your blogs or articles as a free gift, like other free gifts you might offer, is to obtain emails and invite visitors to purchase other products and services from you. It also is a way to develop a relationship and build trust by sending people a series of informative emails, so they are more receptive to your recommendations or buying from you. Then, too, if you include links to your blog, that can help to build your credibility and authority, too.

You can set up your free gift to be provided immediately after a visitor comes to a squeeze page or landing page and provides his or her email. Or you can include a link to a page where the visitor can download your free gift. Another approach is to ask for the email and send the individual a confirming email with the gift PDF to download or a link to a download page. This way the person has to enter a valid email to get the gift.

This free gift is an approach which email and online marketers regularly use to get leads and build traffic. So a first step to using this approach is setting up a series of blog posts as PDFs which you can offer as these gifts. Be sure to include your website and contact information in any blogs you give out, since the printout will be separate from your website. Also, you might want to end each blog with some ad copy that features other offers you have for sale by providing links to other web pages or other details on how to get these offers. Decide on the best approach for you, and use that format to create the blogs and landing page you will use for your gift.

A future book will discuss how to use these blogs to sell your products and services using email and online marketing techniques.

104

BOOK III: CREATING YOUR PRODUCTS: FROM VIDEOS TO POWERPOINTS FOR TRAINING

CHAPTER 1: CREATING VIDEOS FOR TRAINING AND PROMOTIONS

Another key to success is creating your video, or ideally a series of videos. Then, you can upload them to YouTube, preferably on your own channel. You can also put these videos on other places, such as Vimeo, where many professionals put their videos to share privately or make them available for sale by download or streaming through Video on Demand. You can put your videos on PivotShare and offer them for a viewing fee, for free, or include them in a subscriber program for viewers. You can also upload your video onto your website or embed the YouTube link on your site, so people can see your video there. If you want to send your video file to anyone, you can post it on one of the cloud storage sites, like Dropbox, or you can send a link to the file through one of the send-a-file sites, such as Hightail. Or store the video files on your computer until you are ready to upload them to a selected online location.

Setting Up Your Channel on YouTube

When you post your videos on YouTube, you can make them public, private (where only those you select can see your video), or unlisted (where you provide a link for someone to view the video). If you are using videos for multiple purposes, it is a good idea to create separate channels. This way you can send viewers to your channel to view videos in a particular category, since if you have different types of videos in one place, a viewer could be confused or overwhelmed by seeing everything there.

For example, I have one channel for my earlier videos at Changemakersprod, videos for publishing and writing at Changemakerspublishing, and I'm setting up a separate video channel for marketing and sales videos. You can mix public, private, and unlisted videos on the same channel.

To create separate accounts, you need a separate email, and you can name your channel whatever you want. Then, people searching by that name will find your channel, although you won't get a vanity url, such as www.youtube.com/yourchannelname, until you have 25 or more subscribers to your channel. Ideally, choose a name that reflects the brand identity you are creating for that line of products or services.

Once you create the name of your channel, you can customize it with a photo or other image. Use a picture of yourself or choose something related to your brand or niche, unless you are the brand.

For example, this is my channel for films, which features a photo from a film set and thumbnails of videos, including a trailer from the TV series *Death's Door.*

My channel for Changemakers Publishing has a very different look, featuring a photo of books on top, following by a few thumbnails of videos on how to publish and promote one's books.

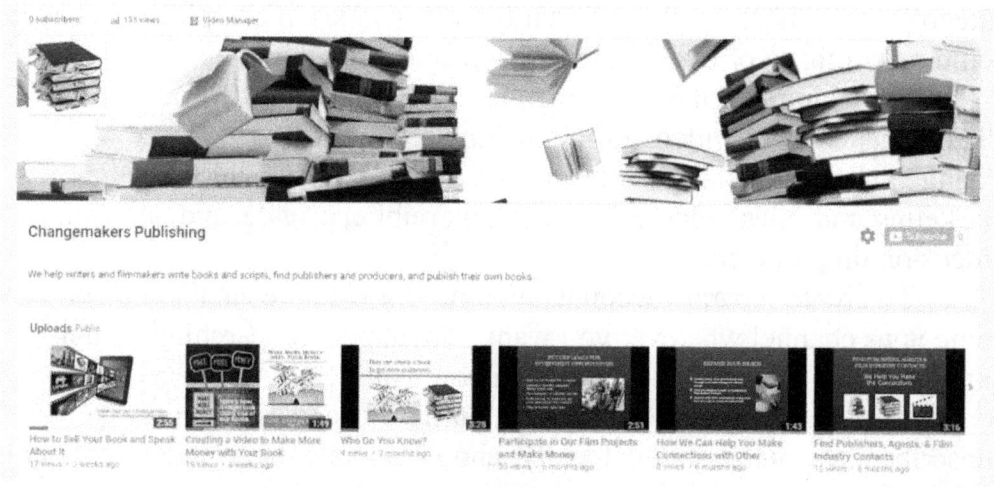

Creating Your Videos

Once you determine where to store or upload your videos, you can create your video and use them in various ways. The purpose of your video will determine your content, as well as help you budget what to spend. Some possibilities include the following:
- A promotional video or video series for your business
- A series of promotional videos for a particular product or service
- A training video series for a course you are developing
- A series of video blogs, where you talk into a camera or smartphone, and possibly include some cutaways
- A video featuring illustrations and photos to promote your work as an artist, designer, architect, landscape designer, writer, or other creative professional
- A video combining two or more approaches.

Different Approaches and Costs

Your costs for each video can range from almost nothing, if you sit in front of a video and talk to the camera, to several thousand dollars for a professional video. Take into consideration the purpose of your video in estimating the costs. The following are different methods to create your video, other than hiring a professional.

Recording Your Own Video

It will cost much less if you can record your own video or get a volunteer to record and edit your videos.

One simple way to make your own recording is to sit in front of a webcam on your computer. Commonly, your computer can record audio directly from its own speaker system, with a built in recorder to your video cam, just as it might be set up to make a call on Skype (www.skype.com), which you can record, as you talk to another person. These webcams can be very inexpensive, as little as $9.99 or $19.99, though a better quality webcam will cost from $40 for a consumer model to $60-$70 for pro versions. These webcams come with built in microphones, so you don't need a separate stand-alone mic.

If you want to edit your recording, which is usually a good idea to minimally edit out any glitches, long pauses, or digressions, you can use a program like Camtasia to edit. There are more sophisticated video editing programs, like Final Cut, which is popular with filmmakers, but that's complicated to learn and designed for editing longer videos and even feature films. For making simple videos, a program like Camtasia is fine. You can try it for free for 30 days with no commitment. Otherwise the software only costs about $200 from www.techsmith.com. I have been using Camtasia for recordings, along with SnagIt for screen captures, and I recommend them both.

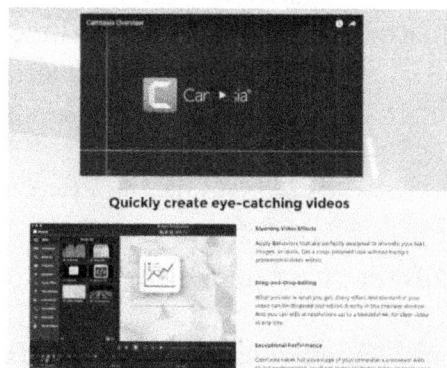

Alternatively. you can record your program directly into Camtasia from your webcam and then do the editing. Before you start recording, set up the frame around the image, and set the recording level for the mic. Select the recording options, press the record button, and test your audio to make sure it is coming through loud and clear or make any adjustments. Finally, start the recording. When it is done, end your presentation and give it a name. Then, you can produce your video as is or edit it.

Another approach is to record your presentation on your smartphone. You can record anywhere, although select a background that doesn't detract from you when you are talking. Speaking against a plain wall where you are standing or seated in a comfortable chair works well. Avoid having a busy background. Alternatively, you can broadcast from the field, such as when you are traveling to other locations. Position yourself so the exteriors don't become a distraction to what you are saying, unless you want to talk about your location such as by describing the beauty of a forest or valley below you. Just be sure you aren't positioned so there are odd images behind you, such as a tree or telephone pole projecting out of your head. Later, you can use the whole video as is, say for a video blog, or you can edit the video, through a program like Camtasia for a short video blog or other types of video.

Working with Volunteers and Video Students

In many communities, you may be able to find volunteers or low-cost video students or recent graduates to help you create or edit your video. While a single individual can use a video camera and record the sound directly on the camera, a better approach is to have a second person capture the sound on a separate recording device, so you can get better quality sound.

To find the video groups and schools in your community, type the words "video" along with "groups" "organizations" or "schools," and your city into a search engine. Then contact the likely organizations that turn up in your search to find out how you might get volunteers or students to help you create your videos.

For example, in the San Francisco Bay Area, I took introductory courses with the Berkeley Community Media https://www.bcmtv.org based in Berkeley, California and participated in film programs with Making Movies Throughout the Bay (MMTB) http://moviemakingbay.com, now based in Rodeo, and Scary Cow, a film collective in San Francisco http://www.scarycow.com. Through all of these groups, I found volunteers who worked with me as cast and crew members for about 50 films I created over a three year period, before going pro and making feature films, TV series, and documentaries.

Creating a High Quality Promotional Video

While the do-it-yourself approach might be great for creating video blogs and your first courses, a high-quality professional video is the way to go to create a professional look for your company, products, or services. Figure on spending about $3000-$5000 for a video done by a professional, much like you might stage a house in order to sell it for top-dollar. Typically, a professional video company will spend two or three hours to take a variety of shots presenting various facets of what you do and how your company operates. Then, it will edit that footage down into a one or a series of short, promotional videos. Commonly, these will be about 3 to 5 minutes, though sometimes they will be a little longer, up to 8 or 9 minutes, such as if these are turned into educational videos for prospective clients or customers.

If you are seeking speaking engagements, especially well-paid ones, for company meetings and corporate events, get a video crew to film you speaking to some organizations. If you are just starting out, you can set up a speaking event and invite your associates, so you can do a talk or perhaps do a series of short segments with highlights from each of the topics you talk about.

Once the video is completed, you can use it in conjunction with an email campaign to invite prospective clients to hire you or to get group organizers to invite you to be a speaker or workshop leader at a future event. That's what I did several years ago, when I created such a video and added it to my website to get clients to hire me as a speaker/workshop leader or get producers to invite me to be a guest on a TV talk show.

After my website introduces people to what I do, they can click on the video to see clips about my work, some of my promotional appearances on TV shows, including Oprah, and my talks on different topics. Since the video is on YouTube, I can readily send an email or include the link on a flyer inviting prospects to check out the video if they want to consider hiring me.

If this is a single promotional video you expect to use for one or more years, it's worth creating a strong presentation with a higher end budget of $3000 to $5000 for a professional job. Check out local referrals and a nearby Chamber of Commerce for leads on who to hire. Then, check out each company's portfolio on their website to look at the styles of the videos they have done for different clients to pick out a video team with the style you like for your video.

A Series of Promotional Videos for a Product or Service

These promotional videos are designed to be a short 30 to 60 second introduction to a product or service you offer. One way to present these promos is to illustrate the different offerings on your website, where a visitor clicks a photo of that product or service and sees a short clip about what it does and its benefits. Or you can incorporate these promotional videos into a campaign where you send out a series of emails about different products or services. You can design a flyer with a brief introduction to each one, along with an invitation to see the video on your website or YouTube.

Alternatively, you can hire a professional to produce a slick series of videos, or you can use various software platforms where you insert a series of photos and short graphic clips, which you can take on a digital camera or smartphone. For example, here are examples of some of my company's promotional videos, grouped together on our YouTube channel for Changemakers Publishing, which features writing and publishing services.

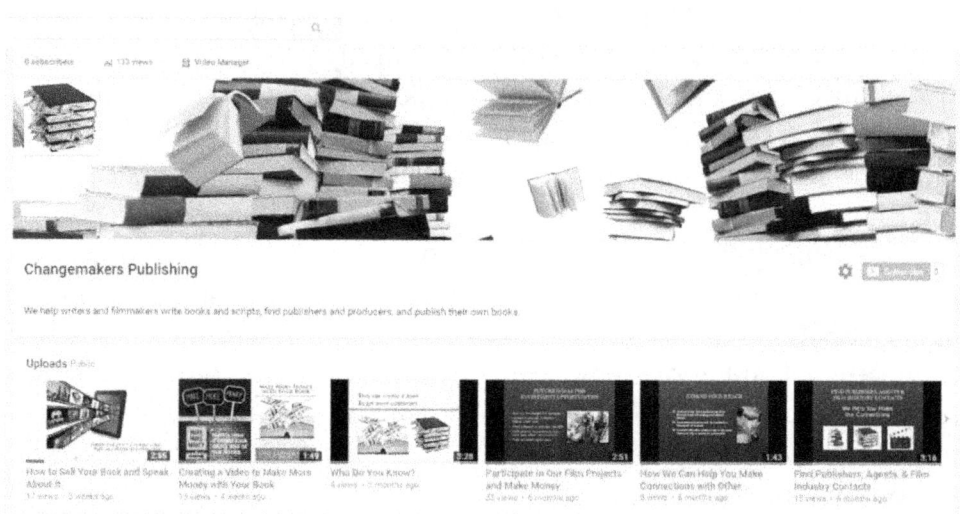

A Training Video Series for a Course

Another type of popular video is the training video modules used for an online course. Some courses are available through live trainings from one of the popular online webinar sites like www.gotomeeting.com or www.gotowebinar.com, where you call in at a certain time to join the webinar. Later, the replays are often in the form of video you can access at any time by clicking on a link and usually entering a password to gain access. In some cases, there is no live course, just a video or series of videos, which you can view at your leisure. Often these courses involve PowerPoints with links to videos, or the PowerPoints may be saved as videos, an option made possible through PowerPoint10 and later versions.

Typically, each module is about 4 to 10 minutes, sometimes as long as 14 to 15 minutes, and you can see a list of modules in the navigation bar, so you can view them in order or skip around. In some cases, the modules are made available over several weeks, where one module builds another, so you are supposed to see them in order – and you can't view the videos for later weeks until they are unlocked each week. That's an approach that ClickBank, a platform for selling digital information products, uses in its ClickBank University course, designed to show new online marketers how to set up an effective digital sales program.

I have been through a dozen of these training programs so far. Generally, they begin with a short 1 to 4 minute introductory video explaining what the course is about and introducing the instructor.

114

Sometimes these videos feature the instructor talking into the camera or they may show PowerPoint slides, where the instructor talks through a voice-over. Or sometimes a thumbnail video insert on each slide shows the instructor talking while the slides present the course. Often the slides feature the text of the instructor's comments or provide an outline of the instructor's main points. Commonly, these courses feature cutaways to photos and videos to support a point the instructor is making.

In many cases, besides viewing and listening to the video, you will have an option to download a copy of the slides or other types of information, usually in PDF, Word, or Excel formats. Sometimes these are a summary or outline of what you have just viewed; in other cases, these are supplementary materials, such as a list of resources with contact information, case studies, or questions to help you think about your priorities and the steps to achieve them.

Whatever the approach, I have found these courses very informative, and in today's digital age, video is a popular way of getting information, rather than just reading a book. The video also personalizes the training, since you have an up-close and virtual encounter with the course instructor. While some introductory classes are offered as free giveaways or low-cost introductions to promote further trainings, others are sold for varying sums – from about $17 on up to comprehensive packages of $297 to $497 and even $697 to $797 packages, depending on the claimed values of the course. Many of the videos offer a way to make or save money or acquire little known information – usually to get even more money. Other popular subjects are health and wellness, and inspirational topics. I'll describe these classes in more detail in the next section on creating your own training and informational presentations.

A Series of Video Blogs

Now many people don't write blogs, or they supplement written blogs with video blogs, because increasingly people get their information via video rather than reading that same information. So just as you might turn any blogs you write into a book, think about how you might turn your blogs into a series of videos or into a course featuring these blogs, and perhaps include some video clips or additional material to download.

Keep these video blogs short – generally 1 to 2 or 3 minutes. Unlike the videos created for courses, which often feature PowerPoint presentations and video clips, most video blogs feature you talking, though you might incorporate some video cutaways. These video blogs don't have to be professionally done – they can be more informal, featuring you talking wherever you are on your video cam or smartphone.

For example, one of my clients used to start his video posts with some introductory comments about what he was doing and his inspirational ideas for the day. Then, he turned the camera on his surroundings when he was traveling to show where he was and what he was doing. Meanwhile, since he was streaming these posts on live video, a stream of blue "like" buttons and "red" hearts streamed across the screen from those who were watching, and later he saved the video to post on his channel and also sent a file to a transcription service – Rev.com (www.rev.com) – to make a copy, so he could later use the transcript in writing a book.

Ideally, it's best to create your own video channel on YouTube, as previously described, and post your videos there. You can create links to these blogs on your website on a separate web page, and you can link to these from your social media pages, such as on Face-book and Twitter. This way you further increase your online presence. Include a brief description with these links, along with a video thumbnail to show what it's about, and encourage others who follow you to click on your video.

If you can, post these video blogs at least once a week, and some videocasters create these blogs two or three times a week or even once or a few times a day.

If you are using a written script or blog to create your video blog, you can easily turn it into a written blog or book. However, if you go from the spoken word to the written word, edit your copy to provide a smooth narrative, since we speak more informally when we talk.

A Video Portfolio of Your Work

Once you have a series of videos, you can create a video portfolio on your website to show of your work, much like a portfolio of photos might do so. This portfolio is in addition to creating a channel on YouTube to show off your videos.

You can structure this portfolio in two ways. One is to create a video from clips of your other videos, or create a series of embedded videos that show off your work, much like you might use photo thumbnails to lead to a gallery of your work. But instead of a gallery of photos, this will feature a gallery of short videos.

Alternatively, you can create a video showing off your work such as if you are a photographer, artist, designer, or architect. In this case, you can create a slide show video, such as with a platform like Animoto (www.animoto.com), where you insert a photo JPEG of each item in a template and select a musical background. Afterwards this becomes a short video – usually about 1 to 3 minutes. If you want, you can add explanatory text, such as where you took the photo or what project each landscape designs was for. Still, another approach is to combine still photos, video clips, text, music, or voice-overs, which you do on Animoto's new promotional platform.

To illustrate, here are a few slides to showcase various books I wrote for clients, along with photos of these books inserted into the video. To make it easy to do this, the program provides a background template, and you incorporate the photos into this layout.

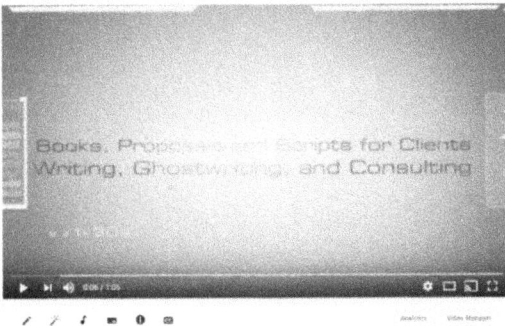

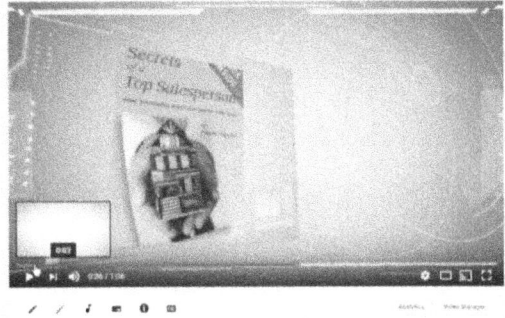

In short, you can create a portfolio in a single video featuring a slide show of photos, illustrations, or video clips, or you can create a portfolio of multiple videos, using a thumbnail from each video to launch the full video. Generally, both the video portfolio and separate videos will be 1-3 minutes.

Videos Combining Two or More Approaches

In some cases, videos involving two or more approaches might be appropriate for your company. For example, if you are doing promotional videos for a particular product, you might incorporate clips from your video blogs, where you talk about the product or feature a clip from an interview with a fan praising the product. If you are creating a training video, you might include clips from your promotional video and video portfolio.

In short, as you develop your videos, think of different uses for them and different ways you can combine them, so they can become part of a product you are selling, such as a training video series, or part of your promotional effort to sell that product.

CHAPTER 2: DEVELOPING POWERPOINT TRAINING AND INFORMATIONAL PRESENTATIONS

One of the most important products you can develop is a training program, which you can create using PowerPoint, videos, or PowerPoints saved as videos. While these programs can be created from books or turned into books, they can be sold for much more than a book with this same information. That's because the training program is viewed like a course with specialized information sold to an exclusive audience, whereas a book is sold to anyone who wants to buy it.

In fact, a book for a limited audience may have relatively small sales at a low price, which is commonly determined by the size of the book, except for a textbook which may be priced much higher, since students in a class where it is assigned have to buy it.

For example, a 300 page book at $19.95 selling to about 1000 readers would gross about $20,000, and if that's a book sold by a traditional publisher, you would probably net about $2 a book or $2000. However, a course with this same information might be priced at $97, and if the same 1000 viewers sign up for the course, that's a gross of $97,000, with almost all of that going to you, after you deduct the costs of creating and maintaining the course on a website hosting service – say about $2000 to create it and $3000 to manage the site and pay the sales commissions to the host of the site – a net of about $92,000.

Should you sell the course through affiliates, they might get a commission of 50-70% or 60% on average, which would leave about $34,000 for you, still much more than a net of $2,000 from a traditional publisher.

No wonder the online training class has become very popular where there is a market for this subject. Some of the most popular topics are ways to increase profits and advice to homeowners, seniors, and retirees seeking to save money, along with health and fitness, diet, and relationships.

Deciding on What to Include in Your Course

If you already have a book or a manuscript on a how-to subject, that can be a good start. However, you don't need a book or manuscript to create your course. In fact, you can develop your book out of your course. You just need to create an outline and script for what you want to say, using a PowerPoint presentation format as a guide.

The type of course that works best in email and online marketing is based on teaching others some kind of skill, so they learn how to do something which will earn them money, save them money, or provide them with more enjoyment and satisfaction. It should not normally be a general interest course, such as on art history or archaeology, which are better left to the universities and college extension classes.

Some popular topics might be:
- how to make more money with your new method,
- how to cook certain kinds of foods,
- how to train your dog,
- how to use a new software to do something,
- how to invest more successfully with a little known approach,
- how to save more money for your retirement
- how to live a healthier, longer life

Whatever the topic, create your course around something you know how to do – and which is new and different from other courses on the topic. With books, you can research what has gone before by searching on Amazon for previous books on that topic, using keywords for the book's title and subject. The research results will tell what was published before, when, the author or authors, the publisher, and the current Amazon ranking of print and Kindle sales.

You can also do a search for previous courses on this topic through a Google search. For example, when I searched on Google for cooking classes, dozens of courses turned up, including some companies that help you create your own online class series or school, such as Teachable (www.teachable.com) and Coursio (www.coursio.com). Once you sign up for Teachable with your email and password, Teachable even lets you create your own school name.

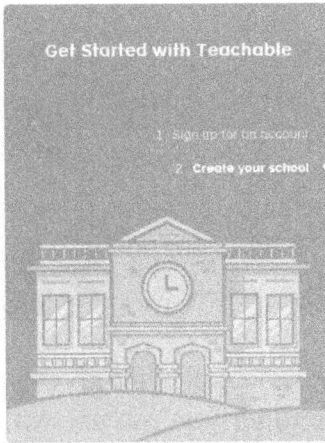

Then, you can create a course, customize the look and feel, create a domain name, and launch your course.

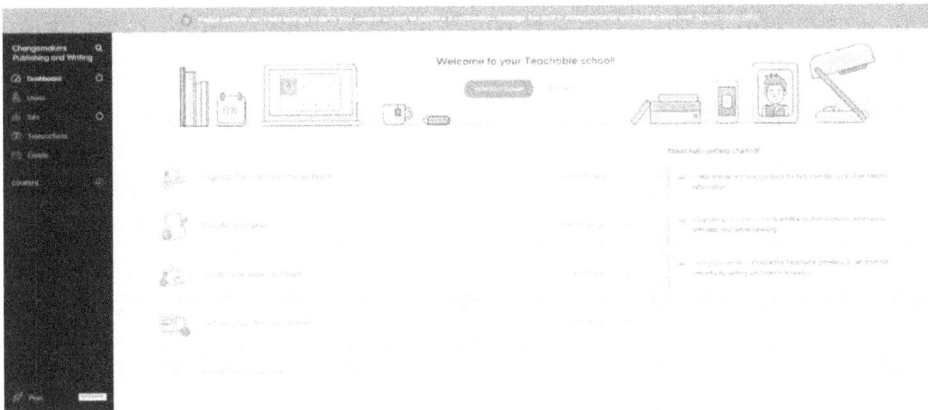

Here's what my school looks like, though it is not yet live, since I haven't created any courses. Once you decide what you want to teach, you can create your own school, as well as offer your courses through various online sales platforms. Then, use email marketing to further let people know about your courses.

An advantage of using a program like Teachable is it gives you an online presence, and it has an attractive site builder you can use with your existing website, or you can create professional-looking pages with Teachable's easy-to-use site builder. You can translate your course into other languages, so you can appeal to international clients in other countries, including France, Japan, and Russia. Then, too, Teachable provides tools to create multimedia lectures with interactive videos, images, text, audio, and PDFs. You can easily import your content from Dropbox, Box, or other online storage platforms. Then, too, Teachable provides demos on how to develop and sell your course.

Looking at the previously published books in your field can help you think about what to cover in your course. This review not only provides a guide to what already has been done, but you might draw on the information in these books, along with your own material, in creating your course. Even if you use other books and courses for ideas and insights, make your course your own by drawing on your own experience, as well as the knowledge you gain from others books and courses in your chosen field.

Organizing and Creating Your Course Materials

Once you decide on what your course will be about, the next step is to pull together the materials you will include in the course, much like you might organize this material in creating a book.

A good way to organize this is to create an outline for the topics you will cover. As needed, create folders for each topic and put your ideas or material to include in each folder.

If you already have a book or manuscript on this subject, that is a good starting point. Use the chapters for the modules or sections within each module. If your book lends itself to multiple courses, divide it up, so a few chapters become each course, and divide those into modules and sections.

Alternatively, as you develop your course, those materials could later be turned into the chapters in your book or series of books.

As you create your outline – whether from a book or from scratch, you might find or develop examples or case histories for each section to illustrate what you are teaching. If you have been keeping a journal, this might be a good source for material. If you have done any talks, participated on any panels, or done any workshops, you can use transcripts from these programs to develop materials for your course, too. If you are using the chapters in your book as the basis of organizing your course, you can supplement what's in your book with other material. Some of this material might work well in a course, but it could too detailed or conversational to work well in a book. Conversely, you might need to add more details to an introductory class to have enough for your book. Consider the different requirements for your course and book and decide what works best where, as you develop materials for each format.

For example, in your course you may want to incorporate video examples and photos, and you might supplement the sequence of steps to do something with stories about what you did and your initial challenges to overcome them in order to complete the project. But in your book, unless it's an e-book, you can't include video clips, and you may prefer to have a more focused step-by-step description of what to do, since a discussion of your challenges and achievements might seem like too much of a digression. But this more personal approach may be well suited to a course, where you want to create a closer connection with the viewer with more personal stories that entertain and inspire as well as instruct.

While your outline of subjects to cover can be as long as you have different topics to cover, combine them into 6 to 12 modules for your course, which could correspond to chapters in your book. Then, take the different topics you have combined to create these modules as sections to be included in each module.

Figure on turning each of the topics in each module into a short video of 2 to10 minutes, and up to 14 or 15 minutes if necessary. The average length is about 4 to 7 minutes for most videos, based on my experience of taking dozens of online classes.

For example, one of the courses I took – *Referral Network Ninja* by

Clarence Fisher, which focused on tips to get more business through referral marketing, was divided into seven modules:

Module 1: Mindset of a Hustler

Module 2: Building Your Referral Network

Module 3: Power Networking CRM Strategies

Module 4: Launching Your Campaign

Module 5: Meeting with Influencers

Module 6: How to Work a Room

Module 7: Following Up Profitably

Each of these modules was subdivided into two to four videos dealing with that topic. For example, the first Mindset of a Hustler module featured videos on: The Strangest Secret in the World, 20 Minutes, Your Top Three, Building Your Belief Systems, and Developing the Mindset of a Hustler. The second module included videos on Building Your Powerbase, Discovering 2nd Degree Connections, and Identifying Power Influencers.

Here's what my screen looked like after I signed in. The navigation bar on the left listed each of the modules. When I clicked, each module indicated the subtopics, each with its own video.

The program began, as most do, with an introduction to what was included in the course, as well as a welcome message from the course developer and teacher, Clarence Fisher.

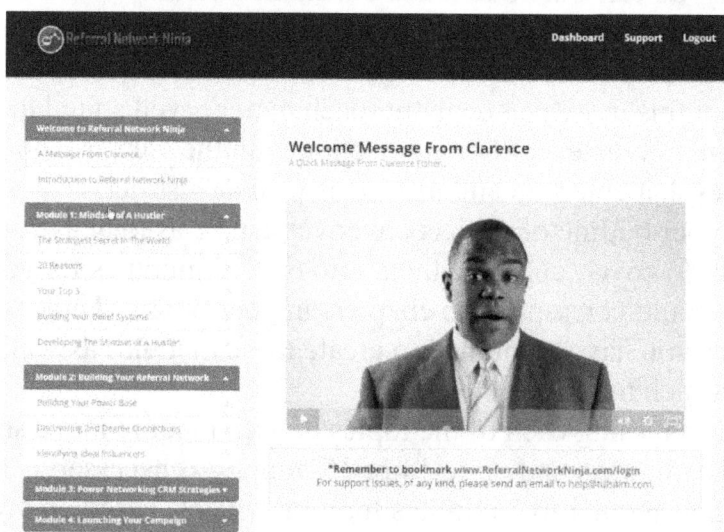

Then, the course features each module with a menu of instructional videos on that topic. The course also provides a way to download each video, audio, or a PDF of the slides in each video. Plus some videos are accompanied by additional resources, including Word and Excel files, PDFs, and links to external websites. The videos also have a similar look and feel, which is common in online classes.

You can easily create your own classes by using a PowerPoint template with a customized design. You modify it with different copy and sometimes different images on each slide, and turn that presentation into a video. Or you can select a theme for your video in a video creation programs, such as Animoto (www.animoto.com).

Here's another example of a course page from the Commission Profit Hack training offered by the Digital Income Academy.

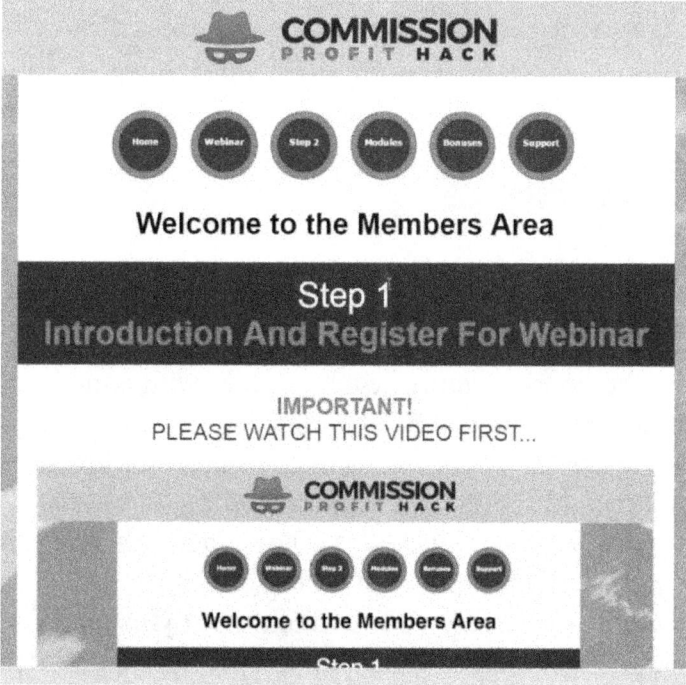

In this case, the class welcome includes an invitation to a webinar about other profit opportunities – notably a course on how they created a sales funnel to generate $150,000 in income a year, and a listing of other bonuses which viewers might obtain from their affiliate partners.

In many cases, these courses promote other courses, products, and opportunities, which you can do if you become an affiliate marketer in addition to offering your own courses and products. Combining the promotion of others' products with your own projects works best if you promote related products and services. Sometimes, as here, the links to other products are promoted first, though in other cases, you might provide links within your course or at the end of it. Also, mMany courses have related Facebook groups and will give you the link, so you can join, as in this Commission Profit Hack class.

In this case, the modules follow in sequence, as you scroll down the screen, rather than listing each module in a navigation bar. For instance, here is the beginning of the six modules in the CPH course.

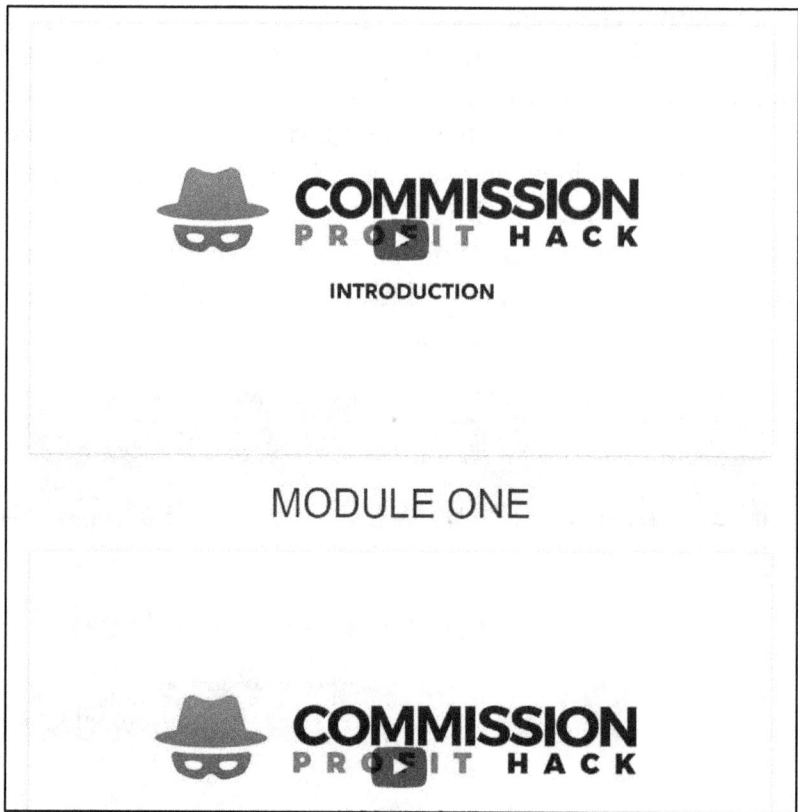

Once you click on the video, you'll notice that the video slides in each module have the same look and feel. Typically each video features a voice-over accompanying the copy on the screen, as in the series of slides in Module #1 illustrated below.

MODULE ONE

✖ Love, Passion or Knowledge
✖ Hobbies, Skills or Interests
✖ Less likely to lose interest

Match your interests to offers!

MODULE ONE

HIGH DEMAND

Give the people what they want!

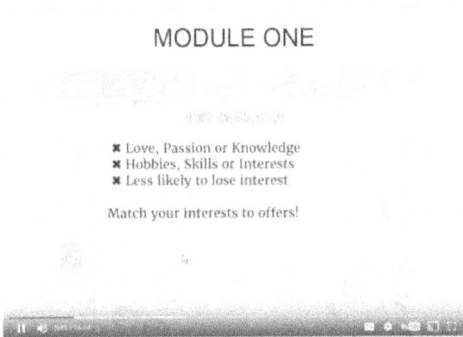

As you can see, there is a fairly simple video interface for the course. It generally involves writing copy on a few PowerPoint slides and speaking with a voice-over. There are a few simple graphics, and each module ends with some links to references and resources cited during the course.

MODULE ONE

MODULE ONE

HEADLINE

Abandon Your Website Now For Your Business To Survive!

SALES COPY/VIDEO

THE SALES PAGE

MODULE ONE

MODULE ONE

Websites

✖ https://www.amazon.com
✖ http://www.ebay.com
✖ http://www.rakuten.com
✖ http://www.clickbank.com
✖ https://www.clicksure.com
✖ https://www.jvzoo.com
✖ https://poetfly.com
✖ https://www.maxbounty.com

Here's one more example of a course design – Email Prospecting Blitz by Tom Gaddis and Nick Ponte, who are based in Hawaii. Their course illustrates an email method that Nick used in getting local commissions for his web design business.

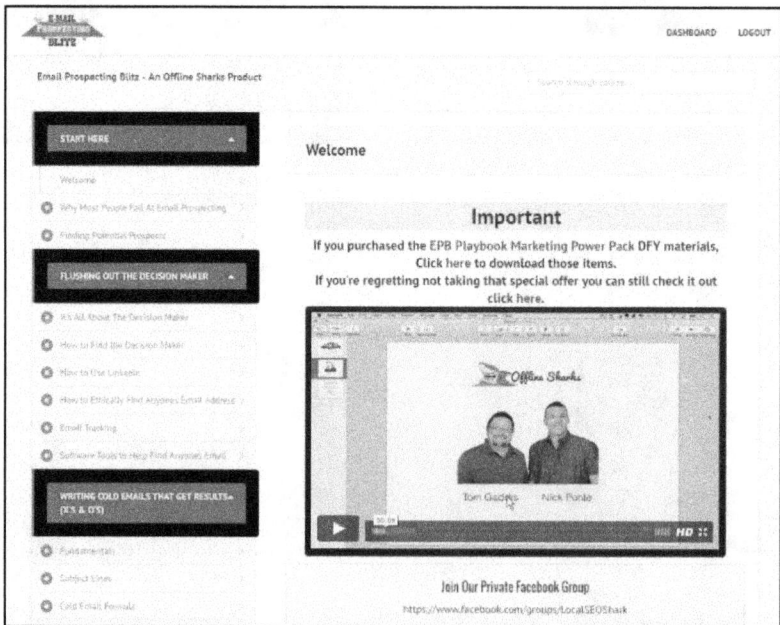

They use the same module format combined with a video, and links to additional resources you can download for future reference, such as templates for writing initial and follow-up query letters and for contacting large companies. They have the same look and feel for each video. Each video starts off with the title of that video both above and on the screen.

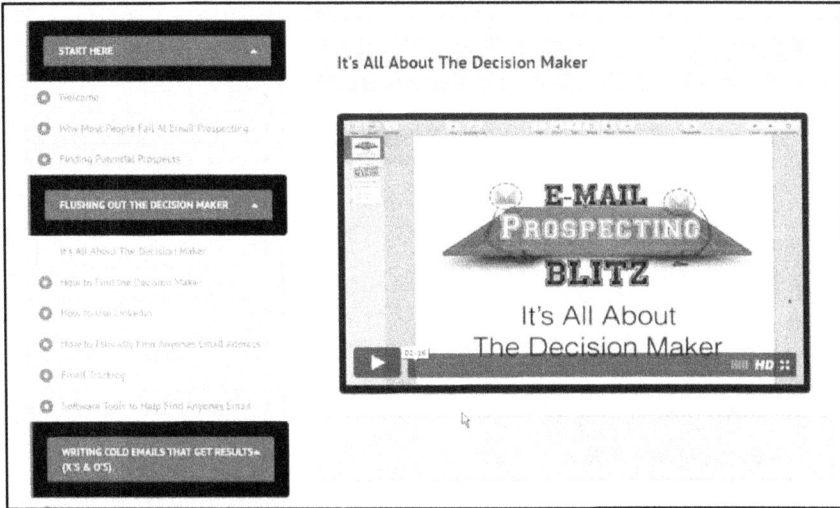

Then, Gaddis and Ponte combine a voice-over with a simple image illustrating what they are talking about, or sometimes they use a list featuring their main points, or they give an example of how they have used a technique. In effect, they have turned a simple PowerPoint presentation with some images into a video with a voice-over.

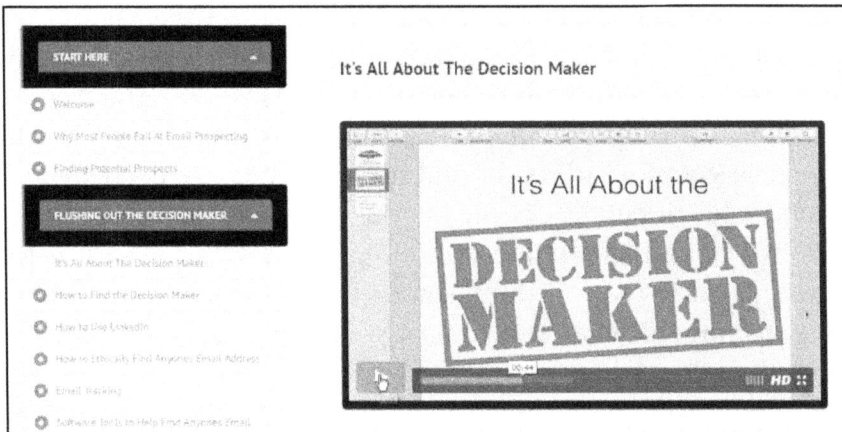

131

It's All About The Decision Maker

How to Find the Decision Maker

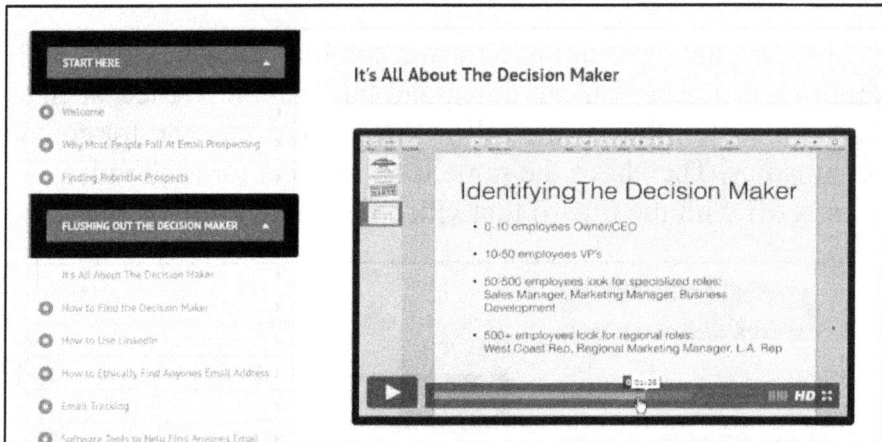

These examples have illustrated some of the ways you can create your own videos. I personally prefer combining modules on the side with videos for the presentation. While video text with a voice-over is fine for many presentations, ideally, I would like to see videos, using more images and video clips to take full advantage of the PowerPoint-Video format.

While these examples provide a basic starting point for creating your video, you can get more ideas for putting your video together by looking at some courses developed by people in your niche market. I have used examples from email and online marketing, since that's what I'm writing about. But if you're writing about some other specialty, such as cooking, gardening, fishing, or whatever, look at what others in your field have done. Don't copy them exactly in style or content; make the course format your own. Let your personality shine through, both in your introduction in the beginning of the course and how you structure each video.

Once your course is complete, you can use various services for promoting it, and you can combine promotions for your classes with your books, blogs, and other materials. You'll see more details about to do this in my book on marketing and promoting your business.

Turning Your PowerPoint Presentation into a Video

An easy way to create your videos for each module is to save your PowerPoint as a Windows Media Video (.wmv) file. In creating this video, you can record and time a voice narration and add a laser pointer, animations, and transitions. You can even include an embedded video, which will play automatically within your video.

You can add the voice-over narration by using a mic to record this as the PowerPoint presentation plays, or record a narrative while you deliver a presentation to a live audience. You can even include their comments and questions. You can also turn your mouse into a laser pointer to highlight text and images in the presentation.

To do so, first create your slide show as you would normally create a PowerPoint. Then, if you want, record and add narration and timings and use your mouse as a laser pointer to highlight things you want to emphasize as you go through the presentation. Next, in the file menu, click "Save & Send" and then "Create a Video."

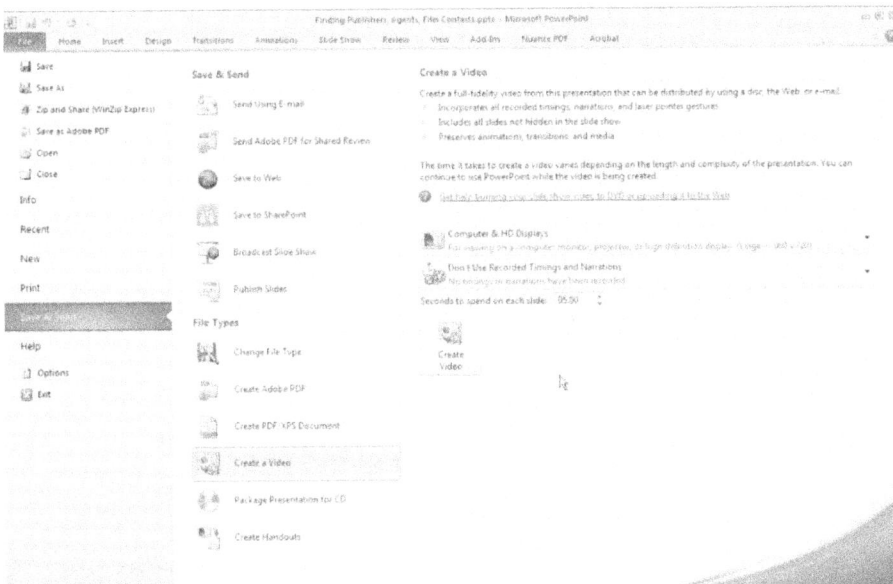

You can also choose the quality of the video – from the highest HD quality to medium quality for Internet and DVD to a lower quality for mobile devices. You can indicate if you used recorded timings and narrations or not. Finally, save the video and double-click the file to play. Afterwards you can burn the file for the video onto a DVD to sell it in that format, and you can upload it to a video sharing website such as YouTube.

Here's an example of how I turned a presentation on Finding Publishers, Agents, and Film Industry Contacts into a video.

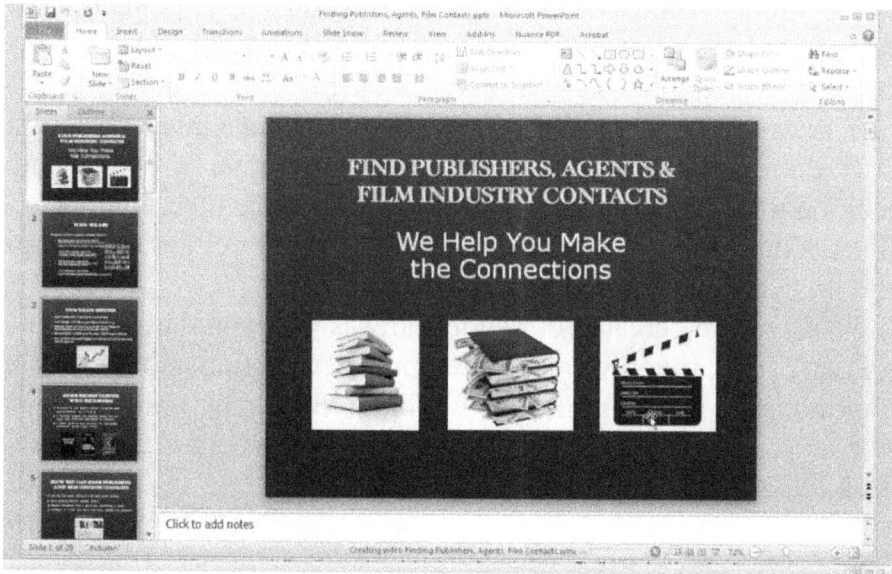

In this case, I created my 20-slide video within minutes, and I could easily add voice-over narration to discuss the major points I wanted to make in my class. I could also, if needed, readily convert a .wmv file created from the PowerPoint into other file formats, such as turning it into a .mp4, a popular video format.

To illustrate how easy this process is, here are some images from my video as it played on a Windows Media Player.

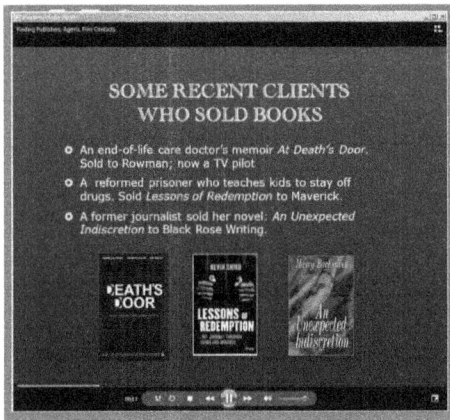

Summing Up

In conclusion, you can easily create presentations using PowerPoints or video programs and turn this into a course. As will be discussed, the videos can also be used to convey a sales message in which you encourage a prospect to leave an e-mail address or buy more – immediately or along the way through a sales funnel.

In using these videos to create a series of modules for a course, you can combine them with a variety of other materials, including PDFs, Word documents, images, Excel files, and even more videos. So while books from traditional publishers may be struggling, there are now many ways to present digital information, and courses have become a key way to spread this information.

136

CHAPTER 3: MAKING YOUR FINAL PRESENTATION LOOK EVEN MORE POLISHED

There are a number of ways to make your presentation look really good, using a variety of graphics programs. Or you can always hire a graphics designer.

Using a Graphics Designer or Graphics Program

Many of the programs already discussed have their own templates and images for creating the cover of your PDF, CreateSpace paperback, Kindle e-book, and ACX audiobook. For an even more polished look, hire a graphic designer or create your design if you're an artist, as a publisher normally does.

If you work with a designer, the designer will generally start with some sketches of ideas. You then provide some feedback on which concept you like best. The designer comes back with a more developed sketch. Finally, after getting your approval, the designer provides some close to final renderings. You have an opportunity to provide more input, and the designer may submit a few more close to final takes, until you give your final approval, and the cover goes to press.

For example, a cover that went through this collaboration and final vetting press is the cover for *When the Rich Kill* by Black Rose Writing. At once on seeing the initial design, I liked the imaginative placement of the hand. But I wanted a larger diamond ring on the woman's finger to show she was a wealthy woman who had been killed.

When you select a graphic designer, look at his or her online portfolio to see if you like that person's style. Choose the designer you like the most, taking into consideration any major differences in costs for the project.

If you are working with a publisher, the publisher normally decides on the final layout, though authors are generally asked for their input.

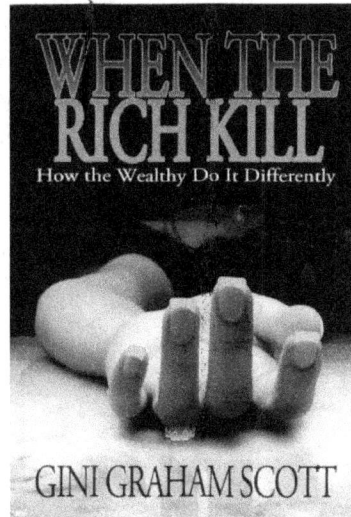

Using a Cover Creator

Another approach is obtaining a template you can modify for your book cover, if you don't use a graphic designer or want to use one of the templates provided by some publishing services, such as CreateSpace. Using a template from an independent service can be ideal for a PDF cover or to modify a design for an e-book or audiobook cover.

For example, one such service is Maggazzine, which offers templates to create high-quality covers without the high cost of hiring expensive graphic designers and writers or getting poor quality PLR (private label rights) covers. As Maggazzine's sales copy illustrates, one can easily adapt these cover designs for not only magazines, but books and e-books. While some of these designs come with interim contents of a magazine on a popular topic, such as health, happiness, and success, you can use these templates to add your own content.

To illustrate, here are some images from Maggazzine's sales page describing the product in detail.

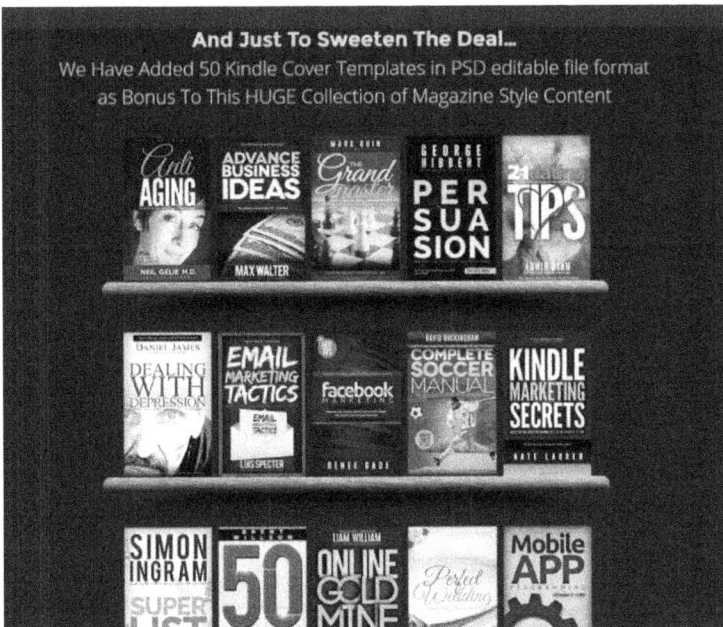
Here's a sneak-peek preview of what you're going to get...

PLUS! Stunning Magazine-Style Templates Makes Hiring Graphic Designers A Thing Of The Past!

And Just To Sweeten The Deal...
We Have Added 50 Kindle Cover Templates in PSD editable file format as Bonus To This HUGE Collection of Magazine Style Content

Besides featuring all of these striking images, the sales copy went on to persuade me that using such images would help me sell more books or whatever products or services I was selling. And to help make this case, the copy explained that the price was only $9.99, reduced from $27, and if I wanted even more exclusive images, the upsell offered them for only $37. Since both the appeal and the images were convincing, I bought them both.

Using an E-Book Creator

While you can readily import a PDF or Word file into an e-book platform, such as Kindle, Smashwords, and Draft2Digital, as discussed, sometimes the conversion can have some glitches, such as graphics that are cut off or appear in the wrong place. But now software programs, such as the Ultimate Ebook Creator (or UEC) (http://ultimatee-bookcreator.com) are designed to fix that.

Ultimate eBook Creator. eBook Creator Software for Amazon Kindle, iPad, Android. Create Fiction, Non-Fiction, Fixed Layout, Poetry and Comic eBooks. Create eBooks in MOBI, EPUB, Word and PDF Formats!

In the Ultimate Ebook Creator, you import your Word document, format it in the platform, and export it into the different e-book formats, which include Mobi, Epub, Word, and a PDF. To get started, insert information about your book's title, description, author, publisher, and keywords on the opening page. In this case, I chose *Turn Your Blogs Into Books*.

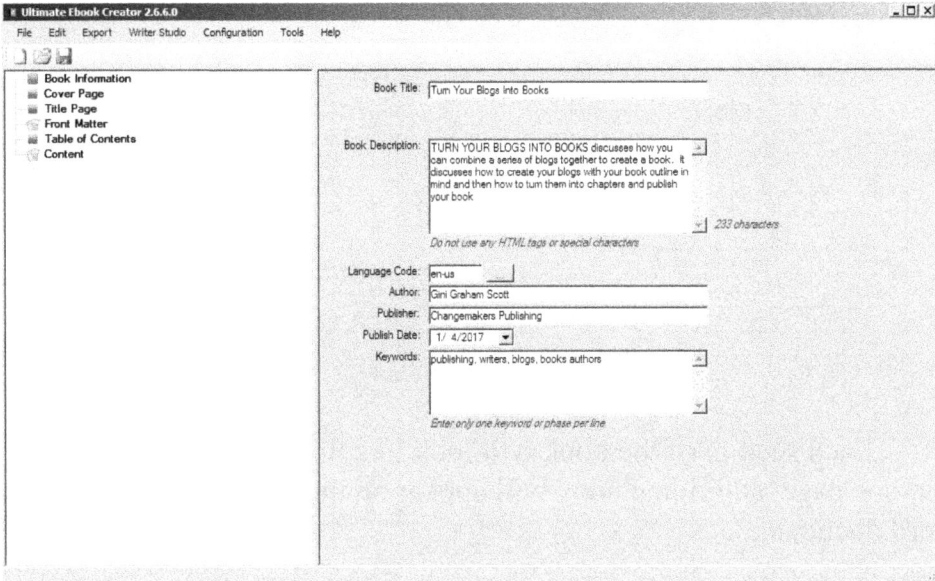

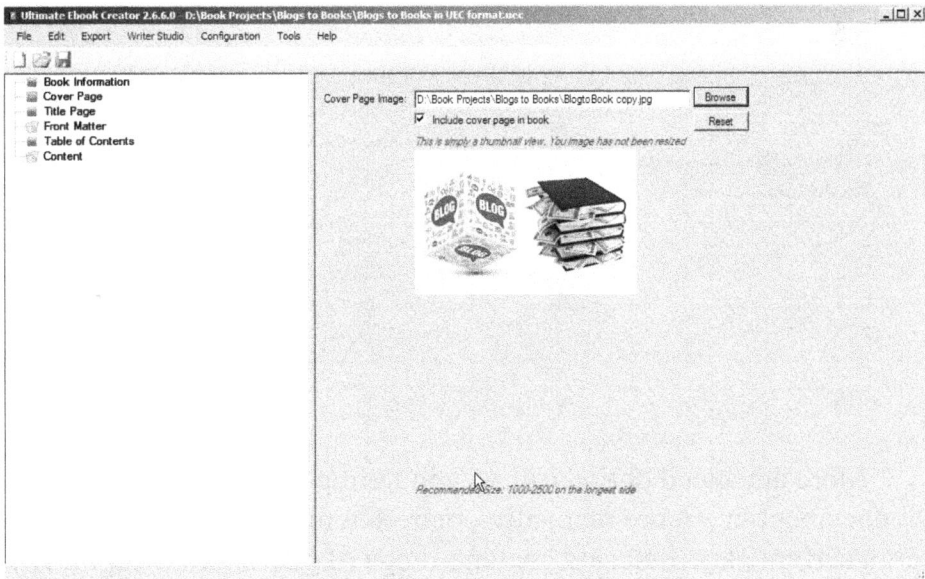

Then, you can import an already created Word document, which will create a Table of Contents with two levels. It looks something like this.

Each section of the book will look like this. If the copy is longer than one page, additional copy will appear on the next page just like in a Word document.

More advanced options allow you to import your text, MS Word, or PDF document in a more manually-controlled manner, whereby you can insert a current page, selected content, range of pages, or all pages. If you want to add images, you can insert four major formats – JPEGs, GIFs,

BMPs, and PNGs, though not all e-Reader platforms support all image formats. For example, Amazon and Kindle only allows JPEG or GIF files, so it is best to only import images in these big formats.

To import an image, go to the page where you want to import it.

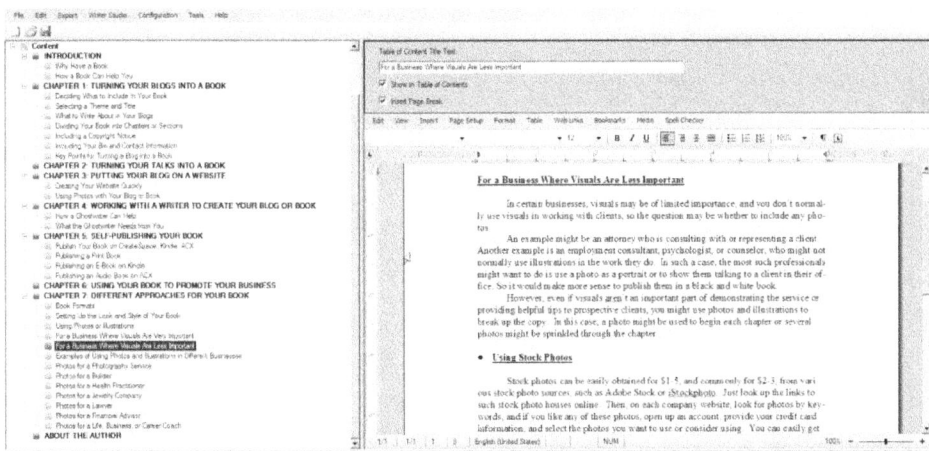

Then, much as in Word, indicate where to import the image. Afterwards, you can resize it to the proper size.

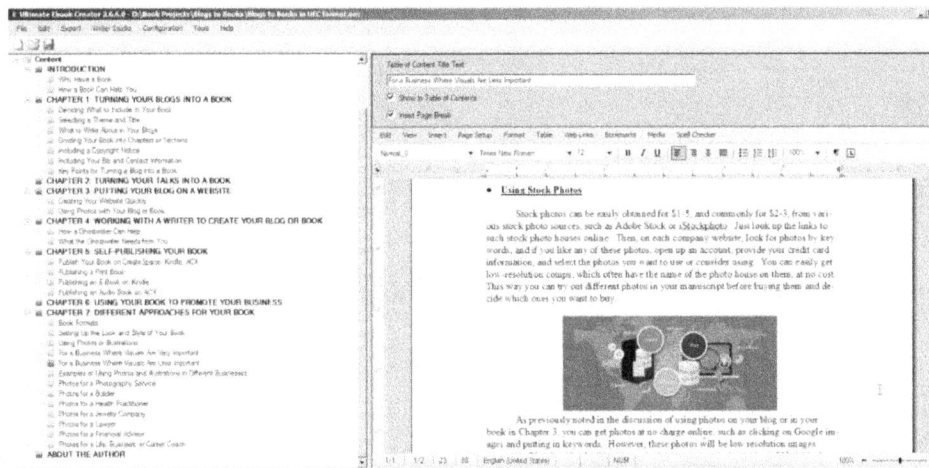

One advantage of using a program like this is that it formats the photos so they appear properly once placed in an e-book document. Otherwise, they may not appear correctly. For example, sometimes adjacent photos in the original manuscript may appear on top of each other in the UEC platform, so you have to adjust them, as in the example below.

For more details, a complete manual describes the various ways you can carefully set up your content. The program for creating your content can easily work with a program that creates covers, such as Maggazzine, where you modify a cover template and use it for the cover of your book. After you have formatted the whole book, you can save it in any of the e-book formats, such as mobi or epub, and upload it into an email sales channel, such as Kindle or Smashwords.

BOOK IV: FINDING EMAILS TO BUILD YOUR BUSINESS

CHAPTER 1: HOW EMAIL MARKETING CAN HELP YOU GET CLIENTS LOCALLY

When you think of email marketing, you may envision online campaigns involving list building and driving traffic to your website. You may also think of creating sales pages, landing pages, and funnels to collect emails and then do email pitches.

While such activities might contribute to a local campaign to get leads to build your business, using emails in local marketing is very different. Here, you want to do more direct targeting to contact a decision-maker in order to set up a meeting and pitch yourself to do some work, perhaps by submitting a proposal for what you will do for how much. Alternatively, you may want to use email marketing along with referral marketing, whereby you go to business networking events and use emails to build a relationship with people you already know. Or you use emails to follow-up with people you have already met at an event or otherwise contacted.

In either case, you use list building to add contacts as you meet them or otherwise obtain their email, but you do so on a local scale. Similarly, you focus SEO or traffic building around becoming more visible to prospects in the area.

Accordingly, in this book, the focus is on how you can use email marketing locally to supplement other local marketing efforts, such as joining a nearby Chamber of Commerce and attending various networking and referral groups.

This book will primarily focus on individuals, company owners, and sales people who are seeking clients and customers, rather than retail stores that depend primarily on local foot traffic, coupons, and other marketing methods to attract customers to their store.

148

CHAPTER 2: FINDING THE RIGHT PERSON TO CONTACT

When you are trying to find clients and customers as a professional, company owner, or sales person, you have to start with finding the right person to contact, whether sending them emails or making phone calls. Then, you have to determine their preferred way of being initially contacted. Some like to receive an initial email, others a phone call, some are open to either approach.

Think of this kind of email marketing as a door opener, whether you initially meet someone at a networking event or social gathering and follow-up with an email, or you send an initial email to someone you haven't met before. Depending on the circumstances, you will use email marketing along with a phone call, brochure, flyer, website, video, or other marketing materials to gain interest in your product or service.

This product or service can be anything you are trying to sell –- from pitching books, workshops, seminars, and coaching to selling a product or service for a large company. The basic email marketing approach is the same. Just adapt the process to your niche and the type of clients or customers you are pitching.

Identifying the Right Person to Contact

Whether you meet someone from a company at an event or have to research that company, the place to start is with the person who makes the decisions for buying your type of product or service. When you meet someone, you need to ask if he or she is the decision maker, and if not, who is at the company. Then, ask to be introduced at the event or later and take it from there. Alternatively, if you are doing research online or in a local directory, you may need to make a phone call or send an email to identify the decision maker.

Who Is the Decision Maker?

The decision maker varies depending on the size of the company, and in larger companies, there may be different decision makers handling different types of products and services. Or sometimes a team of people make the major decisions.

For example, if you are pitching a book, an editor may make an initial decision, but then the book has to be approved by the editorial and marketing committees – though your liaison for the company is still the editor. If you are pitching a software product to a company, you may need to first talk to a certain person who introduces or greenlights these programs, but he or she will similarly need to connect with other people for input. On the other hand, in a smaller company, the president or CEO may make most of the decisions.

Thus, a first step is determining who will make the decision – and what channel you need to go through, as necessary, to reach that person. Some typical titles of this person include the following:

- <u>Very Small Company</u> (1-5 employees) Usually the Owner or CEO.
- <u>Small Company</u> (5-25 employees) Maybe a VP, though the decision could still be up to the Owner or CEO or possibly someone in a specialized role for acquiring new products.
- <u>Medium-Sized Company</u> (26-50 employees) Now a VP or higher-up officer might make the decisions, though there might be specialized roles for certain types of purchases. Some typical titles might be a Sales Manager, Marketing Manager, or Business Development Manager.
- <u>Large Company</u> (51-250 employees). Generally, there will be divisions handling different types of products or services, and you will deal with the heads of these departments. These heads might be in charge of overall functions, such as a Sales Manager, Marketing Manager, or Business Development Manager, or they might be in charge of a special division according to function, such as a Production Manager.
- <u>Very Large Company</u> (250 employees or more) Sometimes these companies have regional divisions, and if so, look for decision makers at this level, such as a State or Regional Marketing Manager or the manager for a particular city or county.

Thus, to find the appropriate decision maker, find out about the size and scope of the company. If it's a large company, learn about its structure and at what level decisions are made and by who. Then, target the person in that position. While ideally, you want to connect with the final decision maker, in many cases, you have to work your way up through channels. Or even if you meet that top person at an event, he or she may direct you down to the appropriate decision-making level for your product or service. So be flexible on who you approach and how.

How Do You Find the Decision Maker?

There are several ways to find the decision maker. Use the approach or combination of approaches that works best for you. These include the following:

- Your Personal Contacts. These are the people you meet through local business networking and referral groups, through the Chamber of Commerce, or through people you have previously worked with both locally or in other locations. Sometimes that contact may be the decision maker, or they can put you in touch with the decision maker in their company or connect you with people who can make that connection.

- Company Website or Listing in a Local or Industry Directory. Sometimes you can find an employee directory online which includes titles of who to contact, and these may even include emails and phone numbers. You can also obtain local directories, such as published by a Chamber of Commerce, or you might obtain an industry directory for your area. For example, in the Bay Area, the *Business Times* publishes a listing of businesses and organizations in different fields in each issue, and then once a year, it combines all of these lists together into the *Book of Lists*. Besides physical addresses, these listings variously include websites, phone numbers, and emails. These directories are an excellent source of leads for business in a particular area or industry.

- Manta.Com. This is a website where you can put in the name of a business and get the company's website, phone number (unless unlisted), and address. To illustrate, I put in my company, and though I never signed up to be listed in the Manta directory, there I am. The directory might also be useful for you to get a listing, since they will post your company name in over 50 places, plus other services.

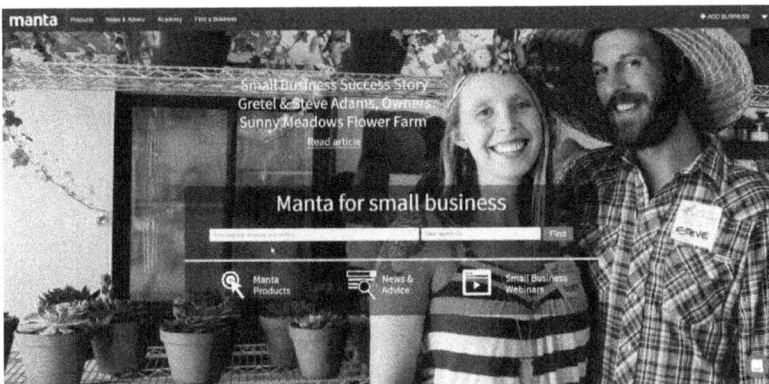

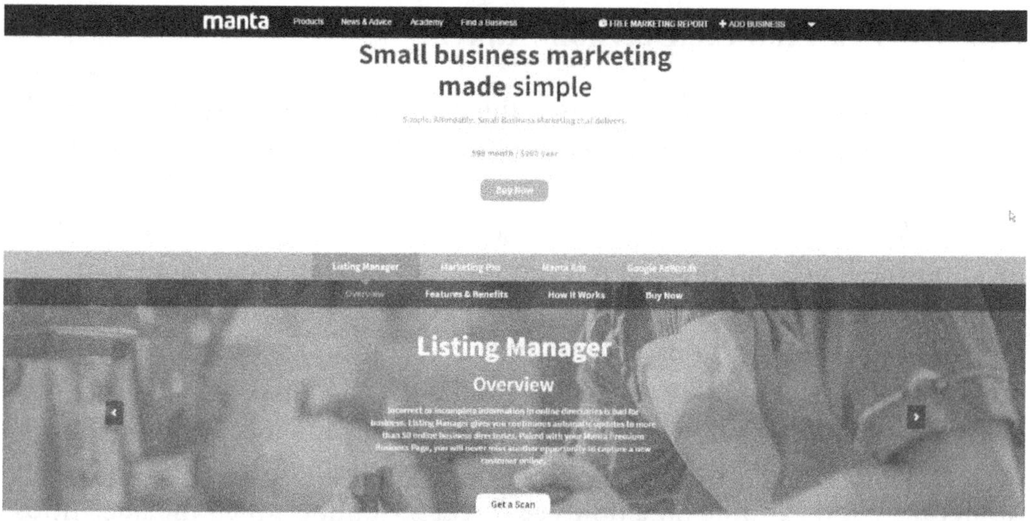

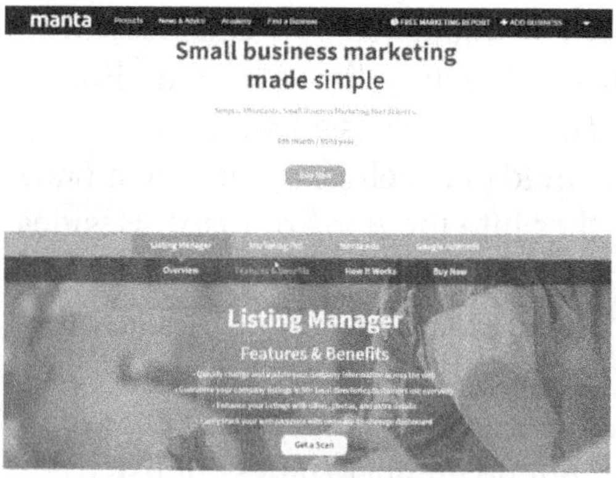

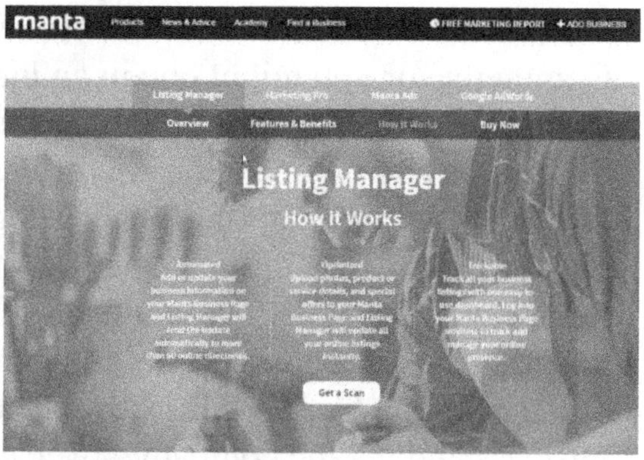

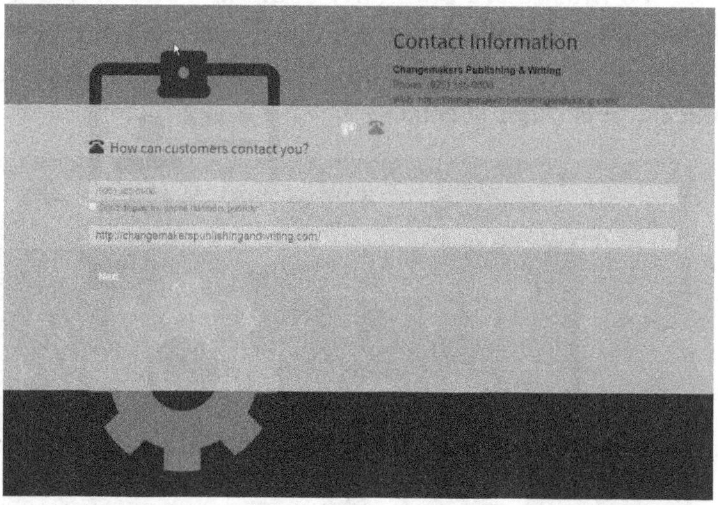

LinkedIn. You can find company information by doing a search of companies which will take you to the company profile page, where you will find contact information, as well as the names of officers and employees.

Following is more information on how to use each of these sources to find decision makers.

Using Your Personal Network

Your personal network includes friends, family members, relatives, and business associates who might be decision makers or might be able to refer you to them. As will be discussed in the book on using emails for referral marketing, your contacts can be divided into influencers, second level, and third level contacts, so you can focus more on the contacts who are best positioned to respond to your product or service or refer you to those who are better able to do so.

Often through your personal network or at business networking meetings, you will not meet the top person or key decision maker at a large company. But if the company is your target market, ask someone from that company who is the decision maker, and if appropriate, use their name as a referral. Having a name of a person in the company is ideal to help to open doors for you, since you are not just doing a cold call, you have a referral from within the company.

When you do talk to such an employee, explain that you are trying to get in touch with the person in charge of making decisions in your area. If you can get a phone number or email, great. Otherwise, you can check on the company website for that information or call. The goal is to get the person's email, so you can use that to introduce yourself and your product or service – rather than directly talking to the person first.

Using the Company Website

You can sometimes find individual emails for people in a company on the "Contact Us" or "Staff" pages on its website. Then, you can email the person who seems to be the decision maker for your type of product or service directly. If you aren't sure, direct your email to several people or to the person who appears to have the higher position and copy the others. Usually, the appropriate person will respond to you or you will be advised who to contact. If there is only an info@ email, you can use that, though it is better to call the main number and ask for information about who is in charge of making decisions in your area and his or her email, so you can send a personalized email to that person. If you can't get the email that way, you can look it up.

Apart from looking for contact information, use the company website to get more information about the company and what it does. This might give you insights into how to best pitch your product or service and show how it will benefit the company. You will also show that you are knowledgeable about the company, which contributes to your credibility and authority.

Using a Business Directory or List

A business directory or list can be a great source of information to get leads. If the directory includes emails linked to a particular name, rather than just an info@ email that's ideal. But often the list will just include the address, phone number, and website information, along with the name of the top person at the company, who may or may not be the decision maker you want to reach.

In general, use this directory or list as a source of information about the company website, where you can get more information on the company. Also, the directory will give you the company phone number you can call for more information.

Calling a Company for Contact Information

Once you have the company phone number, your goal is to get the email of the appropriate person to contact. Even if you get switched to that person, don't try to do a pitch now, since that person won't know who you are. Rather, use the email to introduce yourself. Certainly, a compelling phone call may work with some people. But my usual reaction – and the reaction of most others I know – is to hang up if a phone solicitor I don't know tries to pitch me something.

Instead, call to ask for information. You might start by asking who is in charge of purchasing or arranging for programs for whatever you do. If you can use the name of someone in the company who referred you, say that this person did so and indicate how you know that person. If you have obtained names of various people from the company from a website or business list, you can mention that you weren't sure who to contact and mention a name or two. But don't try to imply that you know those people or say that they referred you, because doing so could backfire in a big way if you are caught in a lie. Then, you probably won't be successful in getting work or selling a product to that company.

If you have reached the correct person, simply ask what email you should use to send some information that will benefit the company. Or if the person mentions someone else in the company, ask what that person's title is and what email to use to send this information that will benefit the company. Also, ask for the name of the person you are speaking to, since you can use that when you introduce yourself to the decision maker.

If during the call, the person who you are speaking to asks for more information about you or whatever you are pitching, by all means tell them with a brief sentence or two, like you are giving a 5-10 second elevator pitch, where you emphasize the benefits. For instance, if I were asked, I would tell someone: "I do workshops for companies on how their employees can become more creative and productive." By putting the benefits first, you show what the company will gain, such as more profits, in working with you.

Should the person want more details, this is the perfect time to indicate that you have some information you would like to send by email and who should you send it to, if not that person.

Once you know the name of the contact person and their email, thank the person you spoke to for his or her help. Sometimes, you will get a direct line to call, so you can follow-up; otherwise, go through the receptionist or voice mail, and if the person isn't there when you call you will often get the receptionist or voice mail anyway.

When you send your email, include the name of whoever referred you or who you spoke to, along with a short description of what you are offering. I'll go into more detail on how to write an effective email and subject line in a future book. Then, two or three days after sending your email, if the person hasn't already responded, you can follow-up by phone to see if he or she got your email, has reviewed it, or wants to discuss it further. If your email wasn't received, send your email again, and follow-up as before. Then, as appropriate, set up a phone conversation or meeting to further discuss what you are offering.

Using LinkedIn

You can use LinkedIn to find more information about a company, much like you might use the company website. Just put their name in the LinkedIn search box. This will give you their company profile, if it has one, and itmay direct to the company website.

For example, suppose I have a product or service that might appeal to banks, and I'm looking for local banks. I found the name of one bank listed in the local chamber directory, Heritage Bank of Commerce. This gives me some additional information beyond the address, phone number and website.

If you have a premium LinkedIn account, that will give you even more information about the bank.

Specialties
Business Banking, Lending, Cash Management, Checking Accounts

Website
http://www.heritagebankofcommerce.com

Industry
Banking

Type
Public Company

Headquarters
150 Almaden Blvd. San Jose, California 95113 United States

Company Size
201-500 employees

Founded
1994

Uncover unique insights about Heritage Bank of Commerce

Try Premium for free

Employee distribution by department

Employee growth rates

Notable leadership additions

Trends in hiring activity

In other cases, your search may bring up the names of different people at different branches of the company, such as this search for the California Bank of Commerce.

The search will also indicate the level of my connection to this person, and when I click on the first person, I can see she's at a nearby branch in Pleasant Hill and is a vice-president and regional manager. I can also discover how I am connected to her. In this case, I have two connections – a commercial lender from a couple of my networking groups, and a real estate broker from a referral group I used to belong to. So this contact would provide an ideal entry. I could mention that I have these connections – though I wouldn't say anyone referred me unless they did. Then, I can phone her to see if she or someone else at the bank is the correct person to contact about my project. If she is the correct person, I would then ask for her email to send her information. If she isn't the right contact, I would ask for the email of the appropriate person. Since I have this information from her, I can now say that she referred me in the subject line of my email, which makes it likely that the recipient will open it.

Additionally, a LinkedIn profile can give me even more information. Besides indicating my connections, it will indicate the groups the VP/regional manager belongs to and the other companies she is following, as well as people similar to her, such as branch managers in other banks. So that information can lead to still other contacts who may be interested in my product or service.

Although LinkedIn gives you the ability to contact someone through LinkedIn's InMail system, it is better to get this person's email from calling the company or using the company's standard email format if you can determine this, such as First.Last@ or First@. It is better to use an email, since a person may not check their LinkedIn account regularly. You can find how recently ad how often they check their emails by clicking the "Send (Name) InMail" button, which will indicate that person's recent activity. Often a person may not have checked their LinkedIn mail for one or two weeks or longer. By contrast, people normally check their email at least once or several times a day.

Alternatively, if you know you want to contact individuals in a certain position in a certain area, you can use LinkedIn to find that information, too. For instance, if I type in "bank manager" East Bay, I will get a number of bank managers in that area. Be sure to put the phrase you are searching for in quotes or you will get a more general search.

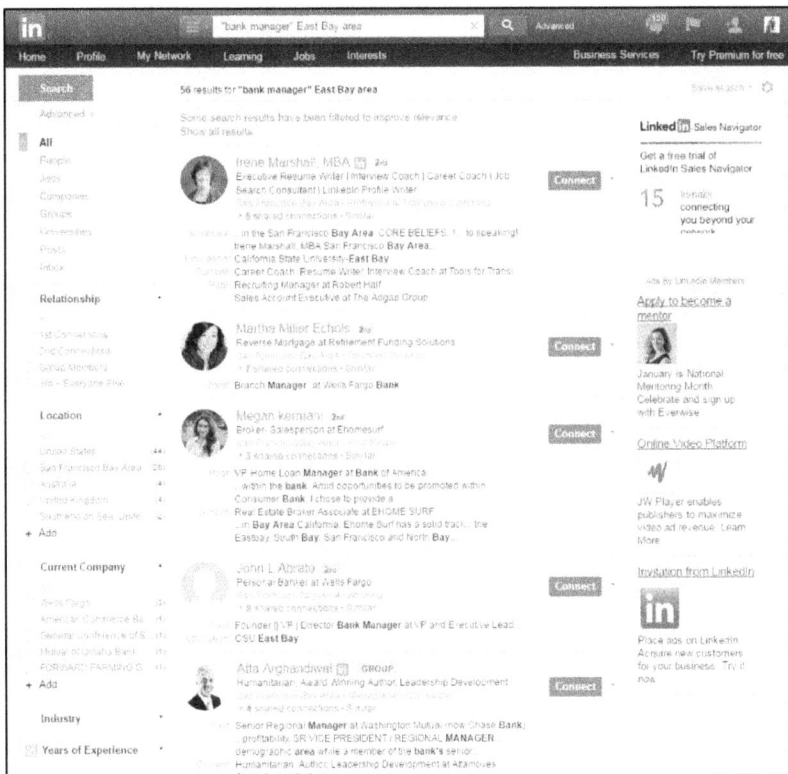

Sometimes you have to experiment to find words that LinkedIn recognizes. For instance, when I put in "bank manager" Contra Costa County or Contra Costa, this wasn't recognized, but East Bay area was.

159

You can also look up people you meet – or anyone for that matter, and see who they are connected to, the groups they belong to, the influencers they are following, and the companies they are connected to. Then, you can reach out to any of these individuals or companies and mention that you are connected to a person they are connected to – but again don't say that this person referred you unless they did. In this way, you can build your own connections, and as you connect to more people, ask them who in their company makes decisions about your product or service, and send your email to that person.

Keeping Track of the Decision Makers You Contact

In sum, you can use all of these techniques to build your network by finding the decision maker, obtaining that person's email, and sending an email message about what you do as an introduction. Then, follow up in various ways, usually by phone or by setting up a meeting.

As you follow these steps, your network of connections will grow, and you will find you are getting more and more clients and customers.

To keep track of this growing network, you need to set up some system, such as an Excel file or a Customer Relationship Management (CRM) system, to be discussed in a future book.

The next chapter discusses still more ways to find anyone's email if you aren't able to find it from the people in your own network, from company websites, or through LinkedIn.

CHAPTER 3: FINDING EMAILS

Sometimes you know someone's name but don't have their business card or slip of paper with their email or you misplaced it. Or maybe you want to contact an individual at a particular company directly, but all you have is an info@ email, and you aren't able to get the email from the receptionist.

Well, there's hope. There are a number of services online which will tell you the email format for a particular company. If employees use several formats, these services will give you the alternatives, too. Then, you can use an online email tester to check if that's a valid email – although you can always send an email to different variations yourself and see what comes back and what doesn't.

The Most Common Email Formats

In big companies, officers and employees commonly use the same format. This doesn't work where people get creative or use numbers along with their name. But otherwise, most people use the company's format to contact people when they know their names.

The five most common formats are these:
FirstName.LastName@
FirstNameLastName@
FirstInitialLastName@
First@
FirstName_LastName@

Finding the Company Email Format

You can find a number of sites which list company email formats if you put the phrase "company email formats" in Google Search. Nearly a dozen turn up on the first page of a search. Here are some of the most popular ones.

One is Email Format (https://email-format.com), where you can search by company name for free, though there is an expanded yearly pricing of as little as $15 a year for more extended searches. Though the service seems to be based in Australia, it has email formats for corporations all over the world, such as when I did a search for the Bank of the West. The results show the most common formats, followed by others in descending order of frequency.

162

Another popular source of company emails is Hunter https://hunter.io. You put in a domain name to find the email format, such as when I put in the Bank of the West. In this case, the service indicated the number of emails found and provides some examples of names from the bank (with some letters covered to conceal the person's full name) and includes the apparent formula for the bank (First.Last@). Besides this free searching, the service offers an account where you get 150 free searches a month, and for a monthly fee starting at $39 for 1000 searches, you can download the results as a .csv (comma separated values) file, if you want to do a bulk personalized mailing to those listed.

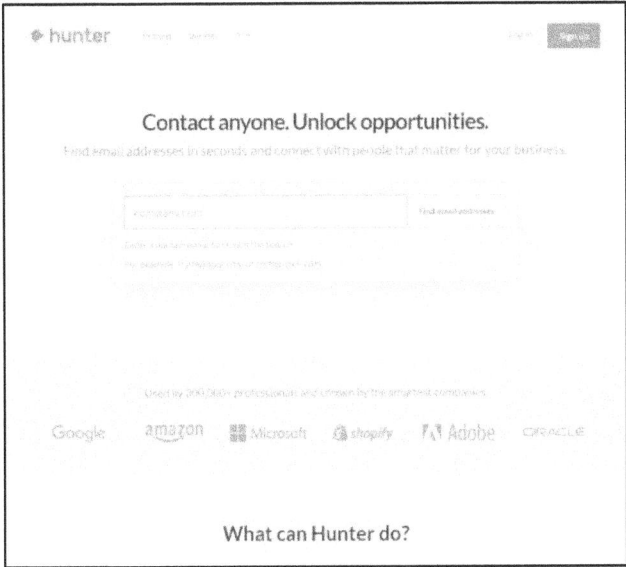

Pricing

Simple and transparent.

Monthly • Yearly

	Free	Starter	Growth	Pro	Enterprise
	$0 / month	$39 / month	$79 / month	$159 / month	$329 / month
			Most popular		
Requests What is a request on Hunter?	150	1 K	5 K	20 K	50 K
CSV exports Download all the results of one or multiple Domain Search(es).	✕	✓	✓	✓	✓

Get started
Start using Hunter today, upgrade when ready.

Sign up and get 150 free requests/month.

Create a free account

Need more? Please contact us at contact@hunter.io

Still another source is Emails4Corporations, which is a free site provided by Google at https://sites.google.com/site/emails4corporations. It includes a breakdown by industry or geographic area, too.

In this case, I didn't find a listing of the Bank of the West. But the site lists many larger banks, such as Wells Fargo and Bank of America.

164

This site is especially useful if you want to target a particular industry.

Still another source of emails is Toofr at www.toofr.com. You put in a website or company name and guess the name of the person you are trying to reach. The company gives you the email patterns and positively guessed emails for millions of domains. It also provides you with a listing of the names of people at that company with that name, such as in the example of a person who works for Uber.

Should you be interested in contacting people at new start-ups, Toofr has lists it can sell, too.

You can test out the service with 12 credits, which means you get back 12 emails that you have tested or guessed which have a relatively high confidence level score of being correct.

Still another testing service is Connect Data.com (https://connect.data.com)

This service is designed to help you contact the right business contacts by company, location, title, or function, and you can try the service out with your first two contacts for free. The service is part of Salesforce, so it is part of a huge network which helps salespeople find good leads in their industry.

Finally, one more source of email leads is Hoovers (www.hoovers.com).

The company not only creates lead lists but provides research on a company. It even has a link to Dun & Bradstreet, which provides very accurate information, unavailable elsewhere.

However, it's fairly pricey, at $1.20 to 1.50 for each lead that includes an email, though an advantage is getting carefully validated current emails.

If you want to target a particular industry, you can get an industry report from Hoovers.

You can search its industry directory.

If you put in an industry you want to target – for instance, I selected the Film and Video Industry – you can get a report, which includes website and media links.

The report itself, which costs $129, looks something like this.

Testing the Validity of an Email

To test if an email you have is valid, you can put it in an email tester, such as MailTester.com (http://mailtester.com). For instance, after I put in one of my current emails – changemakers@pacbell.net, the assessment indicated that my email was valid, along with providing source data about the mail servers associated with the domain that only a computer specialist might care about.

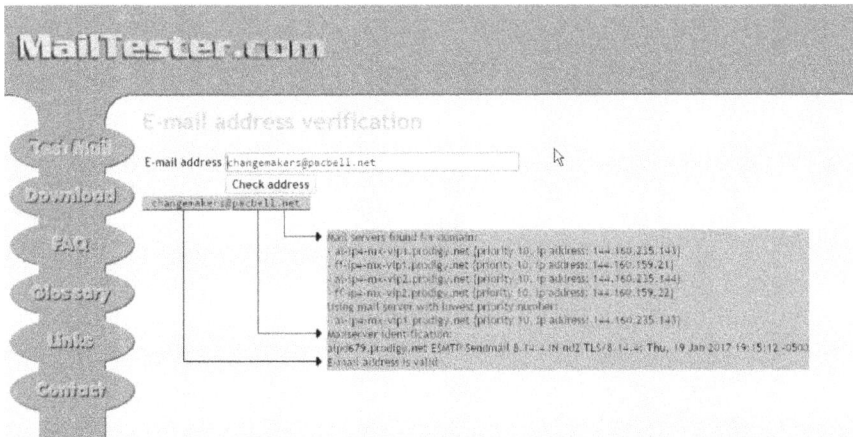

CHAPTER 4: TRACKING YOUR EMAILS

How can you tell if someone received your email. Some software programs can track this, including Yesware, Hubspot, and Boomerang.

Yesware can track who clicks on your ads. It has an email tracking tool that tells you who is opening your messages and lets you check the status of your tracked email from inside your inbox.

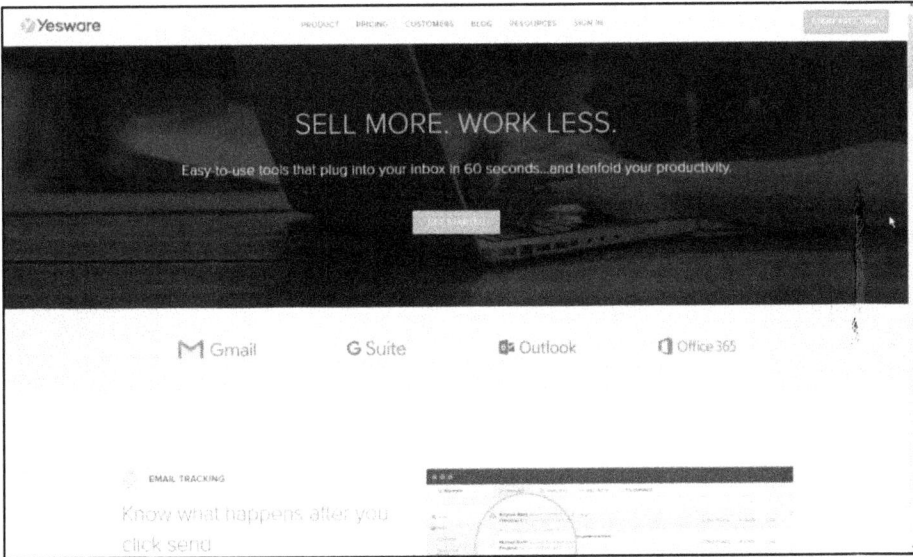

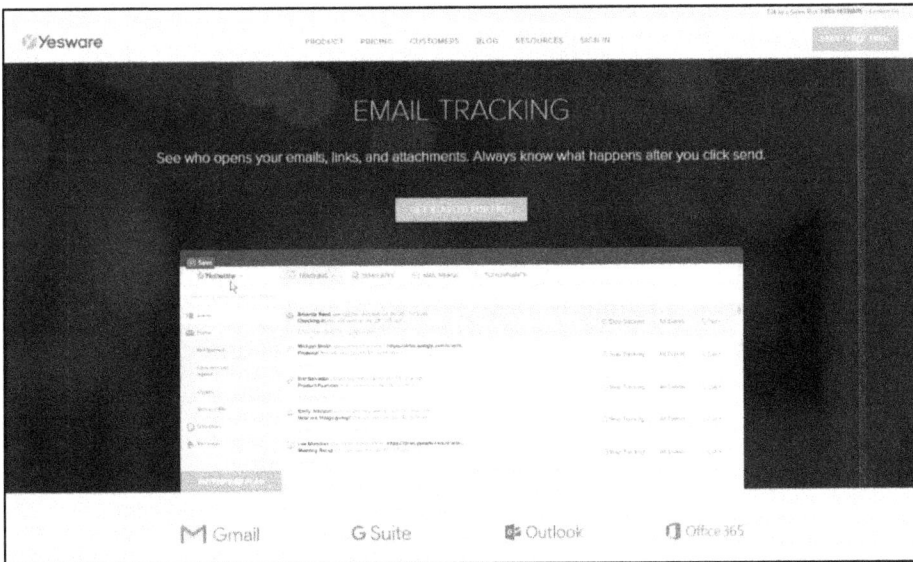

For example, the software tells you if someone opened your message, clicked on a link, or opened an attachment. It indicates if someone viewed a presentation you sent. That information can help you know how someone received your message and how you might better follow up.

The pricing is relatively low-cost, too. You can try it out for 28 days for free, and after that you can sign-up for as little as $12 a month for a single user.

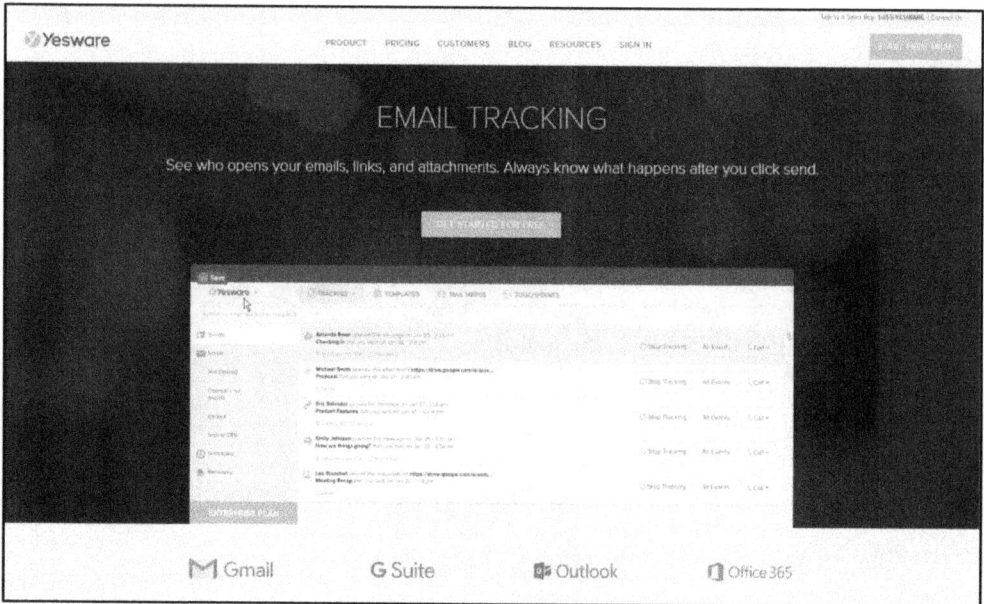

Another platform is Boomerang, which you can use with Gmail, Outlook, or Android phones and other devices, though it's primarily for Gmail. It enables you to schedule emails to go out at certain times, and you can get receipts if someone opens your email, or Boomerang can send out reminders if someone hasn't responded to your email.

The platform additionally has software that can help you write a more effective actionable email, based on its analysis of thousands of emails to see what works better to attract more opens and clicks.

Boomerang is the leader in email productivity software. Since 2010, Boomerang has helped millions of email users focus on what matters, when it matters. From making sure messages receive responses to revolutionizing how we schedule meetings, thanks to Boomerang, effective digital communication has never been easier.

Here's how the app works if you are going to send out a letter in Gmail. You end up writing shorter headlines, include questions to engage the reader, reduce the reading level, and otherwise use tips to create a better letter that will generate a better response.

Like most new software programs, you can try Boomerang for free, in this case for 30 days for its pro-plan. After that, you can continue to use it for free with its Basic Plan of tracking up to 10 messages each month, or you can sign up for one of its Personal, Professional, or Premium plan for

$5 to $50 a month, where you can track unlimited messages. In all of the plans, the site tracks clicks, reads, and responses, and can send out reminders. The more expensive plans have some added features, such as mobile access.

Boomerang for Gmail Plans and Pricing

Try now, pay only if you like it!

All new Boomerang accounts come with a **Free 30-day Trial** of Boomerang Professional. So go ahead and try it before you decide that you want to subscribe. Credit card information is **not required** to get started.

If you don't choose to subscribe to one of the paid subscriptions at the end of the 30 days, you can continue to use the free Basic plan as long as you'd like!

	BASIC	PERSONAL	PRO	PREMIUM
		$4.99/Month	$14.99/Month	$49.99/Month
	FREE	Sign Up	Sign Up	Sign Up
Message Credits	10 per Month	Unlimited	Unlimited	Unlimited
Supported Accounts	Gmail/G Suite (Google Apps)	Gmail	Gmail/G Suite (Google Apps)	Gmail/G Suite (Google Apps)
Send Later	✓	✓	✓	✓
Boomerang Reminders	✓	✓	✓	✓
Response Tracking	✓	✓	✓	✓
Read Receipts	✓	✓	✓	✓
Click Tracking	✓	✓	✓	✓
Mobile Access		✓	✓	✓
Notes		✓	✓	✓
Respondable	✓	✓	✓	✓
Respondable Advanced Machine Learning			✓	✓
Recurring Messages			✓	✓

Should you want to use Boomerang with Outlook or on a mobile device, the platform is free, but you have to have an Outlook365 or Exchange Account, or on a mobile device it only integrates with Gmail, Google Apps, and Microsoft Exchange accounts, though more integrations may be coming.

Another program, Hubspot, has email tracking software, which you can obtain at https://www.hubspot.com/products/sales/email-tracking.

EMAIL TRACKING

While you can get started with a free trial, the email tracking program is quite pricey, because it is part of a suite of services. These include email sequencing and scheduling, email templates, information on what companies are visiting your website, and scheduling meetings at a time that works for everyone. As indicated below, pricing starts at $ for 100 contacts a month, though you need an onboarding package of at least $600. Onboarding is the organizational software which helps new employees acquire the needed knowledge and skills to become effective organizational members, such as formal meetings, lectures, videos, and computer based orientations. If these other features are useful, great. If you just want email tracking, this is too expensive for you.

Still another program is Mixmax (www.mixmax.com), which integrates with Gmail, Google inbox, and Salesforce. Its home page tells you how many emails you sent, as well as how many recipients got it, opened it, clicked it, downloaded anything you sent, and how many replied.

As with other email tracking programs, you can try it for free and then get it for as little as $9 monthly for the basic tracking features. With the more expensive $24 and $49 a month features, you can get templates, CRM tracking, and more.

Another tool to find out the connections of someone on Gmail, LinkedIn, Facebook, and Twitter, is Discoverly, which is an extension you can add to Chrome. It can be used along with other email connection and discovery tools, including Buffer, Boomerang, Hunter, Yesware, Rapportive, and Right Inbox. The direct link is http://discover.ly/

Another useful Gmail plug-in is Rapportive (www.rappportive.com), which will enable you to find the LinkedIn profiles within your inbox. It can quickly tell you what these people do, your shared connections, and where they are, so if they are nearby, you might arrange to meet. Plus, you can readily contact them without leaving Gmail.

Finally, Right Inbox (www.rightinbox.com) is another tool to make email management easier. Among other things you can use it to schedule recurring emails, add private notes to emails, schedule emails to send later, and set up email reminders.

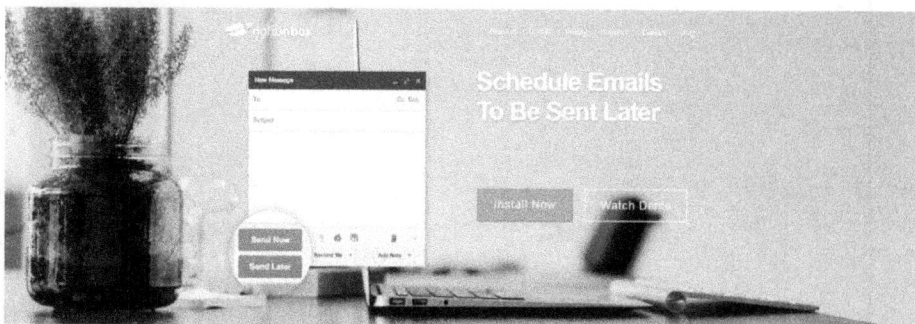

Under a free plan, you can set up these features for up to 10 emails a month. For unlimited emails, the cost is $5.95 a month if paid annually, or $7.95 if paid each month.

So now that you know all these tools for finding emails and tracking your results when you send out emails, as they say: "Seek and you shall find," and "Get tracking." In a future book, I'll describe what to say in your emails for the best results.

BOOK V: BUYING AND VALIDATING EMAIL LISTS FOR LARGE MAILINGS

CHAPTER 1: WHEN TO BUY EMAIL LISTS

Another way to get emails is buying lists, which can range from already created lists based on industry, interests, or geography, to targeted lists which are created for you, based on your criteria. The prices can vary widely from different services. In general, an already created lists costs much less per name, from as little as .005 or .015 a name for the longer lists selling for about $100 to $200 a list to the more carefully constructed lists where you can expect to pay about .45-.50 a name or more.

One caution with the already created lists. You need to run the names through an email cleaning or validation service, so you can clean up the list to get only good emails. The service validates the list by doing its own test to see which emails are good, meaning no bounces. In my experience of using these lists for several clients interested in contacting selected groups, such as CPAs, financial advisers, real estate agents, and other professionals, good emails can range from 25-80% of a list, so you definitely need to clean up these lists with a validation service, or you will find your own email service blocked for spamming by the email servers you use.

Once you clean up your list, you can break it down to target your own city, county, region, or state. To do so, import the Excel or .cvs file you purchased into database software, such as Access. Then, you can do a query on the total database to pull out the individuals or companies in a certain area, and later do a mailing to only that group.

If you obtain customized targeted lists from a more expensive email list provider, you can preselect individuals meeting a certain criteria, including their geographic area. Also, these companies they normally guarantee less than 10% returns, and they commonly offer refunds for any returned email. So these lists could be safe to use without going through a validation service, though perhaps do a check when you first use one of these services to be sure it's assurances are accurate.

With this caveat, buying already created or customized lists can work very well in certain fields, where you want to reach out to a large number of prospects at a time. Then, after an initial mailing, you can do follow-up mailings to these individuals. I have found a good approach after cleaning a list through a validation service is to send out an introduction email in which I briefly introduce my company. I also indicate that I hope to send out emails with information that they may find beneficial for their business (adapted to appeal to their industry), and ask them to indicate any corrections in who I should contact. I have found that most recipients don't respond, though some respond with corrected information. This mailing also enables me to further clean up the list to eliminate any bounces or requests to be removed.

Following are examples of companies which I have used for buying already completed lists or which have contacted me about how I can get more expensive targeted lists from them. You can find many more sources for buying these lists if you do a search on Google for "email lists" or "email list sellers."

CHAPTER 2: BUYING ALREADY CREATED LISTS

The following companies specialize in already created lists, plus some do bulk mailing campaigns, where you not only buy a list, but you can send out a mailing through them. Using the company for a mailing makes sense if you are sending out more than 5000 or 10,000 emails. Even if you use a SMTP service for sending out emails, it takes a long time to send out a very large number of emails, and you risk a large number of returns, even if the bounce rate is only 5-10%, leading to problems with your email service provider. For example, with 10,000 emails, you might get 500 to 1000 back.

I did such a mailing from a company after I bought a list of book readers with one company for a client, paying $129 for 100,000 emails. Then, I paid $99 for a mailing to that list. Since I also got a copy of that list, I could import it into Access and breakdown the contacts by city, county, or state in order to later do more targeted and much smaller mailings myself.

Following are the list providers I worked with and a sampling of the lists available from them. If you go on Google Search and look for "email list," "email list seller," or "email list broker," you'll find dozens of companies listed.

One of the email sellers I used to buy a dozen lists is Emarketing Solutions, http://www.americaint.com or http://www.emarketing-matrix.com, based in Pompano Beach, Florida. The company offers hundreds of lists organized by Industry, by SIC (Standard Industrial Classification – a four digit code the US government uses to classify industries), and by NAICS codes (North American Industry Classification System – a four or five digital standard used by the Federal Government to classify businesses to obtain statistical data, which replaced the SIC code, which is still in use). The NAICS codes are listed at the Bureau of Labor Statistics. https://www.bls.gov/iag/tgs/iag_index_naics.htm

Here's the Emarketing Solutions home page.

You can obtain huge lists of businesses, updated monthly, identified by their SIC or NAICS code, for as little as $99 for 100,000 names, and a few hundred more for up to millions of businesses.

You can get breakdowns by state starting at $99 up to $399 depending upon the number of businesses in that state.

I mainly used their listings by industry or occupation, based on their SIC codes, the default, although you can see a listing by NAISC codes, too. There are hundreds of listings – about 750 in the list I printed out, which range in price from $79 to $199, based on the number of contacts in that category, with most listings priced at $79 or $99. From these listings, I selected Book Publishers, Book Stores, Legal Services, Lawyers, and Professional Organizations, since my client wanted to pitch a book about the criminal justice system.

You can select the most appropriate industry or occupational categories for whatever you are marketing.

Or if you are reaching out to consumers, the company offers consumer lists based on interests, hobbies, lifestyle, and buying habits. I selected "books" and did a mailing through the company for 100,000 book readers. Later, I imported the list into Access and broke it down for a selective mailing.

A second email list seller I used for about a dozen lists was EmailListUS (www.emaillistus.com)

You can target particular industries that are especially popular, such as schools, hotels, restaurants, dentists, healthcare, and real estate.

The cost of these lists, based on the number of records, range from $89 to $180 for a mailing to 100,000 to 1 million contacts.

You can also obtain lists of selected types of businesses, as I did for my client. To obtain still more lists for pitching his criminal justice book, I selected lists for attorneys, county government courts, financial advisory services, fund raising consultants and organizations, human services organizations, public and institutional libraries, psychologists, retirement communities, and senior citizen centers. In this case, there were over 500 categories to choose from. So you can select those businesses or organizations that are a good fit for your marketing campaign.

Finally, the other seller I obtained some lists from was Oddity Software, which has some databases with emails, though their databases range from those with no emails to those with some emails from 10-70%, to some databases with all emails, such as a database for 3.5 million company executives. Thus, you have to check to determine the percentage of emails for the databases that might seem right for your market campaign, and if the percentages are too low, don't get that list.

Here's a sampling of their database download catalog, which includes their top inventory lists consisting of about 600 categories.

If you are interested in a particular category, you can check out the contents of the database to determine the percentage of listings that have emails. For instance, take real estate brokers. They have a high percentage of emails – 86%.

Here's where you find that information in its database of field statistics.

TABLE SCHEMA DATABASE FIELD STATISTICS

Field	Records	Percent	Type	Comment
id	47,510	100%	int(11)	Unique Identifier
con_full_name	43,701	92%	varchar(100)	Broker - Full Name
biz_name	46,050	97%	varchar(150)	Business Name
biz_email	41,019	86%	varchar(75)	Broker Contact Email Address
biz_fax	20,967	44%	varchar(20)	Business Fax Number
biz_phone	44,202	93%	varchar(20)	Business Phone Number
e_address	47,319	100%	varchar(100)	Physical Address
e_city	47,507	100%	varchar(50)	Physical Address City
e_state	47,510	100%	varchar(20)	Physical Address State / Province
e_postal	47,469	100%	varchar(7)	Physical Address Postal Code
e_zip_full	18,371	39%	varchar(10)	Zip +4 for US Physical Addresses
e_country	47,510	100%	varchar(20)	Physical Address Country
loc_county	47,442	100%	varchar(40)	Physical Address County
loc_area_code	47,442	100%	varchar(3)	Physical Address Area Code

195

By contrast, if you want to contact lawyers, only 12% of the lawyers have emails, though it's a very large database of 215,000 contacts --about 26,000 with emails, which might make the list worth getting. The percentage of emails is at the end of the list indicating the types of information in this database.

In getting any of these purchased lists, check on the date of the last update, since the more recent the update, the more likely you are getting a relatively clean list. For example, some of Oddity Software's lists were compiled in 2011, such as its list of 3.5 million business executives or 1.5 million home opportunity seekers. Thus, you might expect a high return rate, since these are over five years old.

You'll find many other email list sellers. It's best to choose those with the higher rankings, such as on page one of a Google Search, since these will be more likely to have more traffic and buyers.

Yet, even if you get these rankings, in buying any of these lists, be sure to run them through a email cleaner or validation service. This way you will be more likely to have good emails and a lower bounce rate, though you often will get some bounces due to servers being down and other factors that are affecting delivery now.

The next section features some email validation services I used.

CHAPTER 3: VALIDATING YOUR EMAILS

Validating your email list before you do a mailing is critical to eliminate any bad emails, because some lists were put together several years ago, so many emails may no longer be current, and you don't want a high bounce rate -- a sure way to get bounced from the email servers and services that send out your emails.

You can find numerous validation services if you do a Google search for terms such as "email cleaners," "email list cleaners," or "email validators." Depending on how many emails you want validated and which service you use, prices range from .002 cents an email to .01 cents, so if you have a large number of names to validate – say you bought a list with 50,000 names, your costs can range from $100 to $500.

Some services have packages, where you buy a large number of email clean-ups to get a lower rate and use them over several weeks for a series of email validations. For example, you might buy a package for validating 200,000 emails at a lower price and apply each mail box validation against that, rather than paying a higher price – say .005 a name – for a series of smaller pay-as-you-go validations.

After you do such a cleanup, However, I recommend doing a further test yourself with the validated emails, where you briefly introduce yourself. Then, check if you have the correct contact information, so you can send them information on different books, programs, products, or services that will help them with one or two benefits for individuals with their type of job, hobby, or interest. And if they are not interested, you can offer to take them off the list.

In this way, you firm up if you have a good email and update it with the latest contacts. You can also remove anyone who doesn't want to be on your list.

Following are the two services I primarily used to do my own list cleanups, followed by services that came up on the top of the list of email validators when I did a Google search.

The Validation Services I Used

The two services I used for validations are Mailbox Validator and Data Validation. Here's more information about them.

I used MailBox Validator (www.mailboxvalidator.com) for several dozen lists.

One thing I liked about them is their plans, which include a free trial where you can send out a 100 queries at no charge. Then, you can determine the best plan for you based on how many emails you plan to validate over a month from 1000 to 1 million, with your price per name ranging from .02 to .0007 cents an email. I usually used their $199 plan where 100,000 emails are priced at .002 each.

The way it works is you upload your original file with emails in a .csv format and indicate which column is for emails. Within about 24 hours, you get back a notice that your files are ready. You get your file with all of your original emails, plus a file of good results and good emails only. You can upload the good results or good emails only into any program for sending a mailing to your list, or you can break down this list by different categories, such as city, county, and state, and mail to a certain area.

For example, here's a copy of my own account, which lists all of the emails I validated, along with files I can download for all results, good results, and good emails.

The other service I used is DataValidation (http://www.datavalidation.com), which works closely with the major email service providers (ESP), which include MailChimp, AWeber, SendGrid, MailGun, MailUp or Emma. Should you use any of these services, you can link your account and monitor your lists at no charge. You can also use an Email Assurance subscription in order to analyze any lists in your ESP account on a daily basis, rather than cleaning your lists every few months.

This regular cleanup helps to protect your deliverabilty and prevents bad email bounces from affecting your campaign statistics.

The way the Data Validation service works is that you get your email list back with a grade for each email, from A+ to F. The A+ emails are those that are not only deliverable, but they have an engagement history based on the recipient's email clicks and opens. The A emails are considered deliverable and safe. The B emails are ones where the host is set to accept all mail, though it may bounce some mail back to the sender, which can affect the sender's IP reputation.

The service recommends that all emails with a B grade should be separated and later retested to make sure they are valid. The D emails are considered indeterminate, meaning that the address has a mail server that is running and accepting connections, but the service wasn't able to connect. Finally, the F emails are considered unsafe. Both the D and F rated emails should be removed from your database or marked so you don't send to them.

One advantage of this service is you can check on the validity of any list, before you decide to pay to validate it, and then that process will tell you the percent of A, B, D, and F files. For example, you can upload a list from a MailChimp account, from your computer, or from another file source such as Evernote or Google Drive.

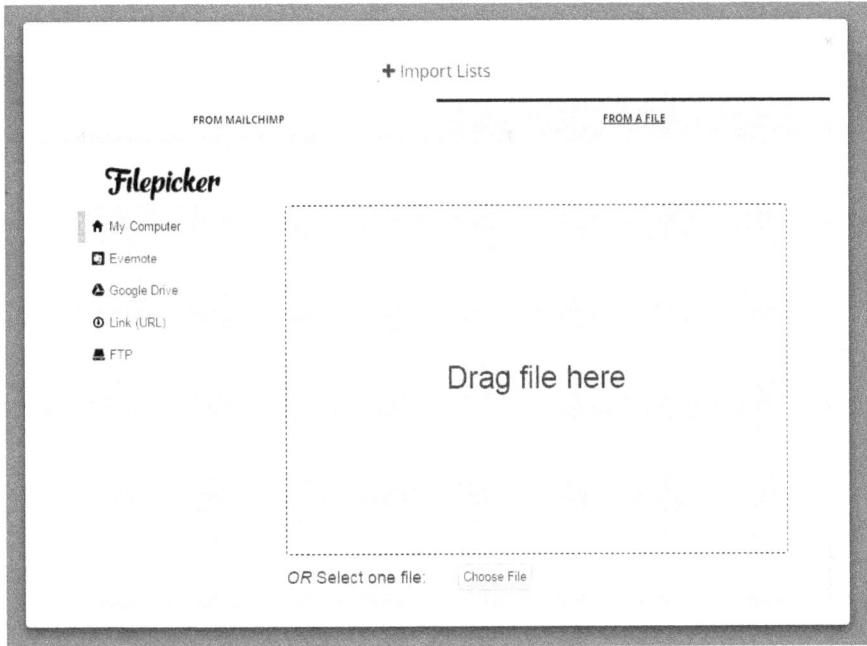

For example, after I selected a file I bought of psychologists, the service imported the file and asked me to indicate which column has the emails (Col 9) and give the file a name (Psychologists)

After an hour or so, I had the results, indicating the percent of A, B, D, and F emails in the list. In this case, there were only 14% As.

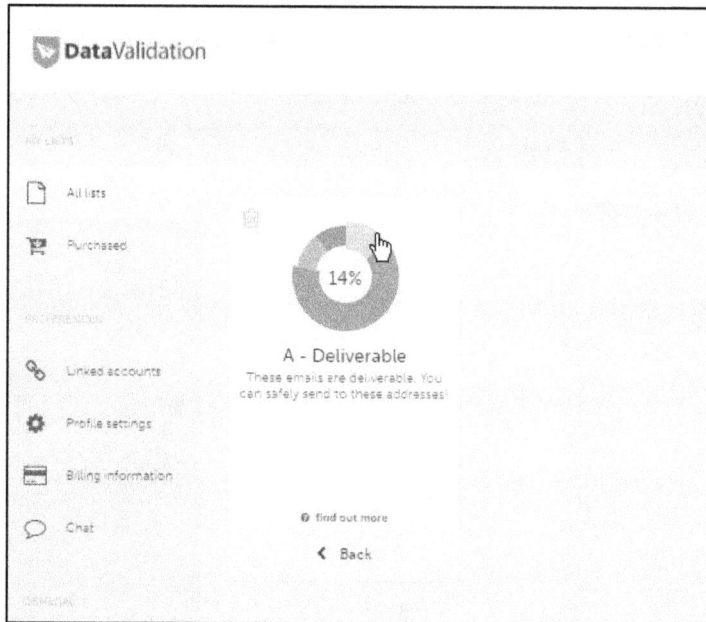

The large blue area refers to 64% Bs, while there are 12% Ds (the orange band), and 10% undeliverables.

An Email Assurance Grades listing explains what these grades mean.

Email Assurance Grades

A+ Deliverable + Engagement Activity: The emails given a grade of A+ have been determined to be deliverable. They also have engagement history concerning email clicks and opens. These addresses are always Safe!

A Deliverable: The emails given a grade of A have been determined to be deliverable. These addresses are also Safe.

B Accepts-all: These emails have been deemed as "Accepts-All". A server that accepts all email means that the hostname has been set to accept any mail. This could also mean the email address in question may be a spam trap. This is commonly seen in business email addresses and in many cases, the server will accept all mail and then bounce it back to sender, which in turn hurts the sender's IP Reputation. We do not recommend sending to the "Accepts-All" category. All emails with a grade of B should be segmented (until later confirmed valid).

D Indeterminate: In checking for an email, we were not able to do anything. The email address seems to have a mail server that is running and accepting connections, but we are unable to connect. We do not recommend sending to the "Indeterminate" category. All emails with a grade of D should be segmented off your list.

F Undeliverable: The emails given a grade of F have been deemed as undeliverable and are therefore, invalid. These emails are unsafe to send to! These addresses should always be unsubscribed from your email database.

After reviewing your Always Free Email Assurance Report you'll be able to make an informed purchase decision. Upon purchase, you will have access to your lists' Address-by-Address Analysis.

After knowing the grading of the list, I can decide if I want to have it validated, with the pricing based on the total number of emails in the list. Or I can get a package for over 3000 emails, and use that for the price of emails on multiple lists.

Pricing Tiers

0-10K	$0.007 / email
10K-100K	$0.005 / email
100K-500K	$0.003 / email
500K-1M	$0.002 / email
1M-2M	$0.0015 / email
2M-3M	$0.00125 / email
3M+	Talk to us!

Signup for Free!

Once I validate a list, I can see the grading for each email and pull out on those emails with an A or A+ grade. Or if I want to take a bit more risk, I can include the B listings. I can also learn about the information used to make up the Email Assurance Grade. Then, I can see how each mail was rated in terms of historical hard bounces, opt-outs, complainers, deceased individuals, historical opens, and historical clicks, all graded on a scale of 1-4, with 4 being the most deliverable.

The advantage of this service is its precision, though it's a little more expensive than the Email Validator service I used the most.

Other Validation Services

Besides the services I used, there are dozens of others. Here in brief are some of the ones with the highest ranks from a search on Google.

Never Bounce

Like other services, Never Bounce (https://neverbounce.com or http://www.neverbounce.com) offers a free analysis of a list, and once you set up your account, you can get a list with up to 1000 emails a month for free. You can check on as many emails as you want in a list to help you decide if you want to buy that analyzed list.

A first step in getting your analysis is to create an account.

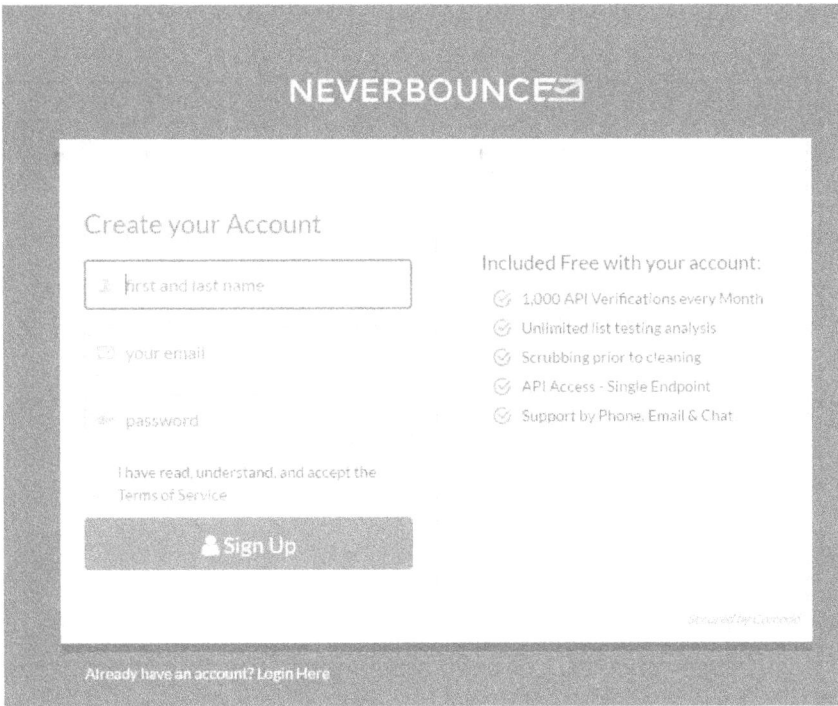

After I have signed up, created an account, and validated it through my email, I can freely analyze any list. For example, here's an analysis of my psychologist list.

Unfortunately, the results aren't very good, as the analyzer advised –

I can expect 13% of my over 4000 emails to bounce.

Should I want to clean up my emails, the cost will be about $35 at the rate of .008 a name.

ListWise

Another cleanup service with a high Google ranking is ListWise (https://www.listwisehq.com)

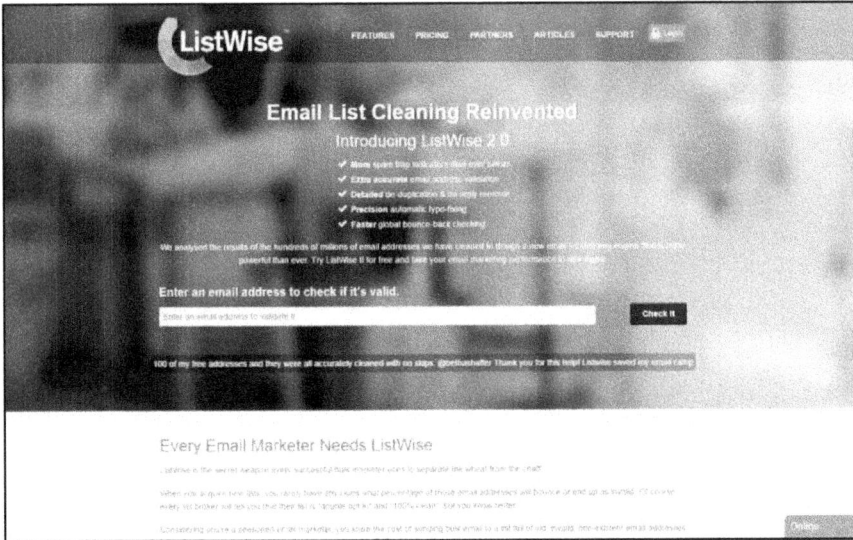

It similarly analyzes a list to indicate the number of invalid emails and bounces.

You can have a free trial of cleaning up to 100 emails. Thereafter, prices range from about .006 for up to 10,000 emails to about .002 for 100,000 emails, and .001 a name for 500,000 or more.

Brite Verify

And here's **Brite Verify** (http://www.briteverify.com)

It does a breakdown into valid, invalid, unknown, or accept all categories.

You can check pricing for the number of emails you want to verify, which is a little more expensive than for other services. It starts at .01 per name to 100,000 names and then costs .008 a name for 250,000-500,000 emails – so prices are about 5 times higher than other services which are about .002 to .003 an email.

Purelist

Another site that came up when I did a search was the Purelist Email List Cleaning Web Application (http://purelist.emailanswers.com), which turned out to be one of the least expensive services, starting at .001 a name for up to 10,000 emails with a minimum order of 10,000, and even less with larger orders of 50,000 or more.

Tower Data

Still another cleanup service is Tower Data
(http://www.towerdata.com/email-validation/validate-email-addresses).

This service is even more precise, since it even corrects the syntax
on up to 15% of your emails. It verifies the domain multiple times over
several days to determine if the domain is really invalid or not and has over
30 email status validation codes to tell you why an email is bad. The
company can even tell you about the activity of that email, such as how old
it is, when a message was last opened, and how active it has been. But it is
more expensive than most other services, since it starts at .01 an email for
up to 100,000 emails and costs .009 for 100,000 to 250,000 emails, with
pricing down to .006 for 500,000 to 1 million emails. So it costs about
three times what many other companies charge.

APC-Lists

Despite its simple home page, the rest of APC-Lists website (http://apc-lists.com) provides some assurance about the quality of the lists. It points out that the lists are relatively inexpensive, since the company is based in Hong Kong and the Philippines:

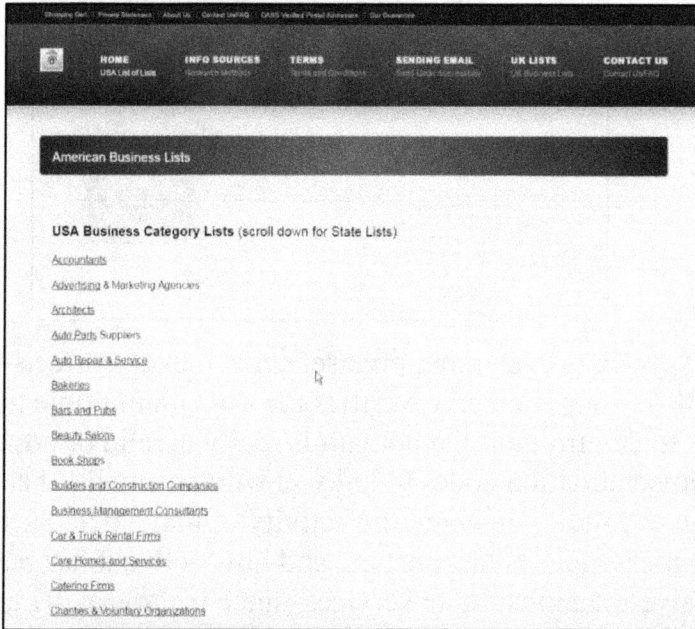

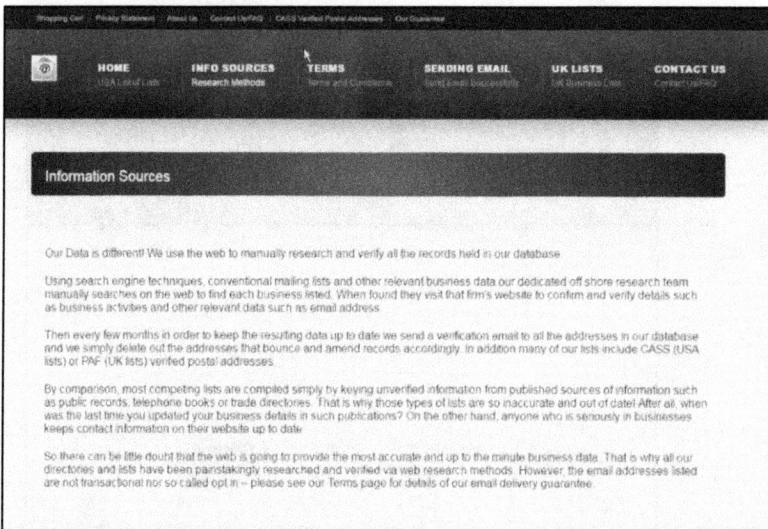

EmailDataPro

And here's the EmailDataPro site (https://www.emaildatapro.com):

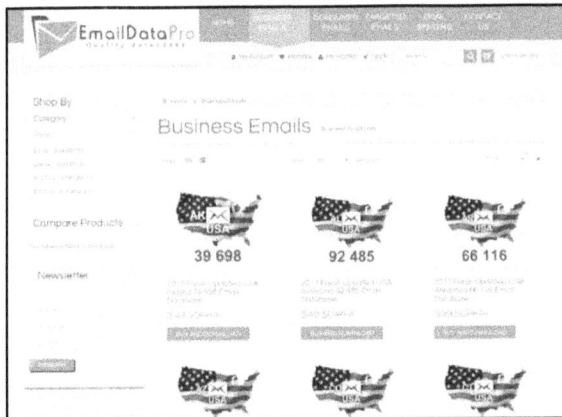

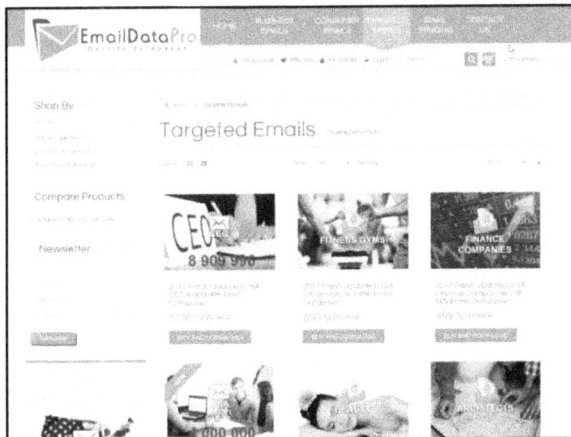

Kickbox

Finally, one last site that was recommended to me by email marketers is Kickbox (https://kickbox.io)

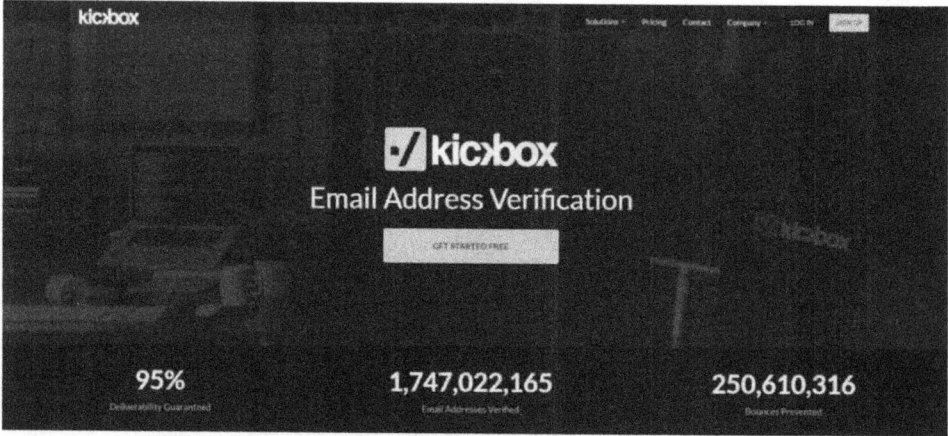

You can try it out with up to 100 emails. It's a bit more expensive than some of the other services, since pricing starts at .01 for up to 2500 emails, gradually goes down to .004 cents at 100,000 emails, and only drops to .002 at 500,000 emails.

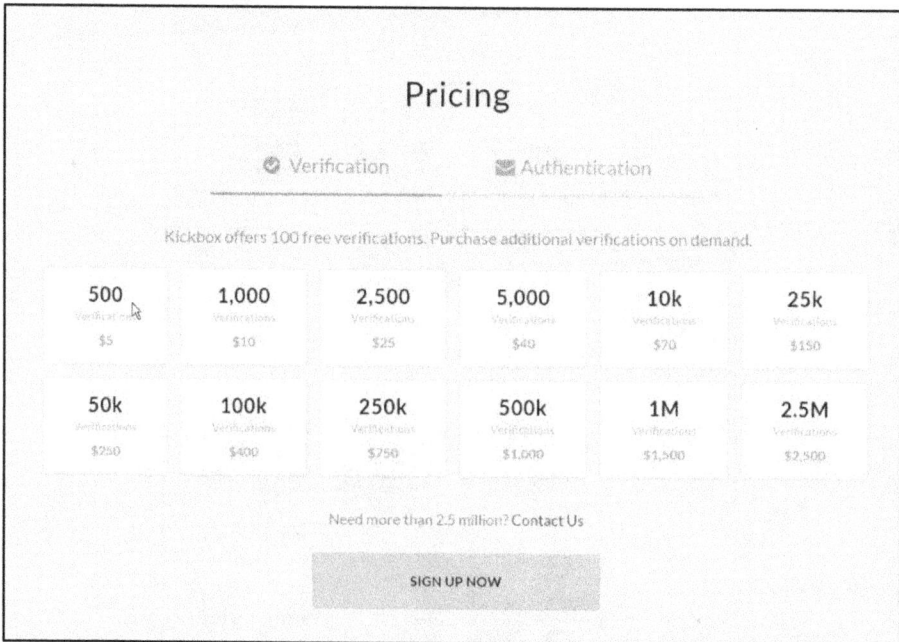

In sum, if you are going to do bulk mailing, you can use any of the above email cleaning services to validate your emails, so you can email to only contacts that pass the validation test. To help you decide which service or services to use, try out the different services with their free email check-ups, free services, or minimal orders. Then, decide.

Most importantly, clean up any bulk emails you buy—and if you haven't used an email list for some time, use a validation service to check out those emails to eliminate any invalid emails from your database, so you don't have a high level of bounces due to invalid emails.

CHAPTER 4: BUYING CUSTOM TARGETED LISTS

An alternative to buying and validating an already created list is getting a customized list which is targeted to a market with particular characteristics that you specify. The cost of the emails depends on the size of your list and the categories you select, but generally the cost is substantially higher using this approach, because these are more carefully curated names and presumably you will have less than a 5-10% return, so you therefore don't have to validate the names. In general, you can figure that the cost per email will be about .40 to .60 a name.

This approach works best if you have a smaller, more targeted group you want to email. Moreover, these are supposed to be double-opt in emails that have been carefully collected by the company obtaining these emails, so you may not need to do an initial mailing to check on the current contact information as when you buy a already created list.

Even so, it is worth doing an initial check when you first get a customized list to be sure these names and emails are as clean as the company claims. You can do this initial check by using an email validation service or by doing your own test with a small mailing to a subset of the list—perhaps email about 100 to 500 names to gauge the response. If minimal or no bounces, proceed with the rest; if not, complain to the company that the list isn't as good as claimed, and work out a settlement with the company on what to do next – from cancelling the order or getting a reduced price to getting the company to give you addition names or further clean up the list.

Although I haven't used this customized approach myself, I have spoken to the sales reps for a few of these companies, received multiple offers from them, and reviewed their websites. So these appear to be solid, reputable companies. Talk to them yourself, and see if their approach would work well for you.

The companies I have been in touch with include Exact Data and InfoUSA. Here's more information about them. Plus you can find others by going to Google Search. Discuss the different options and costs and decide which would be a best fit for you, if you go the customized email list route.

Exact Data

Exact Data is one of the most active and aggressive companies specializing in customized target emails. After six months, their sales people continue to contact me with offers about how much I can benefit from using their service.

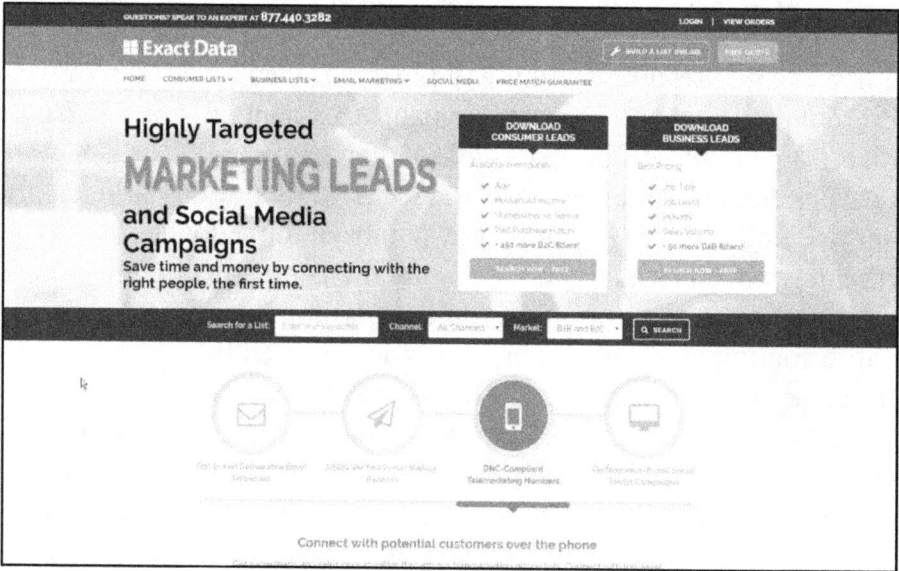

As their website indicates, they can target either consumers or business contacts according to certain criteria. For consumers, you can target your market based on age, household income, whether a homeowner or renter, past purchase behavior, and over 450 other qualities. For businesses, you can base your list based on industry, job title, job level, sales volume, and about 50 other characteristics.

The company promises that all of these leads will have opt-in and deliverable email addresses, as well as verified postal mailing addresses and telemarketing numbers that are compliant with the DNC.—Do Not Call – Registry.

You can start by building a list online and get a quote, or you can request a quote online and get a call based on your criteria. Here are two examples to illustrate, based on seeking a quote for consumer or business leads.

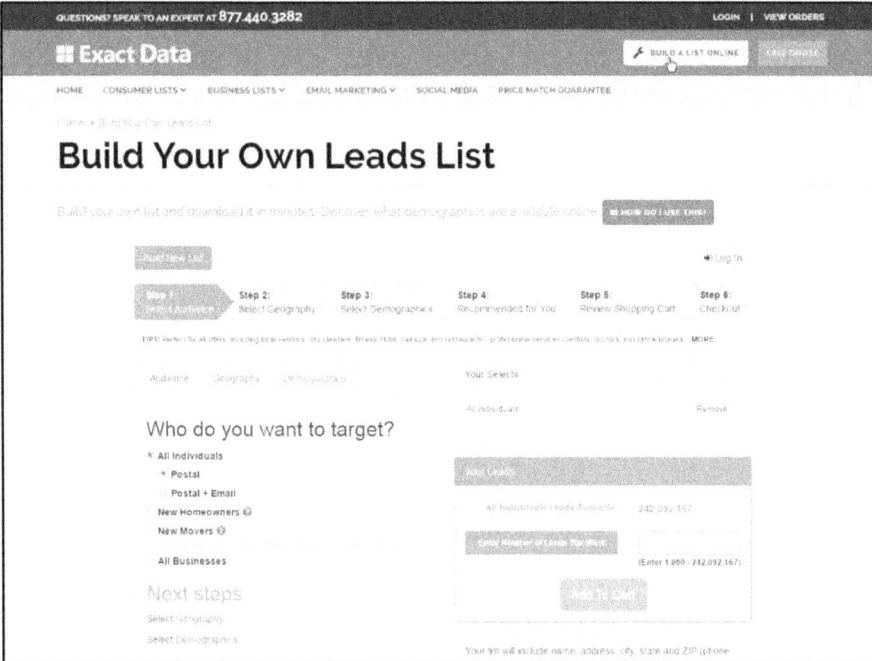

Should you need help, the company even has a tutorial to tell you what to do.

As an example, to get started, I only wanted contacts by emails, which was about 20% of the total list – about 49 million of 242 million individuals. The next step was to indicate the geographic area I wanted to target. If I choose within 25 miles of my location in Lafayette, the list was down to about 517,000 individuals.

If I narrowed down the search further, the list included only about 116,000 individuals.

Should I want to order a subset of that list, the cost starts at about $.18 a name for 1000 leads; $.12 a name for 5000 leads. If I wanted to email everyone, the cost would be about $14,000, substantially more than spending approximately $200 to $300 for 100,000 names from one of the companies with already completed lists.

However, I can specify more precisely who my market is, so I have a smaller more targeted sample. Say I have a diet product that will appeal primarily to women 25 to 55. Once I enter this information, there are now about 29,000 individuals in the list, and my cost for emailing all of them would be about $3500 (about $.12 a name) or $493 if I target 10% of this sample or 2900 individuals (about $.17 a name).

Plus I can specify even more detail about these individuals, such as the house hold income, the number of children, length of residence, type of vehicle owned, and more. Since my target market is professional women who have enough disposable income to buy a nutrition program, if I indicate an income level of $75,000 a year or more, the market is now down to about 16,000 contacts with a cost of about $1100.

So that's how this works for targeting local consumers.

Exact Data also has about 4000 breakdowns based on the types of brands consumers favor, called propensity lists.

Plus they have other breakdowns based on selected categories, such as jewelry, religion, different type of travelers, and real estate agents and brokers, which provide a price per thousand or you can call for a quote. For instance, here's the real estate listing.

For business codes, Exact Data uses the SIC codes, which indicate the number of businesses which have an email address in that category.

To get this information, you have to indicate which SIC code you are interested and enter your contact information, so an Exact Data rep can contact you with more information about pricing. For example, here's the form I got to fill out after I indicated I was interested in printing, publishing, and allied industries.

If you want help in sending out a mailing to a list you have selected, Exact Data has its own email deployment system.

Thus, while it might be pricey to use this service to get lists or send out emails, the company has a highly professional approach to obtaining targeted emails and sending them out. But given the costs, I would recommend using them for more targeted lists of perhaps 1000 to 5000 contacts, which would cost about $200 to $900, about 5 to 10 times as much as obtaining already created lists and cleaning them up. At least, with this targeting and pricing for high quality lists, you shouldn't have to use an email cleaning service, though you might still test out the emails you initially receive by using a validation service. If they come in at under 5-10% all is good.

InfoUSA

InfoUSA is another major leader in the customized target market arena.

Like Exact Data, the company enables you to target businesses or consumers.

The company emphasizes the quality of its lists, noting that its business and executive email addresses are obtained from phone interviews, phone directories, trusted third party sources, and other sources. Then, it tests out the email addresses to make sure they are deliverable and checks the IP addresses to be sure they are legitimate. The company also makes sure to follow the CAN-SPAM laws and get rid of any individuals on the list who want to opt-out.

You can create your own list of businesses by putting in an industry or searching the SIC or NAICS codes, where you will see the total number of emails available for that industry. Then, you can target the list further by geography, size of business, job title, credit rating, and ethnicity, nationality, and religion.

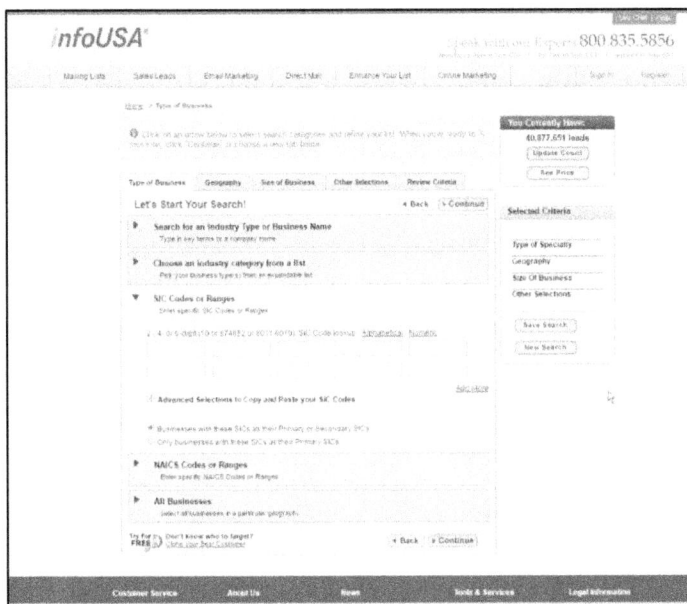

When I did a search for "publishing," I got a list of different types of publishers and related fields.

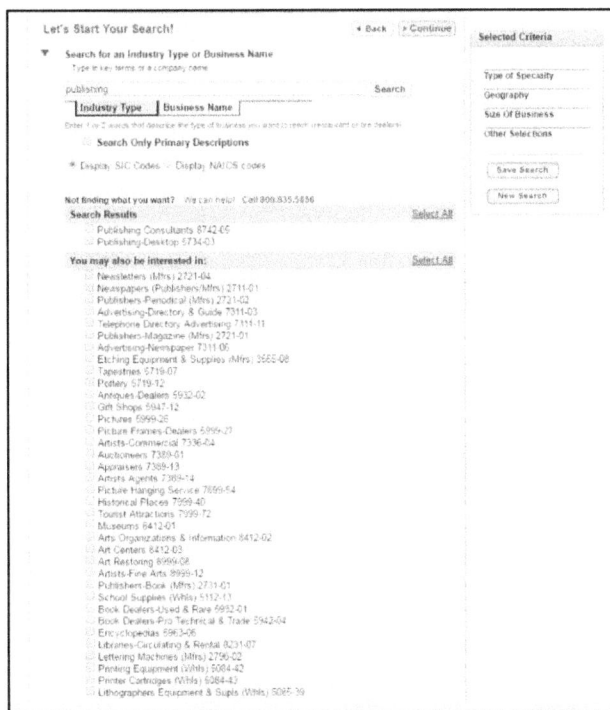

Alternatively, I could select a category and find a specific industry that way.

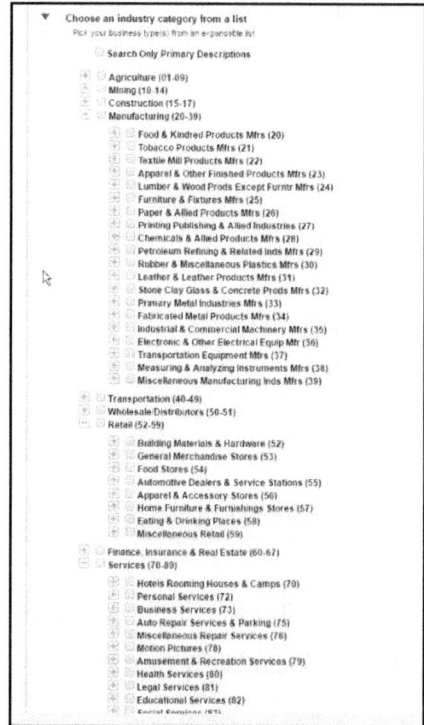

For example, when I did this for legal services, I came up with about 26,000 emails.

If I wanted the whole list, I learned that I qualified for volume pricing, so I should speak to a sales rep. But when I indicated I wanted only 2000 contacts, I got a price for a basic package of about $960 or $.48 for each email with the company and contact name. The cost was $1160 or $.58 for each email for a more comprehensive package with extensive detail about the business, including its physical address, phone, website, sales volume, credit rating and more. Even at 5000 contacts, the cost was relatively high – over $2000, costing about $.43 an email for the basic package, and about $.53 a name for more extensive detail.

The price for consumer leads was substantially less. For example, if I wanted to contact 7900 homeowners within 10 miles of Lafayette, California, that would cost about $.15 a name. Or for only 1000 contacts, the cost would be $250 or .25 a name.

Thus, while this customization might lead to more high quality leads, as with Exact Data, the costs are much higher than when you buy an already created list.

Other Targeted List Companies

Besides Exact Data and IntoUSA, many other companies specialize in targeted lists. I couldn't research all of these other companies in depth because there are so many, but this overview of these two companies will give you a sense of what to look for in assessing a company that creates a customized targeted group. Some things to check out include the following:
- an ability to carefully target your consumer or business market, based on important characteristics, such as location, demographics, interests, and buying habits for consumers; job title, company size, and sales volume for a business.
- the availability of a sales rep or support team to discuss and recommend different email packages for you, based on understanding your ideal target market.
- the cost of reaching that audience and the availability of any special discounted packages based on the size of the mailing.
- the sources of the company's data and how recently the lists have been updated.
- the expected return rate for a mailing, which should be no higher than 5 or 10% or even less;
- the company's willingness to guarantee the maximum percentage of returns;
- the company's ability to provide you with testimonials to the effectiveness of its mailings;
- the company's assurances that these are opt-in and preferably double opt-in emails;
- the company's ability to provide you with the names and titles of individuals to contact, and ideally with other information about the company, though sometimes more detailed information will cost a little more – typically about 15-20% more;
- how the company is different and better from other companies that provide custom emails;
- and anything else you want to ask so you feel comfortable in working with this company.

Some of the other companies with custom targeted lists that you can check out include the following:

-DMDatabases.com (http://www.dmdatabases.com)

-Experian.com (http://www.experian.com/small-business/geographic-targeted-mailing-lists.jsp)

-

DirectMail.com (http://www.directmail.com/mailinglists)

- Mega One (http://www.omegaonemarketing.com)

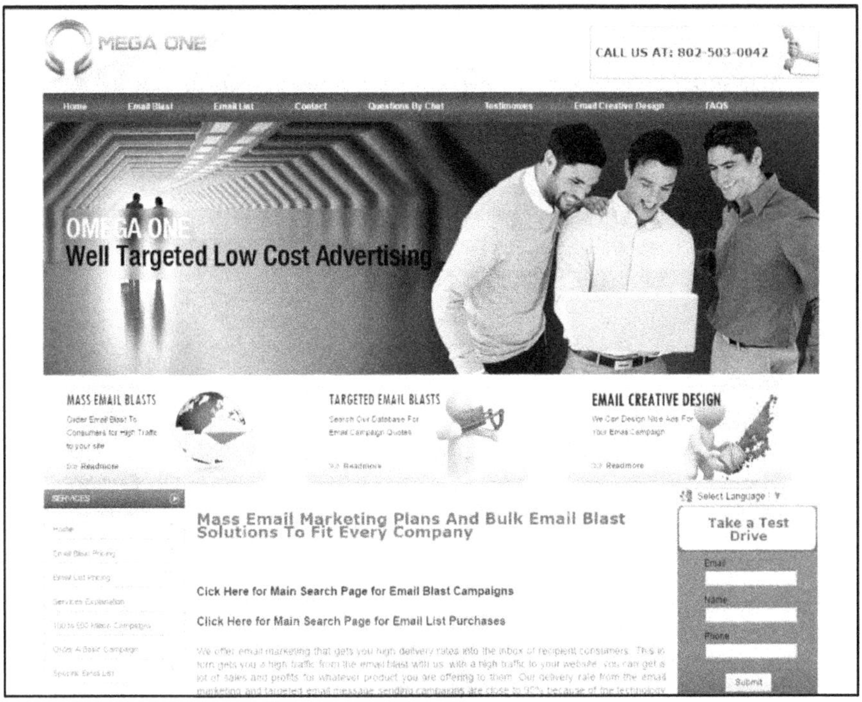

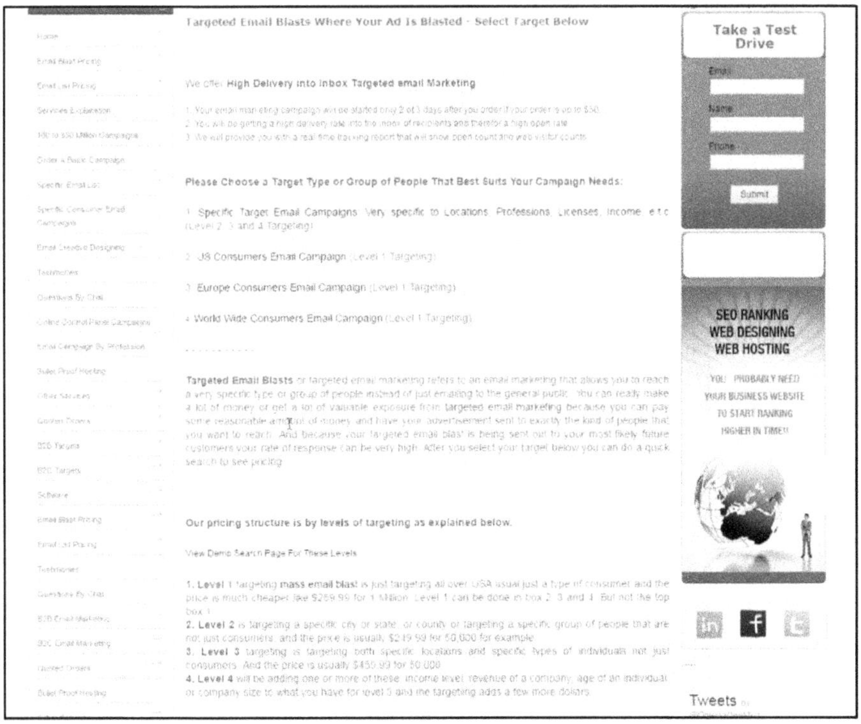

- ETargetMedia.com (http://www.etargetmedia.com)

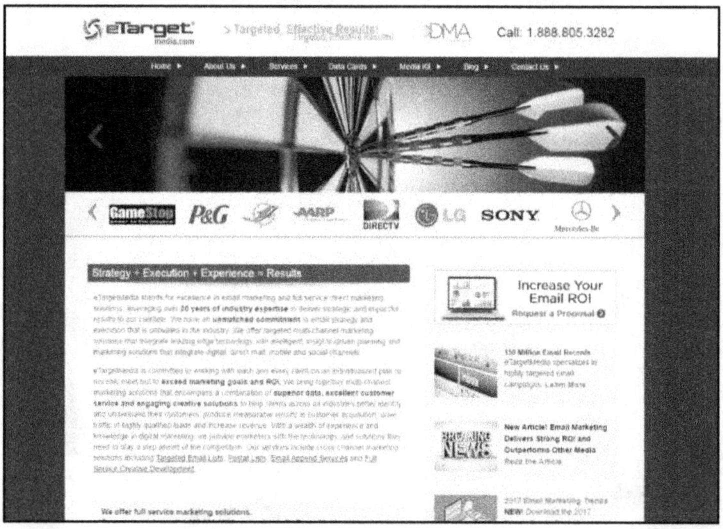

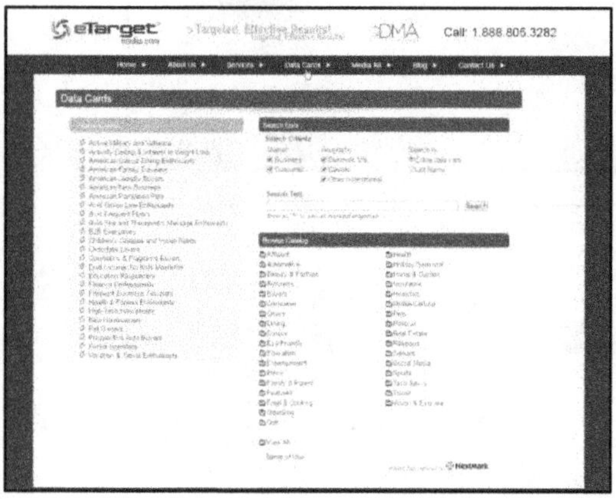

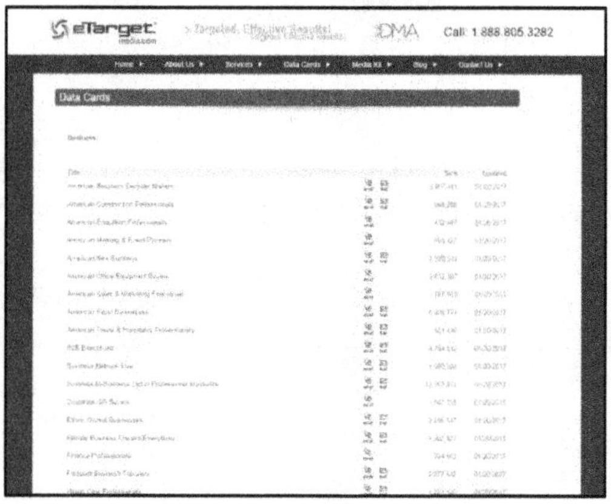

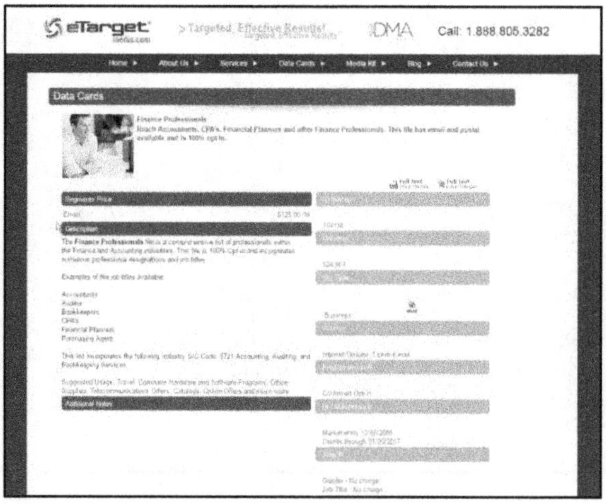

CHAPTER 5: BUYING SPECIALIZED LISTS

In addition to obtaining lists for an already created group or a customized targeted list, you can get specialized lists from a particular organization. I've listed some groups below. In addition, you can do a targeted search on Google, which will turn up some organizations which have lists of their members or companies with in lists in a particular field. For example, a Google search listed these professional organizations or email sources and their websites:

Architects: The Directory of Architects:
  http://thedirectoryofarchitects.com
Dentists: Dentist List Pro
 http://www.dentistlistpro.com
 http://integratedmedicaldata.com
Doctors: IMD (The IntegratedMedicalData.com)
 http://integratedmedicaldata.com
Nurses: Nurse Email List
 http://www.skaiinfo.com/databases/nurse-email-list
Psyhologists: California Psychological Association
  http://www.cpapsych.org
Lawyers: AttorneyListDownload
 http://www.attorneylistdownload.com
Real Estate Agents
 http://realestateagents-usa.com
Health Care
  http://www.definiteivehc.com
Financial Professionals
  WSPonton.com: http://www.wsponson.com
  Reach Marketing: http://www.reachmarketing.com/financial-mailinglists-and-email-lists
Law Enforcement Administrators and Fire Chiefs:
 http://www.safetysource.com/lists
Chief of Police Mailing List
 https://lists.nextmark.com
Police Departments and Chiefs
 http://www.cml-llc.com/datacards/polie-departments-and-chiefs-mailing-list.html

In short, all kinds of lists are available online and some groups in your profession, industry, or related fields may sell lists of their members, or they may have a members' directory, which you can buy to create your own list.

Sometimes these directories are online, and you may be able to download the directory in an Excel file or .csv file, sometimes for free, or you may need to buy the directory or become a member to obtain it, as well as be in it yourself.

While some of these directories are still being published in print versions, increasingly they are published online in electronic form. And even if there is no complete directory to access, you may be able to create one by going through the online directory lists for the letters A, B, C, and so on. Or if you do a search, sometimes you can get everyone in the organization by inserting a single vowel. If so, start with the letter "e" which will be in the most number of names; then "a," and after that "o," "i," or "u." This process of creating a list from an online directory can be time-consuming, but this is often a way to get the very latest updated information for that association.

Thus, in today's information age, there are all kinds of ways to find or buy emails. In deciding whethr to buy a list, consider the time and effort it might take to create this list if you can't readily obtain a downloadable file for that list. Often it may be simpler to buy a list. If you create or buy a list other than from a customized list seller, validate those emails through an email cleaning or validation service. Otherwise you may get lists that haven't been updated in a while.

In the next book, I'll discuss how to send out a large number of emails through bulk mail and other email service providers.

BOOK VI: USING EMAILS TO INCREASE LOCAL AND ONLINE SALES

INTRODUCTION: THE MANY WAYS TO SEND EMAILS

There are many ways to send emails – among them are sending out individual emails, using a platform to send recurring emails, and sending out bulk emails, which can sometimes be personalize or not. Other considerations include what email to use, whether to personalize the email, and whether to include graphics or links and how many to use.

Thus, deciding on the best approach to sending an email can be a complex, in addition to deciding what to say. Which approach to use depends on what you want to say and who you want to target. Knowing the full range of possibilities can help you choose which approach is the best, depending on your message and target.

As a rule of thumb, keep your messages on a topic to a particular email address, so you maintain a brand consistency.

But once you start engaging in an email exchange with an individual after sending a bulk email, you might ask selected individuals to switch to another email used for a continued conversation. This way you can distinguish these emails from all emails in your initial mailing, which has received responses from those interested in learning more and other types of responses, including those who want to "unsubscribe" and automatic emails from those who are away or gone from the company.

240

CHAPTER 1: DECIDING WHAT EMAIL TO USE

You may already have an email that you use for everything. It may be an email tied to your website, such as john@yourdomain.com or marysmith@yourdomain.com, or an email with one of the popular free providers, such as gmail.com, hotmail.com, or yahoo.com.

Whatever your current email, set up multiple emails and where possible, don't use a free email account, for reasons to be discussed. Preferably, use an email linked to your website or linked to your phone or cable company, such as john@comcast.net or marysmith@att.net.

Setting Up Multiple Emails

Multiple emails are sometimes linked to multiple websites which feature different products and services, although you might use multiple emails for other reasons, such as doing promotions for different purposes.

Having different websites can be an ideal scenario for creating different emails for each website. This way it is clear what service or product you are promoting, as featured on the website, and the recipient can always go from your email to your website to learn more about you, your company, and other offerings.

Using an email linked to a website can give you more credibility when contacting a person who doesn't know you, because an email with your domain name looks more legitimate than an email from one of the free services. Having multiple emails for each website contributes to your credibility, too.

Another reason for having multiple emails is so you can keep track of the different people who respond to different orders. While you can create folders in an email and move your emails about a product or service there, this can be a time-consuming operation. Also, you may lose track when you engage in an email exchange with different people in the same email about different topics. And it may be confusing if a recipient changes the subject line to more closely reflect what the conversation is now about. By contrast, when you have multiple emails for different products, services, or types of conversations, you can more easily keep the emails on a particular subject together.

Having multiple emails is also a good idea when you are testing different approaches, prices, subject lines, photos, and other changes. This way, all the responses to one email show a different type of response from those who respond to another email. You can vary your email name and provider for different purposes, too.

You can also prioritize how often you check different emails, based on where you more often get emails, so you more frequently check the emails you use the most and spend less time checking the others. Then, check off each site as you do these check-ups to keep track, so you don't waste time with extra checking again, because you don't recall if you previously checked an email or not.

For example, I have about 25 emails, and check five regularly. I have some emails under my name, some under different company website names, and some are on gmail.com, comcast.net, and yahoo.com. And when I create new project with a new website, I sometimes use a forwarding email to an email I use more often. Because of the nature of my business, it makes sense to have these multiple emails for different products, services, and campaigns.

Decide on the number and type of emails that work best for you.

Deciding On the Your Email Platforms

However many emails you have, a key consideration is what platform to use. The major types of platforms are these:
- an email from your website
- an email from a phone company, such as Comcast or AT&T.
- an email from a free platform, such as yahoo, gmail, hotmail, and AOL (yes, there are still some of those).

Using an Email from a Website

Ideally, if you have a website email, that's a good way to contact people in an initial mailing, although you can easily set up a forward to an email you more regularly use, so you can more quickly see any of these emails. For example, this might be the email on your website when people contact you for more information (such as info@yourwebsite.com, contact@yourwebsite.com, or yourname@yourwebsite.com. Then, that email gets forward to an email you check every hour or two, so you can respond quickly, which shows you are very responsive and customer-service oriented – a big plus when you are trying to gain new business.

Using this website-based email is also good for an initial mailing to prospective clients or customers, since that looks more professional than if you use a free email or email from a phone company. You appear more solid and established, since you have a website. This web-based email also gives a new prospect a chance to go to your website and check it out, because that website is clearly indicated in your initial mailing, though you might later respond from your regular email.

You can also set up multiple emails from your website. Then, if you want to keep them separate, forward them to different regular emails. In fact, if you have multiple officials or employees at the company, forward these emails to each person's personal email and that person can respond.

Another advantage of a website email is it is less likely to be viewed as spam and rejected by the filters and spam bots on some email servers.

Using an Email from a Phone Company

As an alternative to a website email, or if you don't have a website, a phone company platform is a good second choice. This is less likely to run into email blocks than a free email account, but there are some limitations.

Based on my experience, you will only be able to set up a certain number of emails for each phone line (commonly 6 to 10 email accounts, as is the case with Comcast and AT&T. However, if this is important to you, you can always get another phone, and even if you drop that phone or that phone company merges with another, you still may be able to keep that account. For example, I still have my pacbell and sbcglobal accounts, though these companies are long gone, and I still have my att emails, though I dropped by second landline phone with AT&T.

Using an Email from a Free Service

Probably the preeminent free service email is Google's gmail, which is quick to sign up for, though with one caveat. Unless this has been changed recently, you need to have a mobile number where the service can text you a message, and you can only use that same mobile number for a limited number of emails (about six in my experience). So you can only have a limited number of emails associated with a particular mobile phone number. Also, certain generic names can't be used, such as when I tried to create an account for emailmarketing@gmail though I could add a number such as emailmarketing17@gmail or emailmarketing20@gmail, though all of those were taken. But emailmarketingconnection was okay, and this time I didn't get a request for a phone text confirmation, perhaps because this was linked to a series of gmails with the same account.

A feature on many of these accounts is you can connect them to your mobile phone, so you can access your email on the go. And many accounts, such as gmail and yahoo, enable you to move email contacts from other accounts to your new one.

However, one caution in using free emails is that you may run into certain sending restrictions and blockings by servers, because many free accounts have been used for spam. I discovered this while running and later working with an email connection service for over 13 years. About 4 years ago, email protocols changed, so it was no longer possible to send out emails with yahoo.com or aol.com accounts through third parties, such as by using special software and an SMTP server to put any email in the send and reply field, so the email appeared to comes from that email and any replies would go to that email. However, emails from certain platforms like yahoo and aol get blocked, so if you try to send out such an email, you will get back most or all of those emails. For example, if you send out 1000 emails from this third party software and SMTP set up, you may get several hundred emails back, and others may be deleted.

So far it seems like gmail is accepted. But others may not be, so if you plan to use a free emails with a third party mailing service, check to make sure your mails will go through.

The other major caution in using a free email is the reaction of the recipient getting an initial email from you. The recipient may take your email less seriously than if it comes from a website domain, or even from a phone domain, because anyone can easily open up a free account. Thus, the recipient may be more likely to see a pitch for something as an Internet marketing scam or as spam.

However, you might be able to override any such concerns with a very specific subject line about your topic rather than a short and general promotional message, such as "Great New Money-Making Opportunity" or "Discover the Secrets of the Internet Marketing Millionaires." This problem of thinking your message is spam is less likely, too, if your email is associated with a website domain, since this gives you more credibility at the outset. This is the case, since a person can immediately check out that domain, whereas if you send a free email with a link to a domain, recipients can more easily suspect that this is a link to a bogus site or the basis for getting malware or ransomware on their computer. So you have to be careful when using free emails for marketing pitches, especially with the recent news of Internet scams, spams, spoofs, phishing, and other ways of taking advantage of email recipients.

If you still plan to get a free account, I'd recommend gmail, since it is more widely used by marketing professionals than other free accounts. Plus, it is widely used by creative people and entrepreneurs, too.

Choosing Your Email Name

The next major decision in choosing your email name is whether to use your own name, your company name, or a name that relates to your business or industry. There are certain advantages to each, and this is why it may be a good idea to have multiple emails for different purposes and markets.

For instance, you might use a personal email to communicate with people after you have met each other, but use an email with your company name for an initial mailing, since it may look more professional or make it seem like you have a larger company, especially if you are using your name or company name with a phone company or free platform. But if you have a company domain name, using your own name can be fine, since that domain name establishes you as a company.

Since names aren't case sensitive, you can capitalize your name or company name so it more clearly stands out. Using all lower case is fine, too. Avoid ALL CAPS, however, since this is hard to read.

The following sections describe some of the times when you might want to use your own name, a company name, an industry name, or a made up name.

Using a Personal Name

An advantage of using your name with your website domain name is that it is easy to remember. This is particularly useful when you are using an email for referral marketing, after you meet someone at a networking event or get referred to someone. Then, your name provides a more personal touch.

Likewise, if you use your name with a phone company name or free email, it is more personal and memorable.

Using a personal name is also a good idea when a company has multiple officers or employees. In this case, it's good to have a format to identify everyone in the company, since prospective customers or clients can more easily reach a person, when they only have a name. They just need to apply the appropriate names format, as described in Book 4 on Finding Emails to Build Your Business. Common formats are these:

- First Name@companydomain (good if you want to be more informal and personal)

- FirstInitialLastName@companydomain (a more professional approach, used by some publishing and financial professionals)

- First NameLastName@companydomain (a widely used formula, which is ideal to promote both you and the company)

- FirstName.LastName@companydomain (another widely used variation on the firstname/lastname formula)

- FirstName_LastName@companydomain (another variation on the firstname/lastname formula, though less common)

Sometimes if you have a common name, it may not be possible to get that name by itself, when you use a phone company or free platform name. Thus, some individuals use a combination of numbers after their name, such as helensmith241@yahoo or dave.jones.452@gmail. In general, it's a bad idea to combine a name with random numbers, because such a name is difficult to remember and it looks unprofessional. It may be fine for communicating with friends and family members, but it's best not to use this name and number combination in business. An exception might be if you can get a numerical extension that adds a dramatic touch, such as helensmith01@yahoo, helensmith200@yahoo, helensmith2000@yahoo. But if possible, use an initial to distinguish your name which looks more professional, such as helenbsmith@yahoo.

Using a Company Name

When you initially approach a prospect for a cold call, it may be better to use a company name with a phone company or free email, because it sounds more professional and creditable. For example, the new owners who bought my Publishers Agents and Film Business decided to do. They selected pafconnections@gmail, because it makes the new company seem larger, just as I used publishersagents2@yahoo for over 10 years, when I was running the company and assisting the previous owners with writing and consulting for 5 years.

Also, using a company name works well if you are using a phone company or free email platform. Using that name helps to highlight the credibility of the company when you first contact someone, such as I have chosen here for the Email Marketing Connection (emailmarketingconnection@gmail, which is also the name of the Facebook group I set up.

Using an email in your company name is especially effective when your company name indicates very clearly what you do.

Generally, it is best to link together all of the words (ie: emailmarketingconnection) although some company owners separate them by dots, dashes, or hyphens (such as in email.marketing.connection, email-marketing-connection, or email_marketing_connection). But in general I would discourage using dots, dashes, and underlines, since people can forget which to use. Also, if you are choosing that option since the original name is already chosen, it may be better to choose another name or put "the" in front of the name (ie: theemailmarketingconnection) in order to get a .com extension, which is the most common and widely accepted one.

Using an Industry Name

Use an industry name if your company name doesn't readily convey what you do. This is an especially good idea if you are sending out emails to new prospects. This way in cold emailing, much like in cold calling, in two or three words you suggest what your company does, even before someone opens your email.

You can do this with your company domain name or with a gmail or other free account. For example, say you have a soul food restaurant, your company name is Soul Works, and your domain name is soulworks.com. Since it's not immediately clear that soulworks refers to restaurant serving "soul" food, rather than a spiritual practice involving "souls," the reference to "food" in the email name helps to clarify that. For example, your industry related name might be funfoodfacts@soulworks.

Or perhaps you want to reach out to another market, but your name isn't a good fit. An example might be a craftsman who is trying to expand beyond a local clientele, where his folksy name: "FurniturebyPhil" is great for his mostly small town and rural clientele. But now he wants to create wood furniture and other products for retail stores, like Ikea. Perhaps a name like: "woodgardenproducts@gmail" might provide an email that reflects Phil's broader scape for his product.

Using a Made Up Name

Finally, at times you might want to use a made-up name in your email, usually in conjunction with a gmail or free account. This made up approach might work especially well if you are in a creative profession or have a humorous book or product.

For example, one associate uses a term like "sunburst" to reflect his interest in using positive thinking to guide workshop attendees to the light. Another associate uses "astroflyer" to suggest his love of flying and his interest in aviation.

Such made up names can also be useful when you do a product or marketing test where different groups respond to different marketing pitches. Such tests, which involve slightly varying one or two components in an ad or sales promotion to see which has better results, help to show which is the best way to advertise or promote a project. Usually, you do these tests with two target groups at a time to see which approach performs better, and you can do additional tests to find the best approach. Then, you increase your promotional efforts using that approach.

CHAPTER 2: SENDING EMAILS TO INDIVIDUAL DECISION MAKERS

Some of the common reasons to send an email to an individual decision maker are:
- You have a product or line of products to sell to the company.
- You want to provide a series of services or do a project for the company.

In pitching a product, you need to have sales material and be prepared to demonstrate the product and provide cost and ordering information if the company is interested.

In the case of a service or project, you may need a proposal describing the service, deliverables, date for delivery, the cost of different phases of the project, and the like.

In either case, you often start with an email to get the decision maker interested in meeting with you, so you can present your product or service in more detail. Or you may initially meet the decision maker or be referred as a result of attending a networking meeting, conference, trade show, or other initial meeting. Then, you send an email is to remind the person of your meeting and seek a further meeting or phone call.

In some cases, you need to follow up with a video or PDF showing your product or service in action; in other cases, you may be invited to bring those materials to a meeting.

Creating a CRM System

To keep track of who you contact by email, phone, or personal meeting, it is important to create a CRM or Customer Relations Management system to keep track of the people you contact to when you make the sale or find out they are not interested, so you don't go through the process again.

Using a manual system, such as an Excel sheet, is ideal for individual sales pitches. However, you can increase the number of prospects you contact by using special software to send out and personalize your emails. Then, you follow-up individually later, as described in Book VIII on sending emails.

The advantage of a CRM system is you more easily keep track of the email pitches you send to decision makers at different companies. You track the emails you send, the response, the results of any follow-up meetings, and the cost of your average sales based on the time and effort it takes to make sale. This kind of approach is used by successful professional salespeople, and you can adapt it to be used both locally and in other states or countries.

Setting Up Your CRM System

Consider your CRM system like a spreadsheet which you carry around with you on your phone or set up on your computer, so you can record everything that happened during or at the end of the day. You can use a CRM system like a calendar to let you know who to contact to follow-up with on a particular day and time. You can also use the names and contact information for the people you meet to send them emails to follow-up or to send initial emails to start a communication and later follow up. In this way, you record everything as you move from the initial connection, referral, and lead to presenting your offer, any negotiation, and finally note when you close a deal.

Your CRM system should include the following columns, where you can add in this information as relevant in the appropriate column:
- Initial meetings, and where and when they occurred
- Rating prospects from a hot (5) to cold (1) lead or referral, so you can focus on the hottest leads first.
- Phone calls, and where and when they occurred
- Emails sent on what topics and when
- Meetings to present your project
- Follow-up calls, emails, and meetings
- Nature of opportunity for selling products or providing services
- Cost of the sale or deal

Include a section in your CRM where you can record the highlights of any conversation, phone call, meeting, or other activity. Also, include notes and follow-up plans. If someone refers you to someone else, make a record for that new person and indicate who referred you and whether by phone, personal meeting, or email. This way you can keep track of who are your best sources of leads and the type of referral they give you. After getting a referral, plan to follow up within two or three days, let the person making the referral know what occurs with that lead, and use the CRM to keep track of this information. To guide your further follow-up with each person, rate the prospect from hot (5) to cold (1). Plan any follow-up based on responding to your highest priority leads first.

A key advantage of the CRM system is that you can track your sales process, as you start with pitching your product or service in-person or by email. Then, as you get responses after your initial contact, you can increasingly zero in on those prospects that present the greatest opportunity for sales based on their level of interest and likelihood to follow through and buy.

The process works much like an online sales funnel, with certain prospect opting to continue through the funnel with one, two, or three upsells, while some decide not to go through the funnel at all. You want to assess how well that process or funnel is doing, and a CRM system can help you assess what you are doing right and what you should change to increase your potential for sales.

In contacting individual decision makers, start with the most promising leads who are either likely buyers or connectors, who can refer business to you, because they are top influencers in their field. In some cases, you might consider them "power partners," where you work together and refer business to each other.

While sometimes you can set up a meeting on the spot, a more common scenario is to exchange business cards, or at least get their business card so you can follow-up, because if they just take your business card, often they will not contact you. Should they claim no business card, offer to write down or have them write down their name, phone number and email on the back of one of your business cards.

However you get their card or contact information, note what they may be interested in. Then, add them to your CRM contact sheet, along with information about them and their rating as a prospect or source of referrals. Then, follow up with an email or by phone, and decide what to do next, based on their level of interest. While you should plan to follow-up with your highest priority leads first, follow up with everyone over the next few days. If you have less than a dozen or so contacts, you can use individual emails. With more contacts, use an email system that lets you personalize the email using the software and email server approach described in Book VIII.

What to Include in Your CRM System

Whatever CRM system you use, add in the relevant columns for adding information, comments and tips about following up with that person. Preferably use an email rather than a phone call for your follow-up, even with local contacts, since many people don't like to get random calls from people they don't know or have just met during the day. They find such calls disruptive, or you may get caught up in a conversation with their receptionist or assistant. By contrast, when you follow up by email first, they can review their emails when they are ready to look at them and respond. Whichever you do, enter it into your CRM system.

The main categories to include on your spreadsheet, some of which have already been briefly described, include these:
- Name
- Company
- Type of Business
- Phone

- Email
- Address/City
- Best Method of Contact
- Common Connections
- Level of Influence (1-5)
- Level of Interest (1-5)
- Potential Buyer/Referrals to Others
- Special Interests/Hobbies
- Comments
- Type of Initial Follow-Up
- Date of Initial Follow-Up
- Results
- Any Additional Follow-Up
- Date of Additional Follow-Up
- Results
- Plans for Meeting
- Date of Meeting
- Results
- Future Plans/Developments

You may find that other categories are relevant for you, including adding even more follow-up categories, if you are dealing with an especially expensive or complicated product or service. For example, some business associates report they commonly have four, five, or six or more meetings before finally landing a million dollar project in the housing industry. By contrast, others pitching less expensive products or projects, such as installing a floor or selling jewelry at a house party may only need 1 or 2 follow-up calls or meetings to make a sale or set an appointment to sell the product line to a group. Talk to others in your industry to determine what is most common.

Using CRM Software Programs to Track Your Progress

To illustrate how a CRM program might work, here's Pipedrive, https://www.pipedrive.com , which is recommended by some top salespeople. One of the advantages of Pipedrive is that it can synch your email account with the system, and you can send emails through Pipedrive which will be incorporated into the system. For example, you can list your leads, note when you make contact by phone or email, and when you have scheduled a follow-up meeting. If you make a proposal, you enter this into the system, note when you enter into negotiations, and indicate if you make the sale.

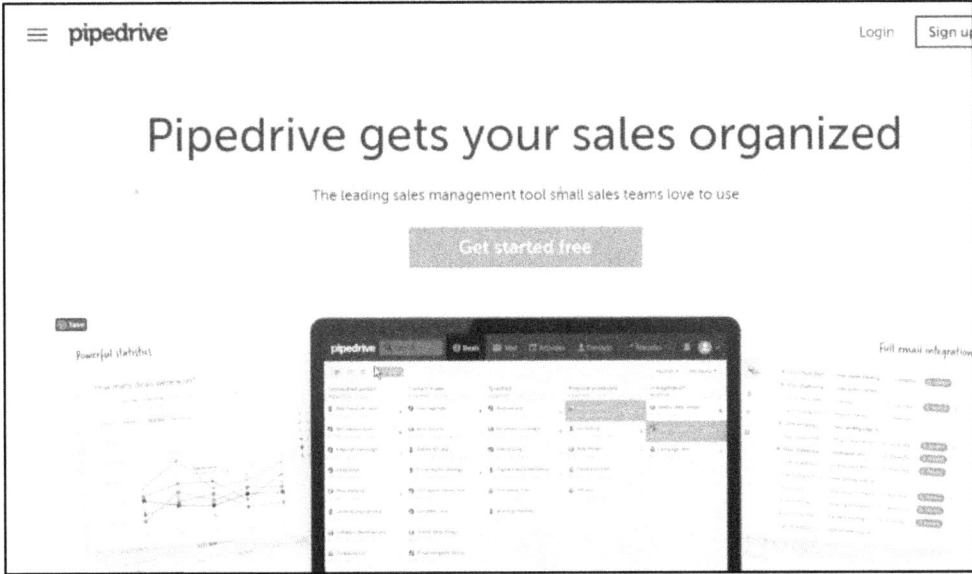

The system also keeps track of the results of following up on a lead. To do so, the system tracks when you make a call, have a meeting, send an email, complete a task, or otherwise follow through until you make the sale or don't.

It includes a calendar so you can schedule an activity. Additionally, you can indicate who the activity is linked to, such as who referred you, what organization they are connected to, and what kind of deal you are discussing. For each activity, you note if it's a call, meeting, task, deadline, or email, and you can enter notes about that activity. As a result, when it comes time to place a call, send an email, have a meeting, or just have lunch, you know what to do.

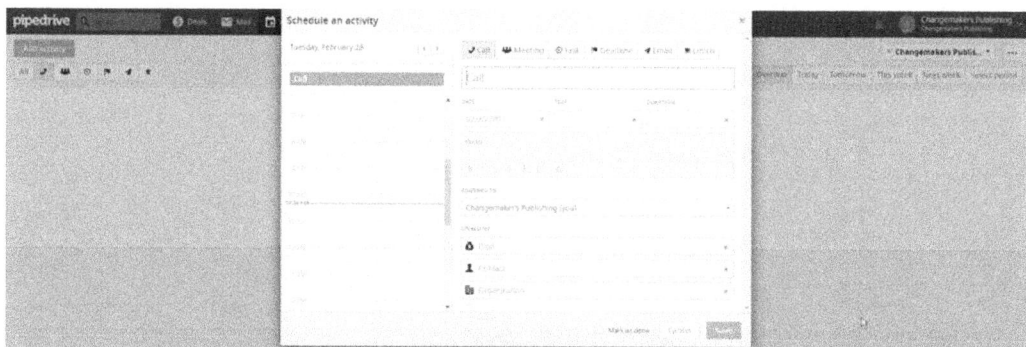

For example, on the following form, you can see how I entered a few activities for a call, sending an email, and having a meeting.

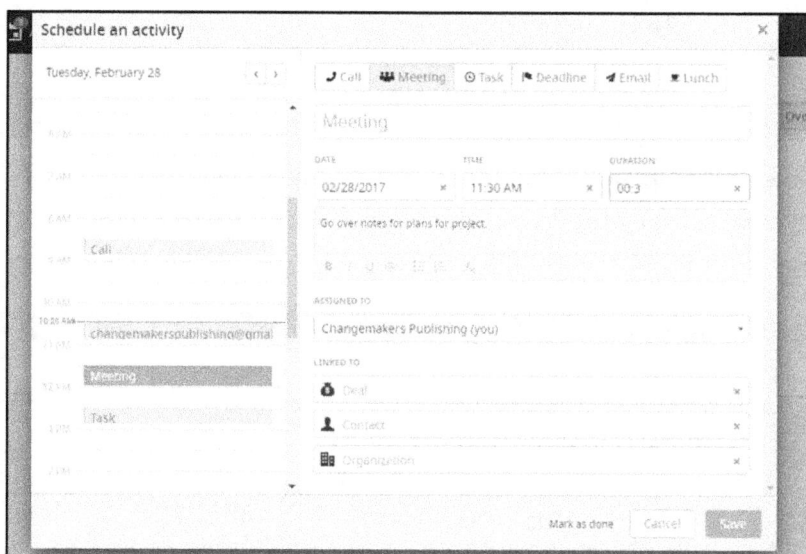

Later, you can see your stats for your deals, activities completed, deals lost and won. Obviously, I don't have any stats, since I'm just using this to demonstrate, but you get the idea.

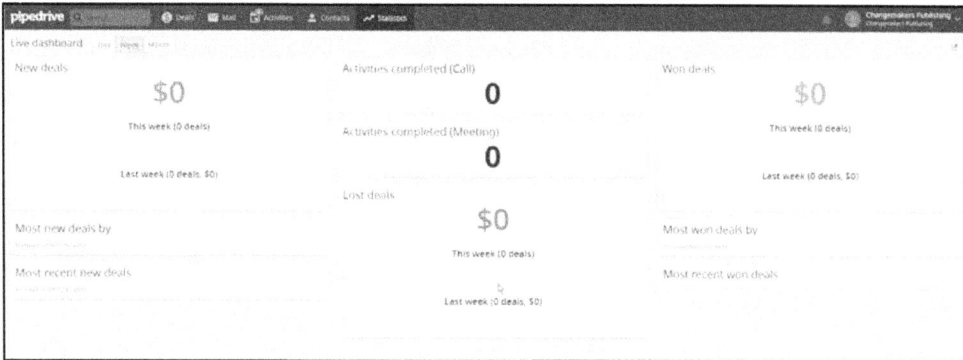

The Advantages of Using a CRM System

An advantage of using this or many other CRM programs is that CRM systematizes the sales and marketing process, including how and when to send emails to initiate a stage in this process. As a result, you are more effective in what you do, leading to more deals and sales.

Moreover, you can synchronize when to send out an email with all of the major email providers, such as gmail and Yahoo, and any cloud-based email services. Also, you can enter information about the main points discussed, when to follow up with a call or email, and the results at each stage of the process.

This system can also assess how well you are doing in monetary terms, so you can see what's working and the value of doing that. Say you usually earn about $2000 a week. If you find that by increasing the number of contacts you are meeting and emailing by 10%, you increased your earnings by 20%, that's a $400 value for a small amount of additional time to send a few more emails or make a few more calls. Then, if you get even bigger deals due to your extra efforts, the value you have gained increases much more.

You can use it to further chart your progress based on the dollar value of each deal and how likely it is to close, so you can prioritize where to focus your attention. Suppose you have a $20,000 deal with a 10% likelihood of closing, that's a $2000 value; whereas a $10,000 deal with a 40% likelihood of closing is a $4000 value. Knowing this, you should put more effort into that $10,000 deal. Of course, you have to accurately estimate the probabilities and the value of the likely deal for this approach to work. Moreover, as you move along through the sales funnel, the probabilities will change as will the value of the deal, so the deal value becomes greater because it is increasingly likely to close. Accordingly, you should put more effort into projects that are further along in the sales funnel.

For example, your $10,000 deal might now have a 60% likelihood of closing after you send some follow-up emails to schedule a meeting, and then follow up by email with a memo on the major deal points discussed at the

255

meeting. Then, if the other party asks to schedule another meeting, the probability might climb to 80%, so your work on this project is now valued at $8000. By contrast, your $20,000 deal might be moving through the system more slowly, so it's value is only 20% or $4000.

On the other hand, if you don't do anything to move a deal along for a few days – unless the other party has asked you to delay further conversations for a couple of weeks – the probability may drop. Thus, in most cases, these changing probabilities indicate that you need to do something to activate any deal in the pipeline, say every four or five days.

For example, one good way to keep a deal active is to do something to provide more value to show how you might help the prospect gain even more. For instance, you might send the prospect a summary of some relevant facts that show the value of acting now to complete the deal.

At the same time, if the deal seems stalled for a few weeks, the CRM system can remind you to make other contacts or follow up on other contacts already in the system. In this way, you get a series of deals working their way through the system, along with reminders of actions to take once you reach certain milestones, such as sending a first follow-up email after one week; sending a second follow-up email after three weeks, and so forth, until you schedule another meeting or two and close the deal. Or alternatively, the system can help you recognize that a deal isn't going to happen, since along the way you see clear signs of a lack of positive responses from the prospect.

You can also add in activity reminders on the day or night before for the following day.

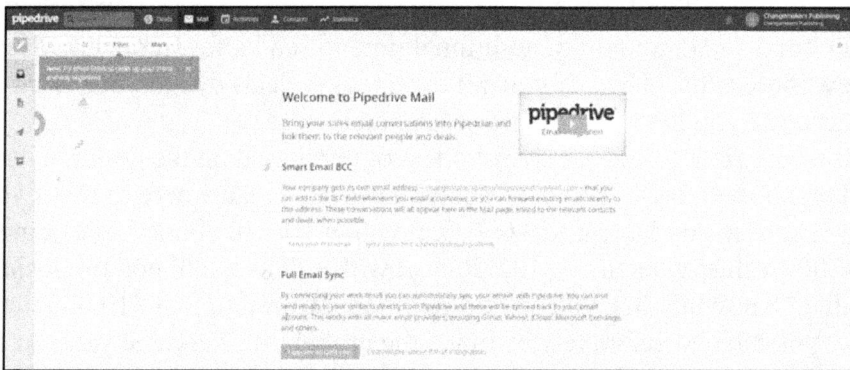

Other CRM Systems

Pipedrive is just one of many CRM systems. I used Pipedrive to illustrate, since it was recommended in one of the email marketing seminars I attended. Also it can be deployed on a computer, since many of the other systems are only available on the cloud or a mobile device.

That being said, the top 10 CRM software programs are the following according to Capterra (www.capterra.com), a major source of business software products. All of them include contact management, customer support, email marketing, interaction tracking, and lead management. They are listed according to how they can be used (1) computer, cloud, and mobile device; 2) cloud and mobile device; and 3) cloud only.

Computer, Cloud and Mobile Devices

Bpm'onlineCRM https://www.bpmonline.com/crm-products

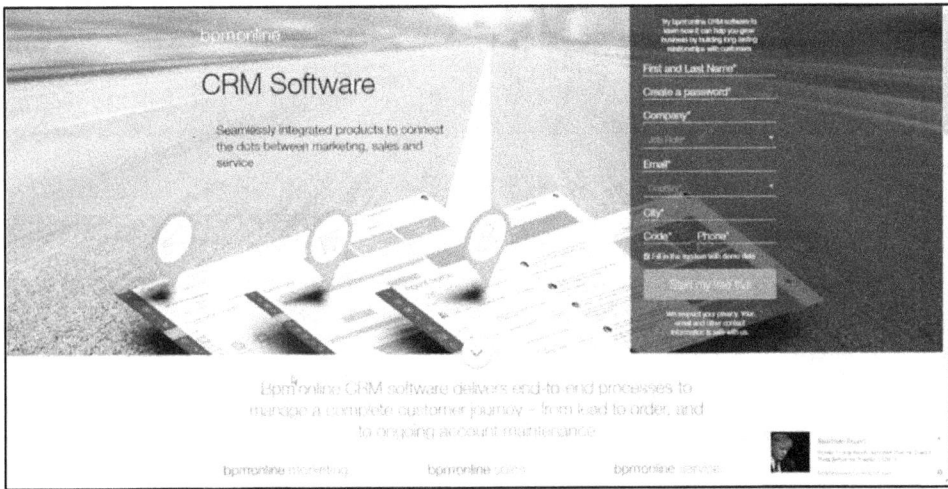

Cloud and Mobile Devices

Insightly https://www.insightly.com

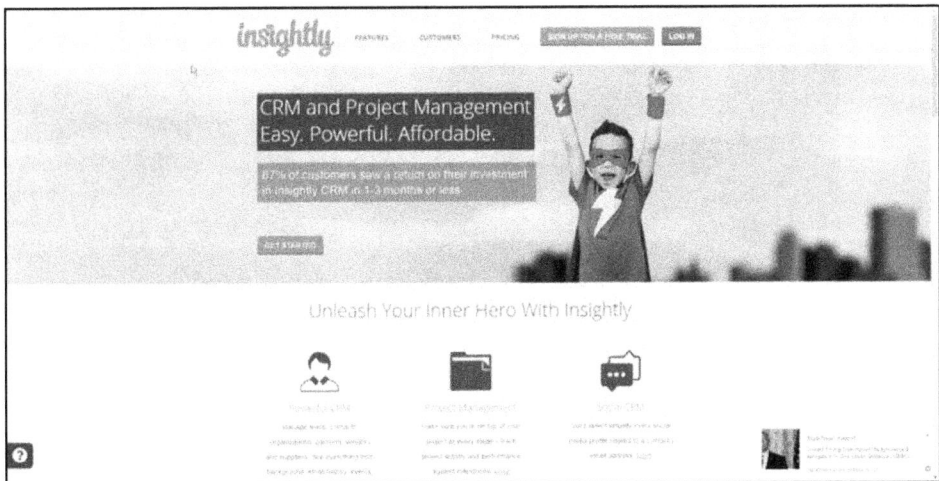

ProsperWorksCRM https://www.prosperworks.com

Marketing360 https://www.marketing360.com/small-business-crm

PipelineDeals https://www.pipelinedeals.com

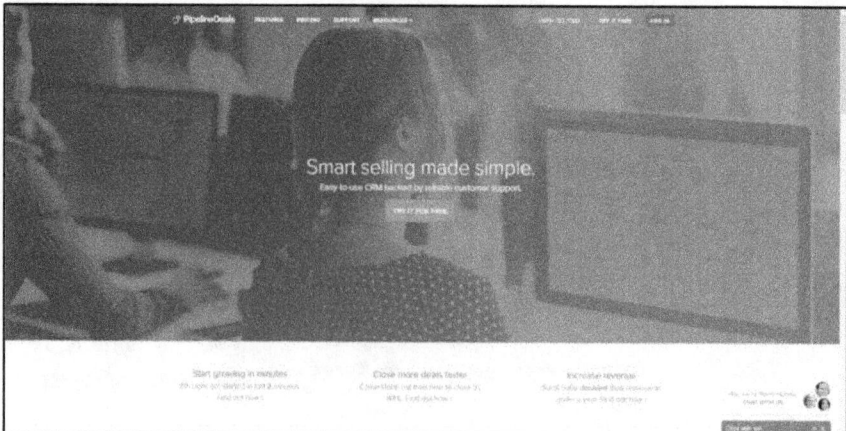

Desk.com https://www.desk.com

Base https://getbase.com

HubSpotCRM https://www.hubspot.com/products/crm

Cloud Only

Freshsales https://www.freshsales.io

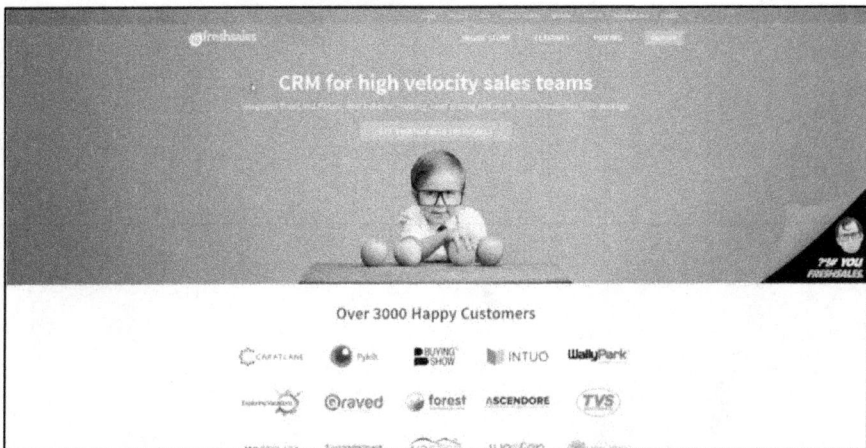

All of these CRM Software programs offer you a free trial for about 30-45 days, so you can decide which program is best for you.

Using a CRM System

Once you choose your CRM system and set it up, use it as a daily guide for what you are going to do each day, enter each new contact you meet, and ote how and when you plan to follow up. As you get other leads and referrals from a follow-up meeting, phone conversation, or email, enter those in your CRM system, too.

If you are collecting a lot of business cards at a meeting or event, there may be too many to enter in the CRM, such as if you collect all the cards from a display at a Chamber of Commerce office or if several dozen people pass their cards around at a business networking group meeting. Perhaps stick most of these cards in a box for further processing, but add the ones which are potential leads or referrals and add those to your CRM system. This way you select the potential buyers or individuals of influence who might be a source of leads and referrals for you.

Then, take those cards you have identified as people to contact – your PTC group, and enter them into your CRM system. Once entered, rate them in terms of their likelihood to be buyers (1-5 as previously noted) or to be a good source of referrals to prospective customers or clients (1-5 as also noted).

You can follow-up using the phone call or email to set up a meeting or more extended phone conversation to pitch your product. Then, enter the follow-up call or email, the date of the meeting, and any further notes on what approach to use in the future.

Because of all the detail you are entering, use your CRM like a daily, weekly, and monthly calendar to keep track of what you do. Later, you can use the accumulating stats for your daily, weekly, and monthly activities as a guide to your usual pattern of activities and what approaches are working the best.

For example, tally up the number of prospects or connections who you contacted by email or phone and note the number of each type of contact that led to a sale. Then, do more follow-up with the individuals in that category. For instance, if your emails are leading to the most meetings which result in the most sales, continue to do that. But if your phone follow-ups produce better results, use that approach. Or if you are doing both – sending an email and following up with a phone call – or making a call and confirming with an email – continue to do both.

In any event, seek to set up a meeting with a likely prospect or connection as soon as possible after you first meet, since you and your contact will better remember your exchange at the meeting, and the person will appreciate your responsiveness, which adds to your credibility. In some cases, you may be able to schedule a future meeting at a meeting, where you and the other party both whip out your calendars to set the date, time, and location.

After you set up a meeting, send a reminder a day or two before to confirm that you are still having this meeting. Also, set a reminder to send a follow-up thank you after the meeting. In this follow up, you might comment on how much you enjoyed the meeting and found it helpful, or you might point up the highlights of what the meeting accomplished. Such information not only increases your credibility and authority, it helps you and the other party know where you are in the deal discussion process, which can help you close the deal. It can also help you make an immediate or future sale, because your conversation at the event will be better remembered; it will have more emotional energy because it is still recent and seems more urgent to further discuss the possibilities. Still, you can later follow up after several weeks by explaining the reason for the delay in a positive way, such as you were involved in looking for the best, new products.

Finally, use the CRM system as a guide or reminder for what you are doing the next day, week, or month. In this way, you can better plan what you are doing each day and control your time. As they say: "You have to control your time to control the results," or conversely, "If you are not in control of your time, you are not in control of the results."

To use the CRM system as a guide and keep what you are doing top of mind, review your next day's activities the night before. This is also a good time to do a quick review of what is coming in the next week or weeks. Then, by knowing what is happening the following day, you can get everything ready the night before or first thing in the morning, so you can be well prepared for any meetings. Also, if you have to make any phone calls or send any emails, you can check when you are doing this and how much time you have allotted for this activity.

BOOK VII: WHAT TO SAY
IN YOUR EMAILS

INTRODUCTION

You may want to send emails for a number of purposes:
- to initiate, follow-up, set up meetings, and close a deal with clients in your area
- to promote a sales opportunity for your product or service
- and more.

BOOK VII on WHAT TO SAY IN YOUR EMAILS provides an overview of what to say in different situations. It includes some basic guidelines to follow no matter what kind of email you are sending.

Obviously, there are a lot of specific details to consider in deciding what to say in your email, such as what kind of person is it going to in that person's role (ie: store buyer, radio show host, potential customer, business associate) and his or her personality or perceptual style. This style affects how he or she likes to perceive and receive information, such as preferring short to-the-point messages or wanting more detail, or responding based on intuition or feelings or being a more rational, logical thinker. Then, there is the style characteristic of those in your industry, as well as your usual style, which may tend to be spare and lean, informal and flowery, crisp and ironic, or have other characteristics.

Thus, you need to adapt your email to the person you are sending it to, taking into consideration common industry practices and your own style.

This book features what to say in your emails in these situations
- contacting and communicating with prospective buyers in your area to set up meetings and close deals for your products or services;
- promoting the sales of a product or service

I'll be providing you with a number of sample templates you can use in different situations. Adapt these templates and make them your own. The emphasis will be on the basic format and content to use, rather than specifics of editorial style and writing copy, which could be several books and is beyond the scope of this book.

CHAPTER 1: GUIDELINES FOR SENDING EMAILS TO PROSPECTS IN YOUR AREA

Your goal in sending out email to potential customers and clients in your area is typically to set up a meeting where you can present your product or service in more depth. Following are a few general guidelines for sending an effective letter.

- <u>Keep it short</u>, up to about 300-500 words. Highlight the main points, such as who you or your company are and where and when you met or how you got referred. Describe how can help that person or work together, based on what you talked about or what that person's company does.

- <u>Don't attach sales materials or other attachments</u>. Unless the prospect has specifically asked you to send something, don't send any sales materials in an attachment in your initial letter. You can always ask if the person wants you to send more information through an online link or file you can send in your follow-up letter. Otherwise avoid any attachments in the beginning, because many people don't open attachments from people they don't know or unless they asked you to send them something, due to concerns about spyware, malware, and ransomware. Then, too, you don't want to come on too strong by trying to pitch something for sale right away. Rather, start with a "get to know you at a meeting" approach, since as they say at business networking meetings, the basis of a business relationship is getting to "know, like, and trust someone." When you send your first email, you are at the "know" phase.

- <u>Don't use technical jargon</u> if you have a specialty product or service, such as a customer management system, computer security software, or health and fitness device which provides computer readings. It can be tempting to explain how the product or service works, but initially you only want to emphasize the results of what the product or service does to help the person's business. In other words, lead with benefits, not features, especially if the features are quite technical.

- <u>Use a conversational style</u>, where you write like you are talking to the prospect to offer your assistance through your product or service. Don't make your email sound like a sales letter. So don't use words and phrases like "terrific," "great opportunity," and "chance of a lifetime." Also, avoid exclamations, phrases or sentences in CAPS, *italics*, or **bold** type, or use a **_COMBINATION_** of these, which makes your letter seem too salesy. And stay away from emojis, such as smiley faces, which seem unprofessional. Rather, in a friendly, but subdued, conversational way, introduce yourself and write your letter.

     - <u>Make any arrangements to meet or talk convenient</u>. Depending on the circumstances, you might suggest an initial phone call or a short personal meeting to discuss your product or service further. If you or the person you are contacting prefer an initial phone call, take the lead and offer to call, unless the person wants to call you, and schedule a time for this. Double check the line to call on, since some prospects may have another phone for the call. Or if you plan a meeting, offer to come to the person's office, though referral groups typically suggest meeting for coffee, and sometimes it may be more convenient to meet at your own office. Work out whatever arrangement seems preferable to the prospect. If he or she wants to meet for coffee, suggest some place near the prospect's office or ask the prospect to suggest a place he or she likes.

     - <u>Don't expect the prospect to respond right away</u>, since the best prospects for your product or service are often very busy. So an email from someone who is not known to them will be of lower priority. Generally, give the initial response about 2-3 days, and if you haven't heard anything, you can send another email to follow-up. If there's still no response, that commonly means the prospect isn't interest, though you can always call to try to reach the prospect, just in case he or she didn't get your email, and then take it from there, based on the response you get.

     - <u>Avoid certain words and phrases,</u> which are variously weak, overused, or seem phony in an initial query letter about your product or service. The words to avoid include "just," "actually," "hopefully," and "kind of," which are weak qualifiers.

     The phrases to avoid include:

        "Thanks for your time" or "Thanks in advance," which seem weak and needy.

        "I thought I should reach out" or "I wanted to reach out to you," which are overly wordy; just start with your message.

        "Hope you are doing well," or "Hope all is well," which sounds patronizing

"Please do not hesitate to contact me," or "Please feel free to contact me at your convenience," which seems to assume the person might hold off contacting you.

- <u>Use a common closing word or phrase</u>, such as "best," "regards," or "best regards." Avoid outdated closings, such as "sincerely yours" or "very truly yours," which are too formal and considered "old school."

- <u>Start off with the person's name or "Dear...." followed by their name</u>. Avoid a generic "to Whom It May Concern." If you aren't sure of the person's name, use the title of that position, such as "Dear Sales Director." Also, use the name people commonly call someone, not their formal name, such as "Dear Tom," not "Dear Thomas."

CHAPTER 2: WRITING AN EFFECTIVE EMAIL

The Goal of a Prospecting Email

The goal of creating a compelling email is so that the prospect will want to talk or meet with you to learn more about how you can help. The advantage of sending an email rather than phoning is to it helps to orient the prospect in a non-threatening way, where he or she can look at your email proposal and decide if interested in knowing more or not. Then, if interested, he or she can choose a convenient time to communicate with you. If you try to call, you may not be able to get through the receptionist who handles the call, or the prospect might be annoyed that you have called at an inconvenient time and brush you off.

For example, I frequently get calls from salespeople pitching web services, paying off student loans, getting a home owner loan or other programs, sometimes prefaced by a recorded sales message. My response is usually to hang up as soon as I realize it's a sales call – and normally I wouldn't be interested in many of these deals anyway, since I'm not interested in a product that's for homeowners or students, since I'm neither, which shows a lack of attention to detail or a lack of marketing knowledge.

Creating a Good Subject Line

Having a good subject line is especially important in your opening letter, since it will determine whether the prospect opens your email or not. There is an art to creating these subject lines, and sometimes marketers do split tests or even three-way tests to see which subject lines gets the best open rate. If you are only sending a few emails to people you have met at events or have been referred to by an associate, you can't do a split test that usually involves 50 or more emails. But you can try a different email for future mailings. For example, if you send out a mailing to a few prospects and don't get a response or get a low open rate, you can try emailing that same person and others with a different subject line.

The basic rule for a good subject line is to focus on the benefits – what's in it for the prospect. In up to 10 or 15 words, highlight the main benefit of your product or service to that individual or company.

For instance, some good subject lines for a company involved with creating websites and social media campaigns might be:

271

"Gain More Leads for Your Campaigns on YouTube and Facebook"

"How you can get more calls from your listings?"

"What are the most effective social media platforms to use now?"

"New software program automates and tracks your calls."

"Per our meeting Tuesday night: Video company tells your story to increase your sales."

You can use either the Headline style where all the words except for prepositions and connectors like "for," "on," and "and" begin with a capital letter, or a Sentence style, where only the first word is capitalized. But unlike a regular sentence, don't end with a period. But you should still use a question mark "?" to end a question.

It's best to keep your subject line specific, so it's directly related to how your particular product or service can help the prospect.

You want to avoid subject lines THAT are so general they could apply to anything or are overly salesy, which is a turn off. For example, some opening lines to avoid are these:

"Do you have time to review this opportunity?" (too vague and salesy – this opportunity could be anything, and "opportunity" suggests an appeal to "opportunity seekers" seeking get rich quick schemes rather than professionals.

"I wanted to connect with you after our meeting." (too vague – what meeting and who are you? Such vague messages are sometimes a source of malware.

"Increase your business with SEO." (too jargony)

Writing the Body of Your Prospecting Letter

Now that you've gotten the prospect to open the letter, a good way to structure an opening email gambit to a prospect is this:

Dear (Name of Prospect):

I'm (your name) from (your company). We met at (or I was referred by) (where, when) and we talked about (the nature of business/a problem of the business). You indicated you needed some help with (the nature of problem/the help needed), and this problem seems to growing for many companies in your field (what you know about the problem).

Well, I have the perfect solution (a way to help you overcome your problem and achieve your goal).

Our company (name of company) helps businesses (people) in your situation. We do (what you do).

And we've helped (number) of individuals/businesses (do what). For example, (briefly note an example of someone you helped, how, and with what results).

Do you have 15-20 minutes next week (later this week) when we could discuss how we could help your business? We could schedule a phone call or meeting at your convenience, and I can come to your office (Or be ready to change these arrangements if the prospect would like to come to your office).

Best,
Your Name

To sum up, the main points of the letter are these:

1) A brief introduction of who you are and how you met or were referred

2) The nature of the business' problem and how more and more businesses have been experiencing this (or other comment to show that you recognize the seriousness of the problem.

3) The solution which you can provide, which can include a link to a website or sales video showing what you do, and may additionally include examples of people you have helped and some testimonials. (However, only include a link after you have explained who you are and how you can help the prospect, so your link seems like it is to a legitimate website or video.)

4) An example to show how you have helped a number of clients over the years or have recently helped a particular client.

5) A request to set up a short phone call or meeting to discuss the problem and how you can fix it.

6) A sign-off with your name, business, and contact information. In a regular letter this might go on the top of the page, but in an email, it is best to put it at the end, where the prospect will see it once he or she is sold on setting up a meeting.

Using Links in Your Letter

You don't want to include any attachments in your letter, since many recipients won't open emails with attachments from people they don't know or if they haven't specifically asked for that information. Or they may open the letter but won't open the attachment.

However, you can use links, once you establish this is a letter from a genuine individual or organization offering benefits to the prospect, rather than from a spammer or con artist sending the prospect to a phony set to get information. So you need to start with a compelling introduction to who you are, why you are writing this letter, what you are offering, and what the link leads to.

Preferably limit the number of links to two, since some email providers may identify those emails as spam, so they end up in a spam folder or get rejected as spam. However, I have also sent out emails with multiple links that have gotten through, so perhaps having a specific subject line and a paragraph or two explaining who I am and what the email is about has helped to overcome any suspicion that such an email is spam or contains malware.

Thus, pick out the links you consider the most important and create those as live links, such as your website and a sales or pitch page, in addition to your email.

When and Who to Copy in Your Emails

Should you send a copy of your initial email to someone else in the company, a business associate who referred you, or someone you want to keep in the loop about your correspondence? That depends on whether you met the intended recipient individually or with others and whether that person asks you to email a copy to someone else. Then, too, you may be unsure whether to indicate the name of those copied in the .cc field or include that person with a blind copy in the .bc field.

<u>When You Make the Initial Introduction</u>

When you meet a person at a business meeting or first contact him or her online, you generally don't need to copy anyone else in the company, unless this person has asked you to include someone else. In that case, mention the person who made the referral to you and copy to that other person in your email.

Another possible situation is if you only have a brief introductory meeting or have found the contact information through your own research, and you aren't sure if you are sending the query to the right person. Then, you might copy someone in another position that seems more relevant, such as the director of development or acquisitions, or perhaps include both or more names in the "to" field.

Generally, you want people in a company to know when you have sent an email to two or more different people. And if you do send to multiple emails, you can explain that you weren't sure who to send your email to, and usually that will be acceptable to most recipients. In this way, you keep everyone informed, and typically the relevant person will respond to your email.

In some cases, you may want to copy others in your own organization to let them know what you are doing. In this case, it's best to include those individuals in a blind copy (bc), so you don't undermine your authority in sending the letter or confuse the recipient or recipients about who to respond to.

When You Are Sending an Initial Query Due to a Referral

When you send your initial query letter due to a referral, include a copy to whoever referred you (with their email in the "cc field") – and indicate the name of the person referring you in your opening sentence and in the subject line. Including this referral information in the beginning is very important, since a referral makes it more likely that the query will be opened and read – and that the recipient will do so more quickly. It doesn't matter if the referral is from someone in your company or from business associates, friends, and family. Indicate the source of the referral and why they did so (ie: "They thought you/your company might want to (buy/rent, sign-up for). Then, describe your product or service and why the person making the referral thought you might be interested in how your product or service can help them.

If you do mention a referral, be sure this is accurate. Otherwise it could blow up in your face if you claim that someone in the company referred you. It could later come out that you claimed this false reference, and that could quickly squelch any deal you thought you had. It could also prevent you from ever selling a product or service to that company again. Then, too, a falsely claimed referral could be immediately discovered if you name someone you found in an online search of companies in an industry no longer works there. Or if you pick up a card from someone you met briefly and claim a referral, that person could later deny meeting or remembering you. So be honest when you claim any referrals – and don't claim one that doesn't exist.

Sending a Follow-Up Letter

What if you don't get a response within a day or two? How long should you wait before sending a follow-up letter or calling to see if the person got the letter? And how should you handle including any copies on this letter?

Typically, if people get their email, they may normally respond within a few hours to a day or two, although in some industries, where an individual may be bombarded by numerous emails (such as an editor or agent in publishing), they may not respond for a few days or even a week or two. So take into consideration a person's position and industry in determining if a response is unusually late.

Before you do follow-up with another email or by phone, two things to consider are these:

- Did your email actually go out? To find out check your send folder, and if it didn't go out, it might have ended up in your "drafts" folder. If so, send the email again. Or if you have used an SMTP provider, you can check what emails went out. If they didn't go out, resend them.

- A lack of response may indicate a lack of interest, which is especially the case when the person is in an industry that gets a lot of emails from newcomers trying to break in, such as publishing and the film industry. In this case, it might be worth it to wait a little longer before responding with a follow-up letter or phone call.

Once you decide to follow-up, follow the practices in your prospect's field. In some cases, either a phone call or follow-up email is fine (such as to someone in real estate or the financial services industry, since they do much of their business on the phone). In other cases, it's best to only send a follow-up email (such as in publishing and the film industry, since editors, agents, and film producers don't like calls from aspiring writers; they prefer to do everything by email or using submittal forms on their website).

If you are following up by email, find your email in the sent folder, which will include anyone already in the "cc" field. If the "bc" field

276

doesn't show up, add their names in another "bc" field. Hit "reply" and begin with a brief note to the effect that "I hope you got my previous email, but just in case I am sending it again." The rest of your message will already be there. If you have a signature line, delete the one in your "reply" message, so the contact can see the pitch for your new product more clearly.

If you are following up by phone, say you are calling to see if the person got your email. Generally, don't go into your sales pitch here, since you only want to make sure the person got your email. If not, you can send it again. Or if the person says he or she got your email but isn't interested, that's your answer, and there's no need to follow-up. Should the person ask you what the email was about, you can briefly describe your pitch, but usually it's best that he or she gets your email, since that will have more details and links to your website or video.

CHAPTER 3: SENDING OUT A PITCH FOR YOUR PRODUCT OR SERVICE

Your email approach should be more direct and specific to promote a particular product or service. In this case, you are sending the email to the individual as a prospect for your offer, rather than as someone where you might work together as partners or make referrals to each other.

A Successful Simple Approach

The approach I use, which has been successful for me and for over 1000 clients in sending out letters for over 13 years has the following structure:

- A specific subject line describes what the product or service is all about.
- The first sentence or two summarize the main story or benefits
- Another paragraph or two provide more details.
- The next paragraph features social proof, such as any PR, social media following, or sales track record of the individual or company sending out the query
- A paragraph features a short bio of the individual or company.
- The last sentence concludes with a call for action which invites the recipient to ask for additional information if interested.

Along the way, a few links might be included to the sender's website or to photos or videos that show off the product or service.

More specifically, this letter should include these elements:

1) A strong subject line to attract interest; it should indicate specifically what your book, script, product, or service is about. Use Title Case or Sentence case; avoid all-caps, which comes across as shouting.

2) A short summary statement of 1 or 2 sentences highlighting what the book, script, product, or service is about and what makes it especially interesting and salable. For a product or service, highlight the benefits

3) The highlights of the project in two to three paragraphs, which describe the plot or main topics covered in a book or the major features of a product or service. You can use bullet points to indicate the major plot points, main topics, or features.

4) A sentence or two about the key selling points of the book, script, product, or service and why it will appeal to the recipient or the recipient's

customers or clients.

     5) A short paragraph about the *background of you or your company*, which features the major achievements of you or your company.

     6) A sentence or two about any <u>PR, promotion</u>, or any significant <u>social media</u> following.

     7) A final sentence or two indicating that if the recipient is interested, you are glad to submit more detailed information (INDICATE THE TYPE OF INFORMATION YOU MIGHT SEND, SUCH A PROPOSAL, TREATMENT OR SYNOPSIS FOR A BOOK OR FILM, A SALES SHEET FOR A PRODUCT, OR A LIST OF SERVICES FOR A PROFESSIONAL FIRM).

     Be prepared to follow up after your mailing within a week or 10 days. You might conclude with a comment about how you hope to hear from the recipient and discuss the project further. Avoid thanking the recipient, since this sounds like you are begging for their attention, rather than offering an opportunity to consider a good and highly beneficial service or product.

     For the most part, I and my clients have used this approach in sending query letters to publishers, agents, and film industry contacts, though this approach has also worked in gaining interest from professionals in other industries.

     While some companies use emails to send out ads with photos, graphics, and embedded videos, as well as links to websites, I have found the personalized letter with text only or with one, two or three photos, posters, and links to be very powerful. The letter provide a more personal touch, since it can be directed to a particular person, whether you send the emails individually or through a special platform that personalizes a bulk mail, as described in Book VIII on Sending Emails. Also, because of fears about spam, ransomware, virus, trojans, and other malicious emails, a simple personal or business email is often more likely to be opened and read, than an email that seems more like an ad with photos, video links, promotional copy, and bright bold type.

     You can also can use the email platform for sending out press releases and product and service announcements, which can be personalized or not. For example, after a subject line with a short headline, a press release might begin: "FOR IMMEDIATE RELEASE." An ad might feature a catchy tag line that quickly conveys what the product or service does, followed by a picture featuring that product or service. However, sending releases and promotional advertising gets into a specialty area, where you might hire a PR or ad agency. So writing a compelling press release or ad is better covered in another book.

Some Examples of this Email Approach for a Product or Service

Following are a few templates I have used for sending out email letters. These include templates for contacting publishers and agents about a book project, contacting professionals about a new service that can help them, and writing a query letter to pitch a product.

Whatever your product or service and target market, keep your query short and to the point -- ideally around 300-400 words, and no more than 500. Fill in the details as indicated, though put the letter in your own words. Use a common font, like Times New Roman, Arial, or Helvetica. Also, don't use **bold** type, <u>underlines</u>, or *italics*, since it is best to send out your query as a text message, which is most likely to be received and read. Use CAPS for emphasis, but only for titles, product names, or a word or phrase to highlight. Don't use these for a full line or sentence which comes across as shouting.

In the following template, the CAPS are instructions to fill in with your own information. Adapt the wording to make it your own.

<u>Template for Writing an Email Query Letter to Publishers and Agents</u>

Subject Line: (HIGHLIGHT THE MAIN POINT OF YOUR BOOK AND BE SPECIFIC; THIS SUBJECT LINE IS VERY IMPORTANT. IT IS WHAT APPEARS IN THE BROWSER ADDRESS LINE, AND IT IS WHAT GETS THE EDITOR, AGENT, PRODUCER, OR OTHER RECIPIENT TO OPEN YOUR EMAIL QUERY; IF YOU HAVE BEEN PRODUCED OR PUBLISHED NOTE IT HERE)

Dear (NAME):

(NONFICTION BOOK/NOVEL TITLE) which is about (DESCRIBE THE SUBJECT AREA OR PLOT IN 25 WORDS OR LESS...POINT UP ANY BIG SELLING POINTS, SUCH AS BEING A MULTI-PUBLISHED AUTHOR OR PRODUCED SCREENWRITER, OR IF YOU ARE OFFERING FILM RIGHTS TO BEST SELLING BOOK, ETC. THIS SECTION SHOULD BE LIKE A LOGLINE OF 1-2 SENTENCES.)

It features (THIS IS LIKE A MINI-SYNOPSIS WHICH DESCRIBES THE HIGHLIGHTS OF THE BOOK IN 1-2 PARAGRAPHS OF ABOUT 5-8 SENTENCES; HIGHLIGHT THE MAJOR SUBJECTS COVERED OR MAJOR PLOT POINTS).

(BOOK TITLE) should be highly marketable in that (GIVE ONE OR MORE REASONS, SUCH AS "IT IS THE FIRST BOOK TO COVER THIS TOPIC FROM THIS PERSPECTIVE." ALSO DESCRIBE HOW YOU WILL HELP TO SUPPORT THE BOOK THROUGH YOUR OWN PROMOTIONAL EFFORTS).

(NOW WRITE A PARAGRAPH ABOUT YOUR EDUCATION, BACKGROUND, EXPERIENCE, ORGANIZATIONAL MEMBERSHIPS, OR OTHER FACTORS THAT SHOW WHY YOU ARE IN AN IDEAL POSITION TO WRITE AND PROMOTE THIS BOOK OR FILM.)

I would be happy to submit a (SYNOPSIS/PROPOSAL/SAMPLE CHAPTER/COMPLETE BOOK, COMPLETE SCRIPT) or other materials for your further consideration. I can also submit (MENTION ANYTHING THAT MIGHT HELP PROMOTE THE BOOK, SUCH AS PROMOTIONAL MATERIALS, LETTERS OF ENDORSEMENT FROM WELL-KNOWN PEOPLE IN THE FIELD, NEWS CLIPS OF PREVIOUS PUBLICITY, A LIST OF THINGS YOU MIGHT DO TO PROMOTE THE BOOK, ETC.)

I hope you will be interested in pursuing (TITLE OF YOUR BOOK/SCRIPT), and I look forward to hearing from you.

Sincerely,

YOUR NAME
COMPANY NAME IF ANY
YOUR ADDRESS
YOUR CITY, STATE
WEBSITE IF YOU HAVE ONE
YOUR E-MAIL
YOUR PHONE NUMBER

Template for Writing an Email Query Letter for a Professional Service

Subject Line: (HIGHLIGHT THE MAIN BENEFIT OF YOUR SERVICE AND BE SPECIFIC ABOUT WHAT THIS IS; THIS LINE IS VERY IMPORTANT. IT IS WHAT APPEARS IN THE BROWSER ADDRESS LINE, AND IT IS

WHAT GETS THE RECIPIENT TO OPEN YOUR EMAIL QUERY; IF YOU HAVE ANY ENDORSEMENTS FROM WELL-KNOWN INDIVIDUALS OR FORTUNE 500 COMPANIES YOU CAN NAME, MENTION THIS IN A FEW WORDS AND DESCRIBE THIS IN A PARAGRAPH LATER.

Dear (NAME):

(NAME OF COMPANY/SERVICE which can help you (DESCRIBE 1-2 MAJOR BENEFITS IN 1-2 SENTENCES). We have helped (MENTIONED THE TYPE OF COMPANIES YOU HAVE HELPED; MENTION THE NUMBERS IF LARGE – IE: OVER 2 DOZEN), since/for (WHEN/HOW LONG; EMPHASIZE YOUR TRACK RECORD). You can see more details/testimonials on our website at (INCLUDE LINK TO SITE; SEPARATELY INCLUDE A LINK TO TESTIMONIAL PAGE IF IMPRESSIVE IN NAME CLIENTS; HIGH NUMBER).

It features (DESCRIBE WHAT YOUR PROFESSION DOES TO HELP INDIVIDUALS IN NON-TECHNICAL TERMS; DESCRIBE DIFFERENT SERVICES YOU PROVIDE. ABOUT 4-8 SENTENCES; USE BULLET POINTS IF 4 OR MORE ITEMS.

Our service should be of wide appeal to your contacts because (GIVE TWO OR THREE REASONS).

(NOW WRITE A PARAGRAPH ABOUT YOUR OWN OR YOUR COMPANY'S HISTORY, OR BOTH, HIGHLIGHING ANY CERTIFCATIONS, AWARDS, ACHIEVEMENTS, EXPERIENCE, ORGANIZATIONAL MEMBERSHIPS, OR OTHER FACTORS THAT SHOW WHY YOU ARE IN AN IDEAL POSITION TO HELP CLIENTS.)

I would be happy to submit more detailed information (INDICATE WHAT, SUCH AS A CATALOG SHEET, ONE SHEET, MORE TESTIMONIALS, PHOTOS OF YOU PROVIDING SERVICES TO A FEW CLIENTS) or other materials for your further consideration. I can also submit (MENTION ANYTHING THAT MIGHT HELP PROMOTE THE COMPANY OR SERVICE, SUCH AS PROMOTIONAL MATERIALS, LETTERS OF ENDORSEMENT FROM WELL-KNOWN PEOPLE IN THE FIELD, NEWS CLIPS OF PREVIOUS PUBLICITY, ETC.)

I hope you will be interested in discussing how I might help you and your company, and I look forward to hearing from you.

Sincerely,

YOUR NAME
COMPANY NAME IF ANY
YOUR ADDRESS
YOUR CITY, STATE
WEBSITE IF YOU HAVE ONE
YOUR E-MAIL
YOUR PHONE NUMBER

Template for Writing an Email Query Letter for a Product

Subject Line: (HIGHLIGHT THE MAIN BENEFIT OF YOUR PRODUCT AND BE SPECIFIC ABOUT WHAT THIS DOES; THIS LINE IS VERY IMPORTANT. IT IS WHAT APPEARS IN THE BROWSER ADDRESS LINE, AND IT IS WHAT GETS THE RECIPIENT TO OPEN UP YOUR EMAIL QUERY; MENTION ANYTHING THAT STANDS OUT ABOUT YOUR PRODUCT AND ANYTHING THAT INDICATES ITS POPULARITY IN A FEW WORDS).

Dear (NAME):

(NAME OF PRODUCT OR PRODUCT LINE) which can help you (DESCRIBE 1-2 MAJOR BENEFITS IN 1-2 SENTENCES). The product has helped (MENTIONED THE TYPE OF INDIVIDUALS OR COMPANIES IT HAS HELPED; MENTION THE NUMBERS IF LARGE – IE: OVER SEVERAL HUNDRED; since/for WHEN/HOW LONG; EMPHASIZE YOUR TRACK RECORD). You can see more details/testimonials on our website at (INCLUDE LINK TO SITE; SEPARATELY INCLUDE LINK TO TESTIMONIAL PAGE IF IMPRESSIVE IN NAME CLIENTS OR MANY ENDORSEMENTS).

It features (DESCRIBE WHAT YOUR PRODUCT DOES TO HELP INDIVIDUALS OR COMPANIES IN NON-TECHNICAL TERMS; ABOUT 4-8 SENTENCES; USE BULLET POINTS IF 4 OR MORE ITEMS.)

Our product should be of wide appeal to your contacts because (GIVE ONE OR MORE REASONS).

(NOW WRITE A PARAGRAPH ABOUT YOUR PRODUCT OR YOUR COMPANY'S HISTORY, OR BOTH, HIGHLIGHING ANY NOTABLE STORIES ABOUT PEOPLE USING YOUR PRODUCT).

I would be happy to submit more detailed information (INDICATE WHAT, SUCH AS A CATALOG OR SALES SHEET, MORE TESTIMONIALS, PHOTOS OF YOUR PRODUCT OR PEOPLE USING YOUR PRODUCT) or other materials for your further consideration. I can also submit (MENTION ANYTHING THAT MIGHT HELP PROMOTE THE PRODUCT, SUCH AS A PRESS RELEASES, OTHER PROMOTIONAL MATERIALS, LETTERS OF ENDORSEMENT FROM WELL-KNOWN PEOPLE IN THE FIELD, NEWS CLIPS OF PREVIOUS PUBLICITY, ETC.)

I hope you will be interested in discussing how I might help you and your company with our products, and I look forward to hearing from you.

Sincerely,

YOUR NAME
COMPANY NAME IF ANY
YOUR ADDRESS
YOUR CITY, STATE
WEBSITE IF YOU HAVE ONE
YOUR E-MAIL
YOUR PHONE NUMBER

Creating Other Pitch Letters

The foregoing letters are just to get you started. Feel free to put these letters in your own words and adapt them to your conversational style. Keep in mind that this initial letter is designed to open the door to further communication. Include a reference to your website, photos, or videos about your product or service if recipients want more information.

The basic goal of this letter is to get the person to want more information or to set up a phone call or meeting with you, where you have an opportunity to sell your products or services. So you want to keep the letter short and to the point. You want a subject line that is compelling to get the recipient to open the email, using the language and trigger points for your type of customer or client.

Then, your letter should build interest so the person wants to know more, and ultimately will want to talk to you and based on that discussion, move to the next level. These levels are essentially requests for more information and involve the following types of requests.

- For a book or film, the request is to see a synopsis, proposal, some chapters, or the whole manuscript or script.

- For a service, you want to set up a more extended discussion, demonstration, or strategy session to convince the person to hire you or your company.

- For a product, the person may want more product information, and then the goal is for the person to place an order for a large number of products for the company or store.

Thus, consider the letter like a first step in a sales funnel, where you give the person enough information, leading to a sale to a percentage of the recipients. Not everyone will be an ideal client ready to buy. Some won't be ready; some won't have the interest or money; and some will want to do more research to decide.

Whatever the outcome, consider each person who expresses interest as a prospective customer or client. Sending an email is like getting out on the stage for a few minutes to gain audience approval to continue your act. Then, if you give a great performance and can show how great your book, service, or product is, you'll make the sale, which is like getting a standing ovation when you really kill it onstage.

CHAPTER 4: TEMPLATES FOR INTRODUCTORY AND FOLLOW-UP SALES LETTERS

Here are some templates you can use for sending initial and follow-up emails to clients about meeting with you to pitch a product or service. Adapt them to your own style and that of your industry and location. Some industries and areas of the country will be more formal and others more casual, and you may prefer a more formal or casual style yourself. Use what feels right for you.

In some cases, you might prefer to make an initial phone call seeking a referral and then provide more information by email. In that case, adapt any of these templates to become a sales script.

Introductory Query Letter to an Individual or Small Company

The following letter provides a way to introduce yourself by showing how you can solve a problem for an individual client or company.

Subject: Some Suggestions on Solving Your (PROBLEM)

Dear/Hi (NAME)…

I noticed that you have (PROBLEM). The (PROBLEM) can be especially bad when (SHOW HOW THE PROBLEM CAN BE EVEN WORSE).

We help (individuals/businesses) by doing (HOW YOU CAN SOLVE THE PROBLEM – THIS IS HOW YOU CAN BRING VALUE)

We have helped to fix this for (PROVIDE SOME EXAMPLES OF HOW YOU HAVE DONE THIS FOR PAST CLIENTS, INCLUDING NAMES IF POSSIBLE – THAT SHOWS YOU KNOW WHAT YOU ARE DOING; IT PROVIDES SOCIAL PROOF).

Can we set up a call or meeting for about 10-20 minutes next week to discuss what we can do to help (you/your company)?

Best regards
(YOUR NAME
COMPANY
ADDRESS, CITY, STATE
PHONE
EMAIL
WEBSITE

Introductory Query Letter to a Prospect in a Large Company

Here's a similar letter, but adapted for contacting someone in a large company.

Subject Line: Some Suggestions on Solving Your Company's (PROBLEM)

Dear/Hi (NAME)…

I'm writing to get in touch with the person who is in charge of (DEPARTMENT/PROGRAM). I am also sending this email to (NAME 2, 3, AND 4), since I wasn't sure who to contact in your company.

I wanted to let you know how my company (YOUR COMPANY NAME) can help you improve (WHERE YOU CAN DO TO HELP) by (WHAT YOU CAN DO TO PROVIDE A SOLUTION).

A few companies we have helped with this include (COMPANY 1, 2, and 3).

Can we set up a call or meeting for about 10-20 minutes next week to discuss what we can do to help your company.

Best regards,

YOUR NAME
COMPANY
ADDRESS, CITY, STATE
PHONE
EMAIL
WEBSITE

Initial Query Letter after a Meeting

It's best to send a follow-up email within a day or two after the meeting, or at most no more than four or five days later.

Subject Line: Meeting with You at (WHERE YOU MET)

Dear/Hi (NAME)…

It was great to meet you (WHEN) at (WHERE YOU MET)

It was very informative to talk to you about (WHAT YOU TALKED ABOUT). I'm sending you a link to a (WEBSITE, ARTICLE, BLOG) that can help you with (HOW CAN THIS INFORMATION HELP THEM)

I hope we can set up a meeting for coffee or a phone call, so I can learn more about your (PRODUCTS/SERVICES) and business and tell you about our company. I think there's a good synergy for how we can help each other.

Here are (SOME TIMES YOU ARE FREE OR A LINK TO YOUR SCHEDULER). (OR: Please let me know when you have time to meet for coffee or just talk on the phone.)

Let me know what time would work best for you, and if you'd prefer to meet or just talk on the phone first.

Best,

YOUR NAME
COMPANY
ADDRESS, CITY, STATE
PHONE
EMAIL
WEBSITE

Query Letters to Potential Power Partners

You may meet people who are potential power partners in business networking and referral groups and arrange to meet with them to discuss how to refer business to each other. You can also reach out to others through emails to discuss strategic partnerships. The following email template provides an example of how you might do this for a product or service.

The basic idea of this letter is to explain how you happened to contact the company through a referral or other source. Note that you are looking for other companies of a certain type where you can be mutually beneficial to each other, and that you would like to set up a meeting or phone call to discuss this further. While a face-to-face meeting is ideal, some individuals may prefer a phone call first to decide if a meeting will be useful. In either case, this letter is designed to open the door to further communication about the potential for working together in some way for mutual benefit.

Subject Line: Referral by (NAME) about how we might work together (OR OTHER REASON FOR THE REFERRAL)

Hi/Dear (NAME):

I was (referred to you by/at a business meeting/looking through (NAME OF REFERRAL, BUSINESS MEETING, OR SOURCE OF INFORMATION SUCH AS GOOGLE/CHAMBER DIRECTORY,TRADE MAGAZINE, ETC.) and wanted to contact you.

I thought we can help each other, since our company helps (WHO, WHAT TYPE OF BUSINESSES) to do (WHAT, HOW DO YOU HELP) by (HOW DO YOU HELP) for (WHAT BENEFIT OR VALUE DO YOU PROVIDE).

We're looking for (individuals/companies) that we can partner with, so we can refer business to each other, since we're in related industries.

I'd love to have a further discussion with you about the possibilities. Can we set up a meeting or phone call (later this week/next week) to discuss this further? I could come by your office or we could meet at a nearby coffee shop or just talk on the phone to see if this would be a good fit for you.

If you'd like to talk about this further, please reply to this email or give me a call so we can arrange for a meeting or phone call.

YOUR NAME
COMPANY
ADDRESS, CITY, STATE
PHONE
EMAIL
WEBSITE

Query Letter in Response to a Referral

In some cases, you might get a referral from a business associate you know, sometimes as a result of being in a business networking or referral group. Whether you get the referral by an email, where your associate introduces you to each other, or a conversation, here's an example of an email you might send – and generally copy the person who referred you. The one exception might be if that person mentioned your name as a good contact at a group meeting, so this wasn't a personal referral to you.

Subject Line: Referral by (NAME) about (REASON FOR REFERRAL)

Hi/Dear (NAME)…

I was referred to you by (NAME OF PERSON GIVING YOU THE REFERRAL) when (HOW THAT PERSON HAPPENED TO GIVE YOU THE REFERRAL). He/she thought (WHY DID THAT PERSON REFER YOU; OR IF YOU HEARD ABOUT THIS PERSON AT A GROUP MEETING, NOTE HERE WHAT THAT PERSON SAID THAT LED YOU TO REACH OUT TO MAKE A CONNECTION).

Do you have a few minutes to talk on the phone so we can discuss how we might work together? (ALTERNATIVELY: Would you like to set up a meeting to talk about how we might work together?)

If you'd like to talk about this further, please reply to this email or give me a call so we can arrange for a meeting or phone call.

YOUR NAME
COMPANY
ADDRESS, CITY, STATE
PHONE
EMAIL
WEBSITE

Follow-Up Email after an Initial Email Query

If you don't hear anything after your initial query, here's a way you might follow-up. After your follow-up letter, include a copy of the original email you sent. As appropriate, send a copy to those copied (either .cc or .bc) on your initial query.

Subject Line: FW: (ORIGINAL EMAIL SUBJECT LINE)

Hi/Dear (NAME)…

I didn't hear back from you last week when I sent this email about (IN A FEW WORDS SAY WHY YOU SENT THE EMAIL, so I wanted to follow-up to make sure you received this.

If you are interested/if you'd like to talk more about this, please send me an email or give me a call.

YOUR NAME
COMPANY
ADDRESS, CITY, STATE
PHONE
EMAIL
WEBSITE

Making an Initial Query by Phone

Here's an example of how you might make a phone call if you have been referred by someone else. If you don't have a particular person who referred you, it is generally best to use an initial email query to introduce yourself, although some people like to make phone calls first when they find out about the company as a good prospect for working together.

Hi (NAME)...

This is (YOUR NAME). I was talking to/met with (NAME OF BUSINESS ASSOCIATE, FRIEND, FAMILY MEMBER) last week/the other day/yesterday, and he/she suggested I contact you about (WHY ARE YOU CALLING).

He/she thought we can help each other, since our company helps (WHO, WHAT TYPE OF BUSINESSES) to do (WHAT? HOW DO YOU HELP) by (HOW DO YOU HELP) for (WHAT BENEFIT OR VALUE DO YOU PROVIDE).

We're looking for (individuals/companies) that we can partner with, so we can refer business to each other, since we're in related industries.

I'd love to have a further discussion with you about the possibilities. Can we set up a meeting or phone call (later this week/next week) to discuss this further? I could come by your office or we could meet at a nearby coffee shop or just talk on the phone to see if this would be a good fit for you.

Would you like to set up a meeting or phone call to discuss this further?

(IF YES) Great! What's a good time for us to meet/have a phone conversation later this week/in the next few days/next week/in the next week or two?)

Alternatively, if you found their name from other sources than a direct referral, you might say something like this.

Hi (NAME)

I was (at a business meeting/looking through/at a presentation (NAME OF REFERRAL, BUSINESS MEETING, SOURCE OF INFORMATION SUCH AS GOOGLE/CHAMBER DIRECTORY,TRADE MAGAZINE, ETC.) and wanted to contact you.

I thought we can help each other, since our company helps (WHO, WHAT TYPE OF BUSINESSES) to do (WHAT? HOW DO YOU HELP) by (HOW DO YOU HELP) for (WHAT BENEFIT OR VALUE DO YOU PROVIDE).

We're looking for (individuals/companies) that we can partner with so we can refer business to each other, since we're in related industries.

I'd love to have a further discussion with you about the possibilities. Can we set up a meeting or phone call (later this week/next week) to discuss this further? I could come by your office or we could meet at a nearby coffee shop or just talk on the phone to see if this would be a good fit for you.

Would you like to set up a meeting or phone call to discuss this further?

(IF YES) Great! What's a good time for us to meet/have a phone conversation later this week/in the next few days/next week/in the next week or two?

Creating Your Own Templates for Queries

Besides adapting any of these templates, you can create your own. Write down what you want to say in an email or by phone, save it, and print it out, so you can use that as a guide for future emails or phone calls. That way you don't have to start from scratch each time.

You might also experiment with different approaches to refine your message and come up with an introductory email or phone query that works best for you. However you say it, you want to open the door to a future meeting or a more in-depth phone call to discover how you might work together or refer other business to each other.

CHAPTER 5: USING AN EMAIL TO SELL A PRODUCT OR SERVICE WITH A SALES PAGE

Sometimes you want to send an email to get prospects to visit your sales or pitch page for your product or service. In this case, you need to create a powerful sales page to sell your product or service.

Sometimes, too, you want to start with a thank you page, where you provide a free gift in return for an email, and then that page links to your sales page. That's the sales funnel approach to online marketing, which could be another book. Here I'll just tell you about how to create a good sales page.

Creating a Sales or Pitch Page

If you use a sales page, also known as a pitch page, make your description of your product or service as compelling as possible. Besides any written copy and photos, ideally include a sales video, also known as a video sales letter or VSL.

While some people spend several thousand dollars for a sales video, an alternative is to create a PowerPoint presentation with eye-catching headlines, short snappy copy, and photos or graphics. For instance, you might limit the copy to a header and a few sentences or bullet points on some slides. Then, turn the finished PowerPoint into a video which you narrate as a voice-over, or you can include clips of your speaking directly to the viewer.

An inexpensive way to create a video is to do a screen capture of the PowerPoint as you go from slide to slide, and narrate as you do so. Afterwards, you can edit this to cut off any segments you don't want, such as in the beginning or end, or spots where you have made mistakes.

Once your video is completed, upload it onto YouTube or a webpage where you can copy the link to the video, so you can embed that video link on your sales page. This way, though the video is still on YouTube it will play on your sales page. Used in this way, the video helps to add a compelling narration to support any written copy in your letter or on the sales page you have linked to.

Using Video Capture Software

One cheap and easy way to create a video for your sales page is to use video capture software, which turns a PowerPoint into a video and enables you to add a voice-over narration, and you can later add video clips with an editing program.

The two popular video capture software which I have used are Screencast (www.screencast-o-matic.com) and PowerPoint with the Camtasia Add-In. Then, use Camtasia (www.camtasia.com) for any final editing.

About 10 years ago, I took an editing class using Final Cut Pro which made this whole process seem very complicated – and after six weeks of three hour classes, I still found editing an extremely detailed, difficult process.

But these new programs make any editing very easy and quick to learn – perhaps 5 minutes and you can be up and running. The software is very inexpensive – you can make short narrated videos of up to 15 minutes with Screencast for free, and a pro upgrade is only $15 a year. This allows you to make longer videos and include audio from your computer as well, so you can include a musical background or other sound effects if you want. And if you want to be on the camera, you can easily use the camera on your computer or record the video on your smartphone to film yourself. Then, import the video of you speaking into one of these programs, edit it, or combine it with your PowerPoint video.

In short, other than having a professional create a high-octane sales pitch for you, you can use these programs to create an effective video from a PowerPoint presentation – and if you want to add in a video of you speaking, such as with your smart phone video app, that's easy to do.

The following illustrates how to use these two software programs – Screencast and PowerPoint with the Camtasia Add-In.

Using Screencast

The basic way Screencast works is that you do the following:
- Open up the software,
- Open up the PowerPoint you want to record in Slide Show view,
- Adjust the frame around the first PowerPoint slide,
- Make sure the audio is on to record your voice-over narration,

- Hit the record button and record
- Save your recording as a mp4 file.

You can always stop the recording and then continue it. Or you can edit the recording after it is completed to eliminate sections of the video you don't like. You can make any corrections after the video is completed and shared by pulling it into the software and reediting it.

To illustrate how easy it is to use Screencast, go to the home page of Screencast (www.screencast.com or www.screencast-o-matic.com/home) and start recording. The recorder looks like the small recorder on the left of the screen.

Once you hit the "Start Recording" button, you'll see a brief description of how the recorder works and all the ways you might use the recorder, such as to record workshops and webinars. You can also record your pitch for your product or service, featuring you, your PowerPoint presentation, or both.

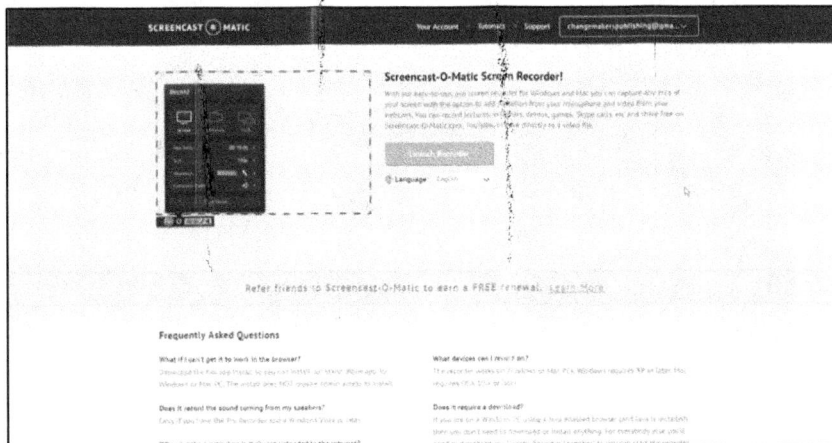

You can launch your video pitch from your browser or download an app to your computer and launch it there. Once you do, you will see a frame which is around anything you see on the screen, and you can make that frame smaller or larger. You'll also get a message to make sure the green bars are flashing as you talk to make sure the narration is working from your computer mic, though if you have the free version, you can't use your computer audio.

To illustrate, here's how I began recording my video, using a PowerPoint I originally used for a presentation to a business networking group on writing for clients. I opened up the PowerPoint presentation and adjusted the screen to get everything set to record.

Though the recorder box appears over the platform, the recorder will record everything behind it, once I click the record button. When I'm recording, the recorder box disappears, but I can see what is happening in the small box below. I can see the mic vibrating to indicate it is recording, as well as see the number of minutes and seconds of the recording.

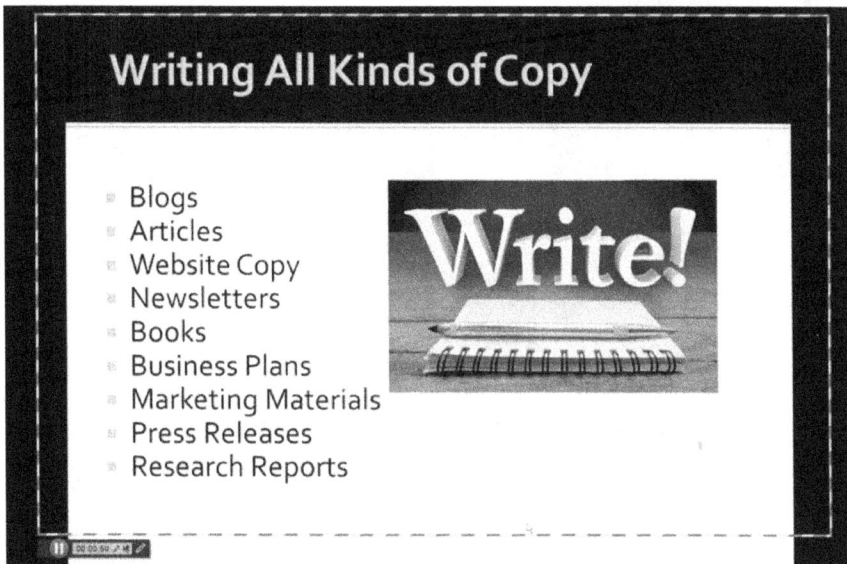

The recording continues until I click "Done." Once I do, I'm back at the beginning screen, and I can see how many minutes have elapsed, along with the audio track.

I can then edit if I want, and I can upload the recording to Screen-O-Matic or save it on my computer as an MP4 video file.

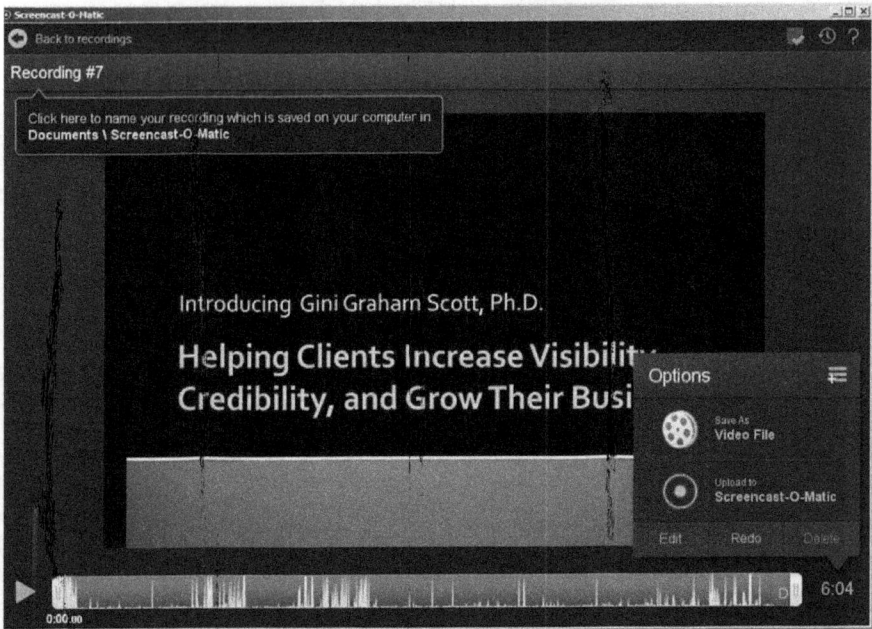

Should I want to edit, I can then do so.

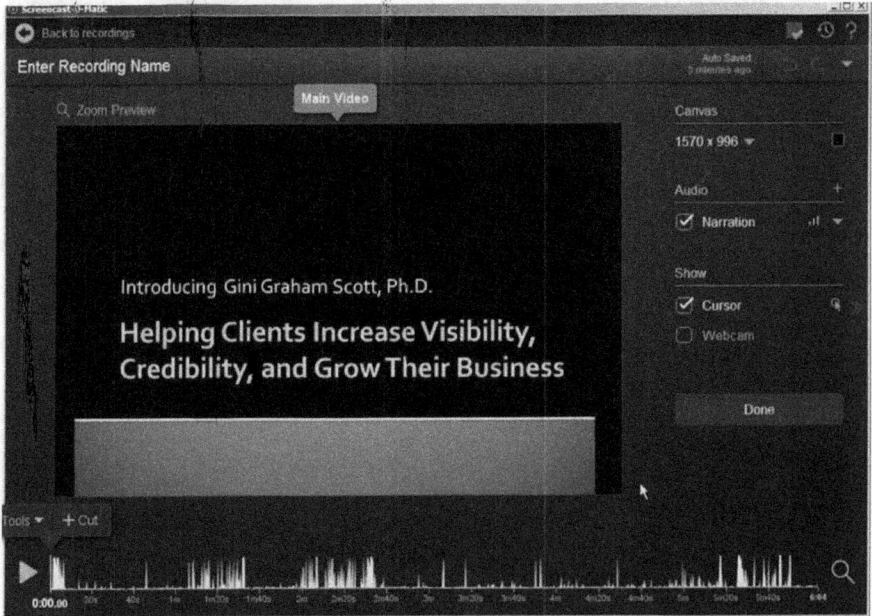

The program includes various editing tools to do so.

Thus, turning a PowerPoint into a video is a fairly straightforward process. If you can do the presentation straight through like you would at a business meeting, you can have your video ready to upload to your website or sales page or embed it from YouTube. Then, you can add a link to that sales promotion in your letter.

Using Power Point with the Camtasia Add-In

      The other program I recommend using is the Camtasia Add-in to create a narration with your PowerPoint slide. If you later want to make any adjustments to the video you have created, you can use the Camtasia editor. You can easily cut off the beginnings and endings and any glitches along the way.

      To begin, go to Camtasia Add-ins to access the recording toolbar. The initial slides from Camtasia will tell you what to do, as indicated below.

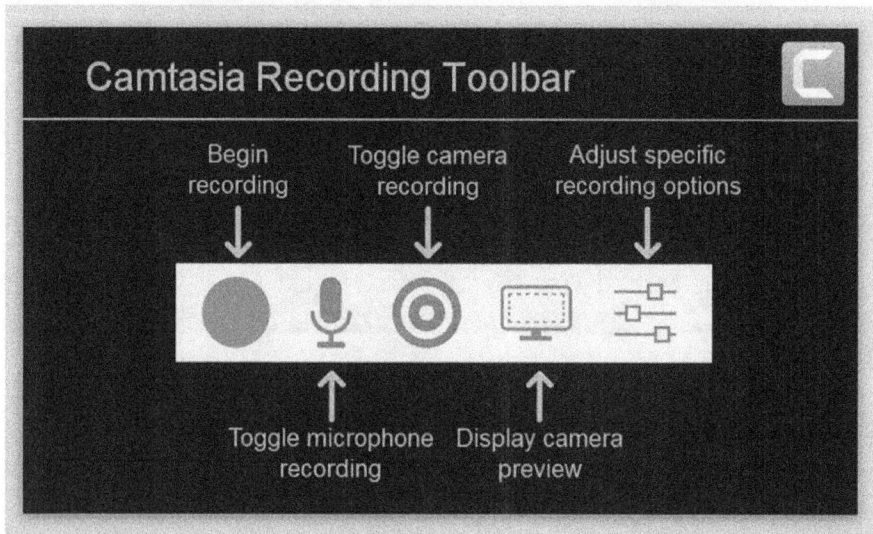

Start a Recording

1. Select recording options
2. Press the record button
3. Test your audio and then start your recording

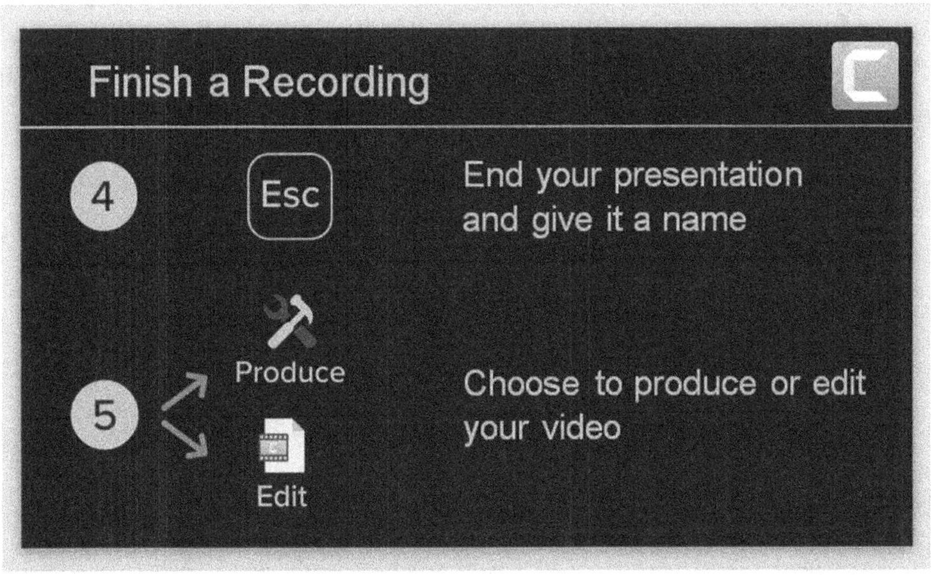

Finish a Recording

4. End your presentation and give it a name
5. Choose to produce or edit your video
   - Produce
   - Edit

You'll see this set of instructions each time you open PowerPoint after you get the add in, until you feel ready to get rid of this opener. Here's an example of how I did this.

After I open my presentation in PowerPoint, I click Add-ins, and the Camtasia recording toolbar appears.

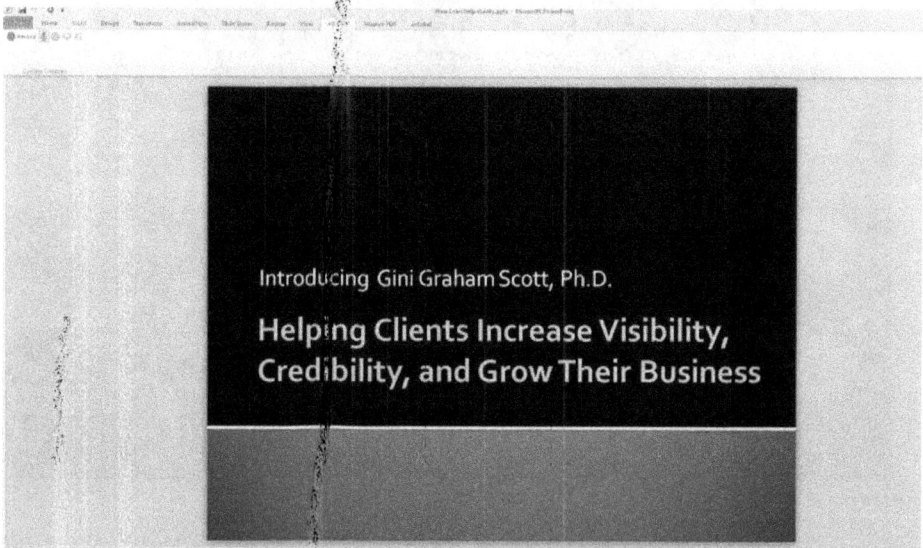

Once I hit "Record," the Camtasia recording screen appears on the bottom right of the PowerPoint.

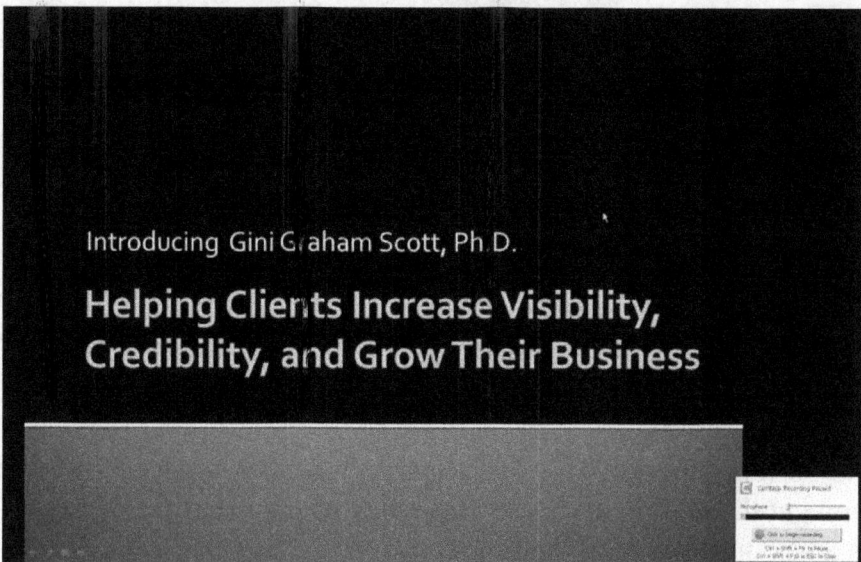

I can then narrate as I go from slide to slide at any pace I want. Thus, I can spend more or less time in talking about a particular slide, just as I might at a slide presentation at a business meeting. Then, I go on to the next and the next, until the whole presentation is done.

While I'm recording, the recording box disappears from the bottom of the screen as I go along. Here's what the screen looks like as I record a couple of the slides. On the top left, as I record the screen, there is a stop recording button, so I can end the recording at any time.

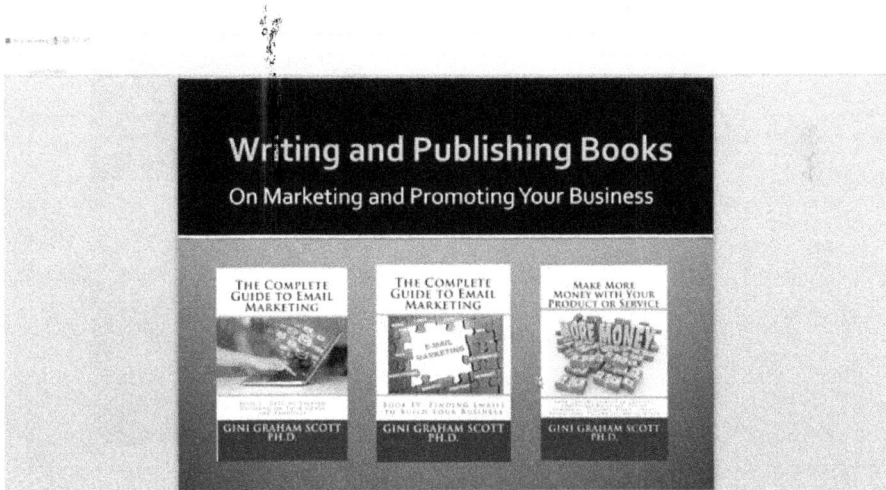

Once I end the presentation, I can stop the recording or continue it if I want to say more.

After I stop the presentation, I save it.

Then, I can produce it or edit it.

If I want to edit it, I go to the Camtasia video editor, which I have already installed. This editor is designed to edit an already completed video, so if I have other video footage, such as a video where I am talking to the camera on a smartphone, I can combine them first.

If I opt to produce it, I end up in the Camtasia Production Wizard.

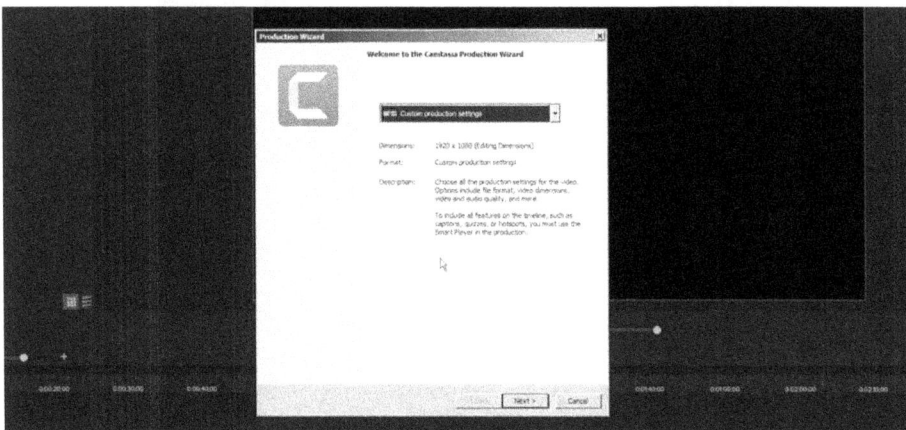

Then, I can produce the video in various formats – the recommended one is the most popular MP4, though I can produce it in other formats, such as an WMV or Windows Media Video.

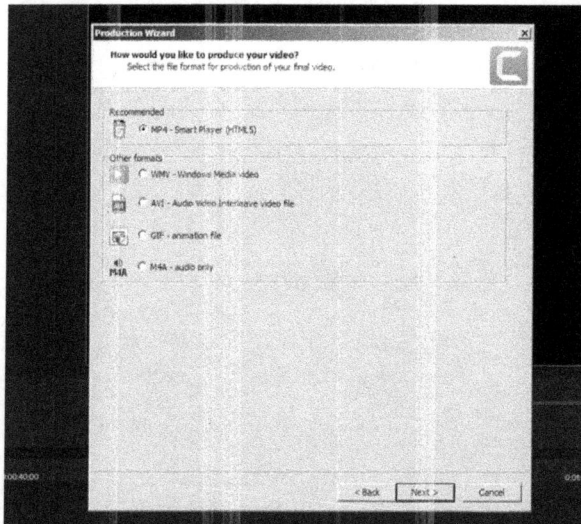

I next have a series of options about the size of the video, settings, audio settings, and other options. Among these are whether the video should start automatically, the size of the video, the frame rate, the audio rate, and whether to include a table of contents and make this searchable. I opted for the default settings, but if you are so inspired and technically inclined, you can experiment and make your own choices.

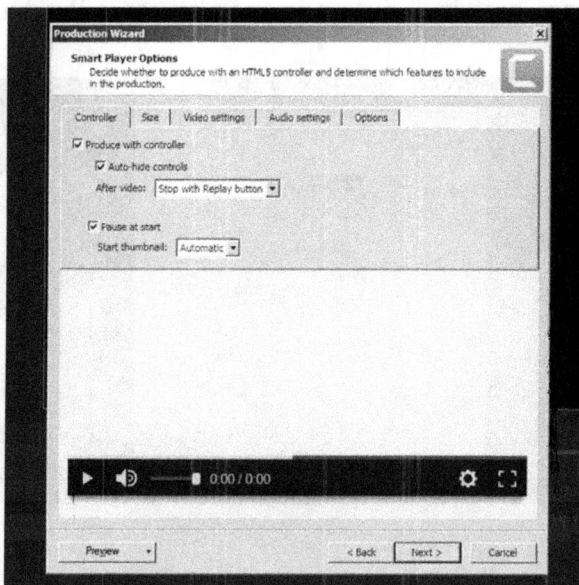

Later, should you want to open up a Camtasia account to do additional editing, get your account on Camtasia and download the software.

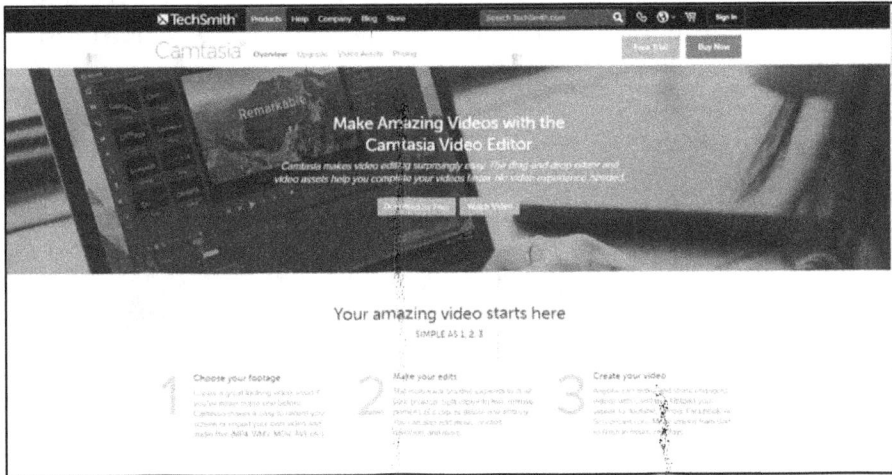

After you open up the software, start a New Project. Any recent projects you have done are indicated, so you can easily locate and further edit them.

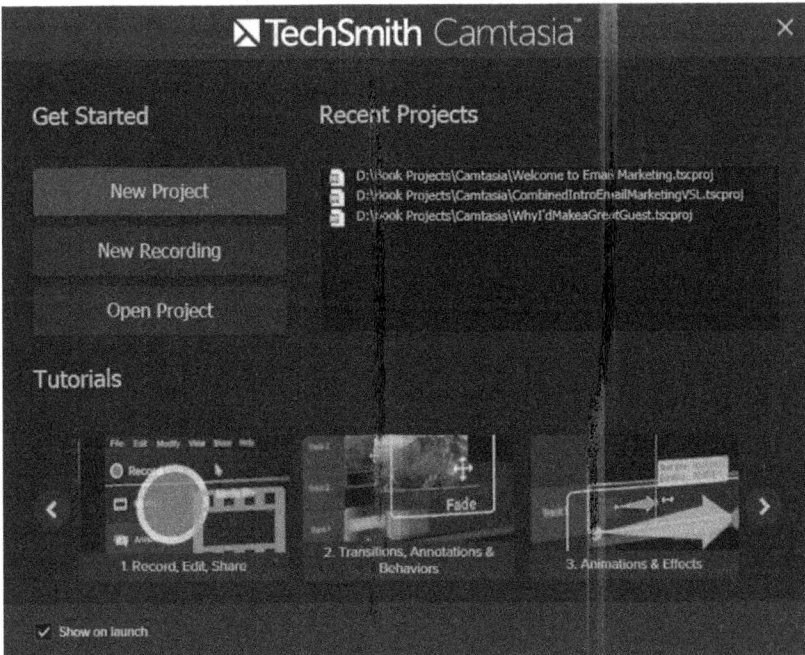

You'll then see a screen where you can import other media to edit it or add a narration. For example, I used this to record a narration to a PowerPoint, much as with Screencast. In this case, a first step is to turn the PowerPoint into a video file, which you can do in PowerPoint10 and above. You simply save it in a MP4 or WMV (Windows Media Video) format.

Once you import any media, you add it to your media bin.

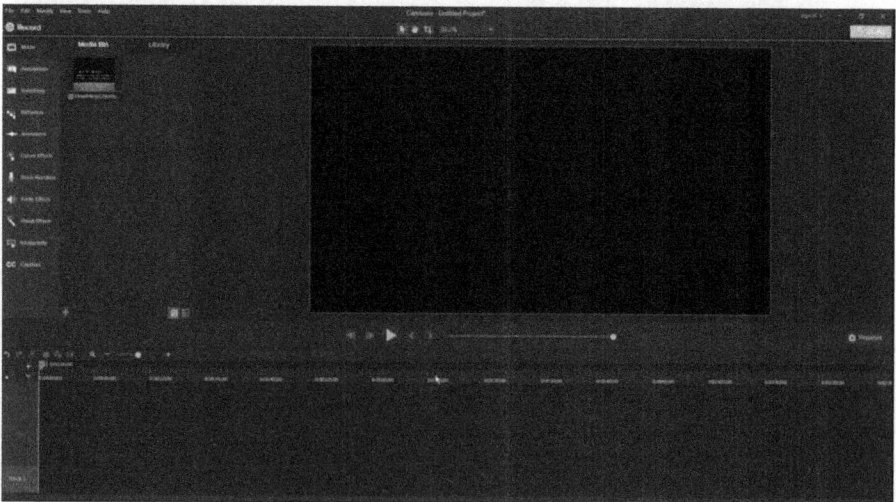

Then, move it into the video screen box, where it becomes Track 1.

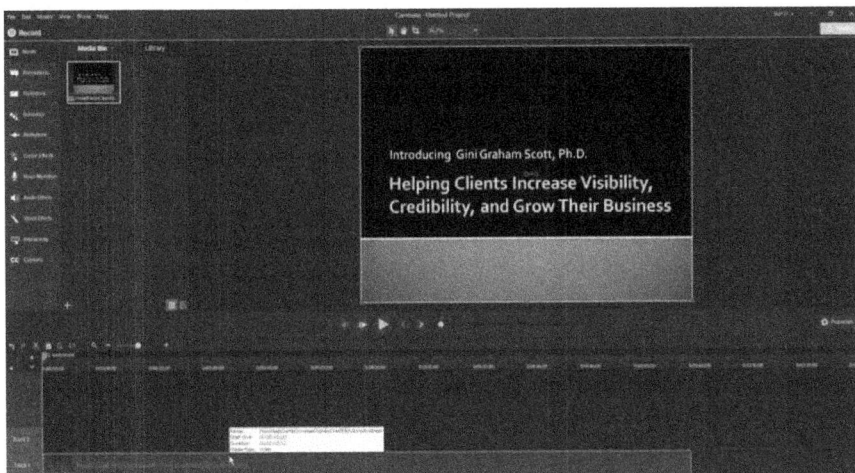

After that, as you play it, you can move the little levers on the timeline to select sections to cut. You can also insert additional videos, as described in Book III on creating Videos and PowerPoint Trainings. The difference here is that you are using your video as a sales video to support your query letter with a link that leads the prospect to this video.

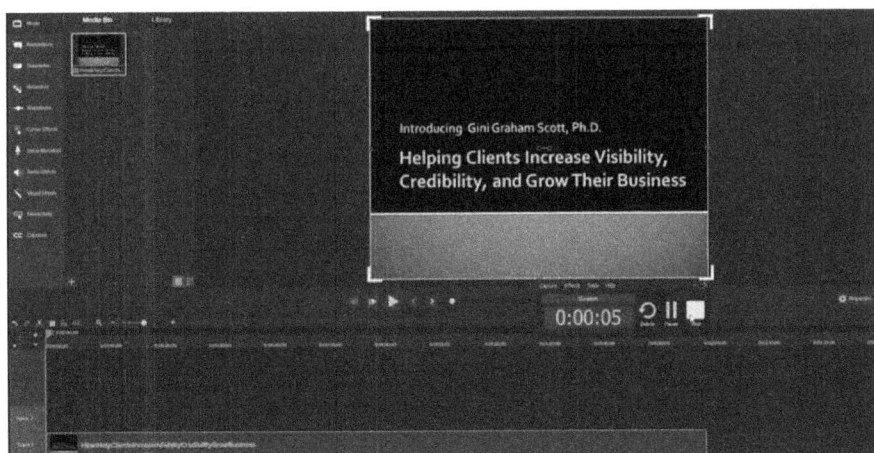

Finally, once your edited or combined video is completed, you save your final video and you can upload it to your website or save it on YouTube.

BOOK VIII: SENDING EMAILS

INTRODUCTION

Virtually everyone with an email account – which includes almost everyone on the planet today – knows how to send individual emails. In *Book VII: Using Emails to Increase Local and Online Sales*, I discussed how using emails to increase local and online sales, and send individual emails to get sales and clients through referral marketing, primarily in your own location.

But there are many other ways to send multiple and personalized emails at the same time to prospects, or to send recurring communications like newsletters and announcements to your email list. At times you may send out promotional queries to email addresses you have collected, or you may want to mail to contacts on lists you have bought and cleaned up.

Thus, there are many ways to send emails, depending on:

- who you are emailing,
- the number of emails you are sending,
- whether these emails are targeted to a particular group,
- whether these are recurring emails.

Book VIII: Sending Emails provides an overview of the many different ways to send emails effectively. It features chapters on these topics:

- Using mailing services to send out high-volume promotional emails for sales and publicity,
- Using software to send out targeted and personalized promotional emails through an SMTP server,
- Using an email sending platform for opt-in emails, like Mail Chimp or Constant Contact

The book includes numerous illustrations to help you evaluate the various programs and services. The emphasis is on deciding your best approach and putting it into practice to increase your sales and clients.

CHAPTER 1: DISCOVERING THE MANY WAYS TO SEND E-MAILS

The Beginnings of the Email Connections Business

I discovered the power of sending out multiple emails with the aid of new technologies about 20 years ago. Even before the Internet, back in 1984 until about 2001, I began sending out multiple queries, pitching books to publishers and agents with lists of proposals for new books. Then, if the publishers or agents were interested, I sent them a proposal by mail. The result was some of my first book sales, *Strike It Rich in Personal Selling* to Avon in 1985 and *Mind Power: Picture Your Way to Success in Business* to Prentice Hall in 1987.

But back then, these mailings were a slow, tedious process that involved physically printing out lists of proposed books, writing a cover letter, putting a set of these letters and lists in a stamped envelope, and mailing them to an editor or agent. Then, if an editor or agent was interested and mailed a letter or called for more information, the next step was sending a physical book proposal with sample chapters or a complete manuscript in a large envelope, and awaiting a response.

In the late 90s, around 1997 or 1998, this all changed with new technologies like Microsoft Office 98 and the beginnings of email used in commerce, making it possible to contact publishers and agents by email. I began doing this in 2001, when I teamed up with a woman who had started sending out emails to film producers to pitch scripts for herself and clients. She used an email server and a new software program from an Irish company called Group Mail, which I'm still using today – though in a much evolved technology. After I contacted her about pitching some of my scripts to producers and she learned how I was contacting publishers and agents with postal mailings, she indicated that she would like to expand into the publishing industry. So a partnership was born.

We developed a database of publishers and agents who had emails, and I began sending out query letters by email with short descriptions of new books to those in the industry who were receptive to receiving emails, while I continued to send postal mailings to others. Today, when almost everyone in the industry uses emails, it's hard to imagine the early resistance to change, but it took another five years or so until email pitching began to catch on. Before then, people wanted to see hard copies, like these were the real thing.

In any case, after a couple of difficult start-up years, I took over the business of sending emails to publishers and agents myself in 2003, and the company exploded. Articles appeared in *The Wall Street Journal* and *Contra Costa Times* about this new way to contact publishers and agents by email, and soon I had hundreds of clients each year. After a few years of just targeting the publishing industry, I expanded into contacting film producers, agents, directors, distributors, casting directors, and others in the film industry. Additionally, I began to do mailings to those in the speaker industry, games and toys industry, music industry, and venture capitalists. I chose markets where I wanted to pitch my own books, scripts, games, songs, and business ideas. Then, after I collected information on company emails and the company official to contact and did my own mailings, I expanded this service to others who wanted to contact companies in these industries.

The Growth of the Email Connection Business

The result was phenomenal growth – from about $16,000 my first year to nearly $100,000 five years later. But despite this success, since I wanted to focus

on writing and filmmaking, I sold the business in September 2008, just before the Great Recession. In 2013 I restarted the business after my 5-year non-compete clause ended, and the software developer who bought the business decided to close it, since he hadn't marketed it or kept the databases updated. So he was earning about a third of what I did my last year in the business. But recognizing his mistakes, I resumed marketing the business. Since I already had updated databases I used for myself, it was an easy relaunch as Publishers, Agents, and Films (to reflect the service's connections with the film industry).

Along the way I had a brief one-year partnership with a business associate, took it over myself in December 2013, and a few months later, created a spin-off service, The Professional Connection, which connects professionals in different industries with each other. Then, in November 2012, I resold the business once more to new owners, and I still work with them to help them promote and grow the business, while taking over the writing for them through a new company I set up called Ghostwriting Gurus (www.ghostwritinggurus.com).

This experience with creating an email based business helped me learn about the email marketing industry, and during this time, the technology has advanced, making email more powerful than ever. As a result, the business not only uses software and special email service companies for sending out emails far more quickly than when I first started doing this, but it has all kinds of tracking tools to indicate how well each email blast is doing. For example, you can know how many recipients received and opened your email, how many emails bounced and which ones, and how many recipients clicked through links in your emails. Additionally, you can learn your percentage reputation based on the number and percent of good emails you send out compared to the number of bounces, dropped emails, and spam reports.

In setting up the Professional Connection, I also learned all about buying and cleaning up email addresses from services that sell hundreds of email lists and getting more expensive targeted cleaned up lists. Then, one can send out emails to these cleaned up lists, using the software and email service providers. Or one can use special mailing services that send out large targeted emails to selected contacts in different industries and locations, as well as to consumers based on their interests and demographics. I also started developing programs to use recurring mailings with services specializing in sending these mailings to opt-in lists.

Thus, this book is designed to draw on what I've learned in over 20 years of running a growing email business that specializes in sending targeted emails using either software and email service providers or sending out large bulk mailings through the services that specialize in doing this.

CHAPTER 2: PREPARING EMAIL LIST FILES FOR EMAIL SENDING PROGRAMS

With many programs to send emails to your email lists, you have to have the files in .csv format, and sometimes you can use Excel (.xls or .xlsx) files. (For those unfamiliar with these common file formats, .csv refers to "comma separated values," where categories are separated by commas, while Excel is a spreadsheet application in the Microsoft Outlook suite of programs.) When you purchase emails, they often come in .csv or Excel formats, and you can easily convert or save the files in one format to that of the other.

You may need to convert them, since you may have obtained the files in one format, but need to convert them into the other format to send them out in a particular software program. But that is easy to do. You either save an Excel file into a .cv format, or you import a .csv file into an Excel spreadsheet.

In general, it is better to have the files in an Excel format if you want to make any changes, such as deleting records or organizing the files into subgroups. You can import either file format into a database program, such as Access. Then, too, when you create lists in many programs, such as in using Cision (www.cision.com) to create media lists based on certain criteria, you can export a file in either or both formats. However, many email sending programs, such as GroupMail 6, require you to have a .csv file.

Converting to Excel or .CSV Files

If you have an Excel file you can easily convert it into a .csv file by simply opening the Excel file and saving it as a .csv file.

Conversely, if you have a .csv file, you can open it up in Excel as an Excel file and then save it as an .xlsx file.

Thus, you can readily switch from one file format to another as needed.

Using a Database Program to Create Targeted Lists

A database is ideal for selecting the list you want to send a query to from a larger list based on certain selection criteria – such as by city, county, state, or country; by demographic categories, such as age, sex, education, occupation, or other factors.

While you can do some filtering in an Excel file or in using data collected through a customer relations manager (CRM) program, it can be easier to work with those files by importing them into a database program. Then, you can export any subfiles you create as Excel or .csv files, or turn any Excel files you export into .csv files to send out the emails.

Alternatively, you can enter the information you gather, such as from business cards or online data listings, into a database to begin with. In working with a database, I have used Access, which is the most commonly used desktop database application in Windows. It comes with the Microsoft Office suite, and it is inexpensive and accessible from most Windows laptops and workstations. It has also become accessible through the Internet, and many e-commerce and content management systems are powered by an Access database running on Microsoft's web server platform.

There are other database programs, which I'll briefly describe at the end of this chapter. But since I have used Access, which is one of the most popular programs, I will use that to illustrate how to work with these databases to create targeted lists for sending out emails to multiple contacts through various software programs.

At a certain point, you may become big enough to outsource your database management and mailing to a company that specializes in such operations. But when you are just starting to send out mailings, you will generally handle these mailings yourself or with an associate in your company. So that's what I'll describe here.

Creating Subfiles by Selecting or Excluding Certain Categories

As your lists get bigger, you will likely want to do separate mailings to groups with different interests, or you might want to create a split test to see the responses to different mailings, where you make changes in your copy or offer. This way you can compare which mailings resulted in more replies, sign-ups, sales, or whatever measure of success you are using.

Additionally, you might want to divide up your list to reduce the size of a single mailing. For example, instead of doing a single mailing to 10,000 contacts, you might select subgroups based on certain criteria, such as the regions of the United States, so you send out four queries to no more than 2500 contacts at a time. While this division into subgroups can give you insights into the responsiveness of different categories to your query, your initial intention is to create a more manageable mailing to a smaller group.

To illustrate, this is what I have done with the contact information obtained from business cards I have collected at business networking mixers, and with the information about publishers, agents, film producers, and other film industry contacts obtained from numerous industry publications. Later, I have used keywords to create queries on the database to select a sublist of targeted contacts to export as a .csv file, rather than exporting the whole database as such a file.

Whatever your motivation, here's how creating the sublists in a database works. You use keywords to either include contacts in a certain category, such as in states in the South, in the Pacific Northwest, and so on, or to exclude contacts in a category, such as all academic institutions with an email ending in ".edu" or all publishers in the UK, Canada, and Australia.

For example, after purchasing a number of databases for a client interested in contacting attorneys, CPAs, doctors, and other professional groups, I imported the original .csv files we bought that had 50,000 or more contacts each to create a database in Access (in an.mdb or .accdb file, depending on whether it was an older or newer version of Access) with all of these records. Then, since the client wanted to first contact professionals in certain areas, I created a series of queries on the database for selected states, such as California and New York, and for selected regions, such as all the states in New England and in the South. Then, I exported each of these subfiles into Excel and turned them into .csv files, which I could later import into the software used to send out the emails.

Here's an example of the initial database I created after purchasing a file from one of the companies selling databases, as previously described in *Book V: Buying and Validating Email Lists for Large Mailings* on buying email lists and cleaning them up in an email validator called Mailbox Validator (www.mailboxvalidator.com).

There are a number of services which work in much the same way to send you back a file of all the valid emails or give you files which rate your emails from A and A+ emails (which are definitely valid) to B files (which are likely to be valid) to other emails with D or F ratings, due to bounces and other reasons for rejection.

In this case, the files came back as a file with all the good results in one .csv file, a file with only the good emails in another .csv file, and my original file with all the results and about a dozen columns which indicated the basis for determining the ratings of each email based on using a series of true and false tests.

I then imported the good results file into an Access database, which resulted in an original file with about 15,000 emails being reduced to about 12,000 good emails due to people moving, changing their emails, retiring, and other factors.

After that, I created a series of subfiles to target specific states and areas of the country and reduce the number of contacts for each email. Each one was created by selecting certain areas of the state and doing a query on the database which indicated the counties I selected in the "Counties" column. You can see the list of sublists created on the left. Here's an example of one of these sublists for the California Bay Area, which I created by selecting all of the Bay Area counties, such as Alameda. Since I was only interested in the contact's email, first name, and last name, I only included those categories in the query.

Likewise, you can create your own subfiles, by selecting to include or exclude certain categories. For example, in Access, I select the fields to include in a query. Then, in each field I indicate what categories I want to include by using those keywords with an * at the beginning and the end of each keyword or phrase I select and the connector "or" – such as in *Vermont* or *New Hampshire* or *Maine* or *Connecticut*. Or I indicate those items I want to exclude by using the word "not" before each keyword followed by the connector "and." For example, if I wanted to exclude certain states in a mailing, in the state field, I would write: not *Vermont* and not *New Hampshire* and not *Maine* and not *Connecticut.*

Exporting the Files to Create Excel or .CVS Files

Once I have created all of these sublists, the next step to prepare them for a mailing in bulk mail software is to turn them into Excel or .csv files. In an older version of Access, I could export a list into a .csv file directly, though now I have to export it into an Excel file, and then save it as a .csv file.

To export the file in Access, you click on the "External Data" tab, which provides various options, including exporting as an Excel File.

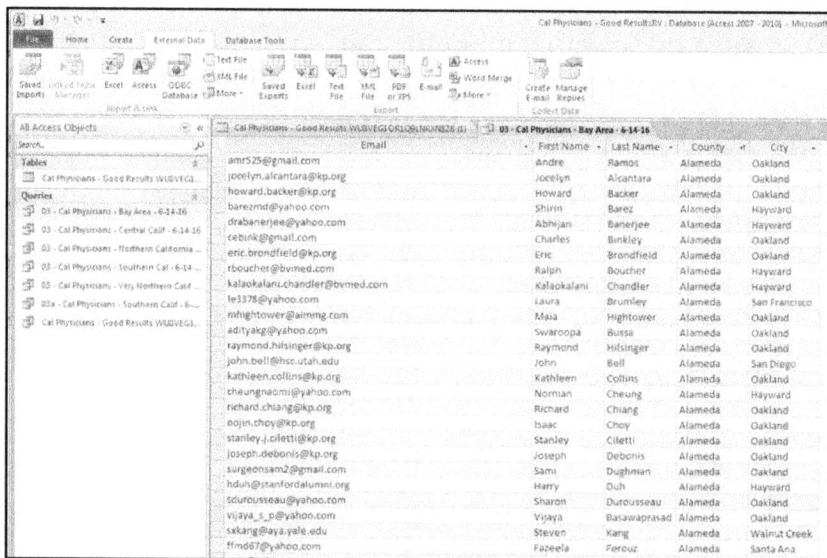

When you click on an Excel icon, you get a dialog box indicating the name of the file (in this case it's the Cal Physicians in the Bay Area with the date I created the file) and the file format (Excel Workbook - .xlsx). You indicate where you want the file to go by clicking "Browse." You want to keep the same formatting and layout, so click that.

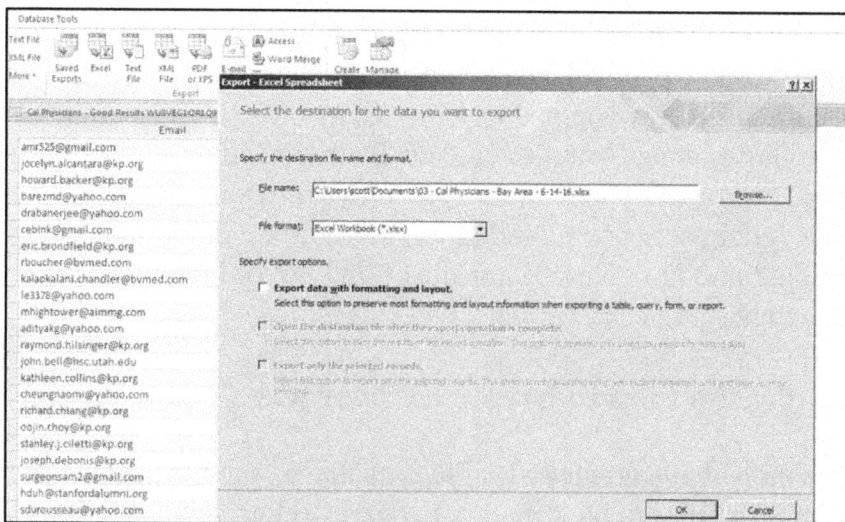

To illustrate, when I click "Browse," here's what it looks like on my computer after I indicated that the file should go in the folder: "New Data – Prof Connection – 11-3-16."

And that's it. Once the sublist is saved as an Excel file on my computer, I save it as a .csv file. Here's where the file is saved.

And here the file opened in Excel.

	A	B	C	D	E
1	Email	First Name	Last Name	County	City
2	spunkymeadow@yahoo.com	Gregory	Chen	Alameda	Oakland
3	amr525@gmail.com	Andre	Ramos	Alameda	Oakland
4	jocelyn.alcantara@kp.org	Jocelyn	Alcantara	Alameda	Oakland
5	howard.backer@kp.org	Howard	Backer	Alameda	Oakland
6	barezmd@yahoo.com	Shirin	Barez	Alameda	Hayward
7	drabanerjee@yahoo.com	Abhijan	Banerjee	Alameda	Hayward
8	cebink@gmail.com	Charles	Binkley	Alameda	Oakland
9	eric.brondfield@kp.org	Eric	Brondfield	Alameda	Oakland
10	rboucher@bvmed.com	Ralph	Boucher	Alameda	Hayward
11	kalaokalani.chandler@bvmed.com	Kalaokalani	Chandler	Alameda	Hayward
12	le3378@yahoo.com	Laura	Brumley	Alameda	San Francisco
13	mhightower@aimmg.com	Maia	Hightower	Alameda	Oakland
14	adityakg@yahoo.com	Swaroopa	Bussa	Alameda	Oakland
15	raymond.hilsinger@kp.org	Raymond	Hilsinger	Alameda	Oakland
16	john.bell@hsc.utah.edu	John	Bell	Alameda	San Diego
17	kathleen.collins@kp.org	Kathleen	Collins	Alameda	Oakland
18	cheungnaomi@yahoo.com	Norman	Cheung	Alameda	Hayward
19	richard.chiang@kp.org	Richard	Chiang	Alameda	Oakland
20	oojin.choy@kp.org	Isaac	Choy	Alameda	Oakland
21	stanley.j.ciletti@kp.org	Stanley	Ciletti	Alameda	Oakland
22	joseph.debonis@kp.org	Joseph	Debonis	Alameda	Oakland
23	surgeonsam2@gmail.com	Sami	Dughman	Alameda	Oakland
24	hduh@stanfordalumni.org	Harry	Duh	Alameda	Hayward
25	sdurousseau@yahoo.com	Sharon	Durousseau	Alameda	Oakland
26	vijaya_s_p@yahoo.com	Vijaya	Basawaprasad	Alameda	Oakland
27	sxkang@aya.yale.edu	Steven	Kang	Alameda	Walnut Creek
28	ffmd67@yahoo.com	Fazeela	Ferouz	Alameda	Santa Ana
29	cycx@yahoo.com	Tyler	Kang	Alameda	Antioch
30	melnyko@sutterhealth.org	Ostap	Melnyk	Alameda	Antioch
31	ronbo84@yahoo.com	Ronald	Olson	Alameda	Walnut Creek
32	miriam_rhew@yahoo.com	Miriam	Rhew	Alameda	San Leandro
33	zhangd@sutterhealth.org	Douglas	Zhang	Alameda	San Leandro
34	zekensophie@yahoo.com	Amy	Halio	Alameda	Oakland
35	karlhkim@gmail.com	Karl	Kim	Alameda	Oakland
36	kate.kasberger@kp.org	Kate	Kasberger	Alameda	Oakland
37	tlgashkim@yahoo.com	Tami	Gash-Kim	Alameda	Emeryville
38	scott.abramson@kp.org	Scott	Abramson	Alameda	Oakland

H ◀ ▶ H 03 - Cal Physicians - Bay Area

Ready

Then, you save the file as a .csv file, as I have done here.

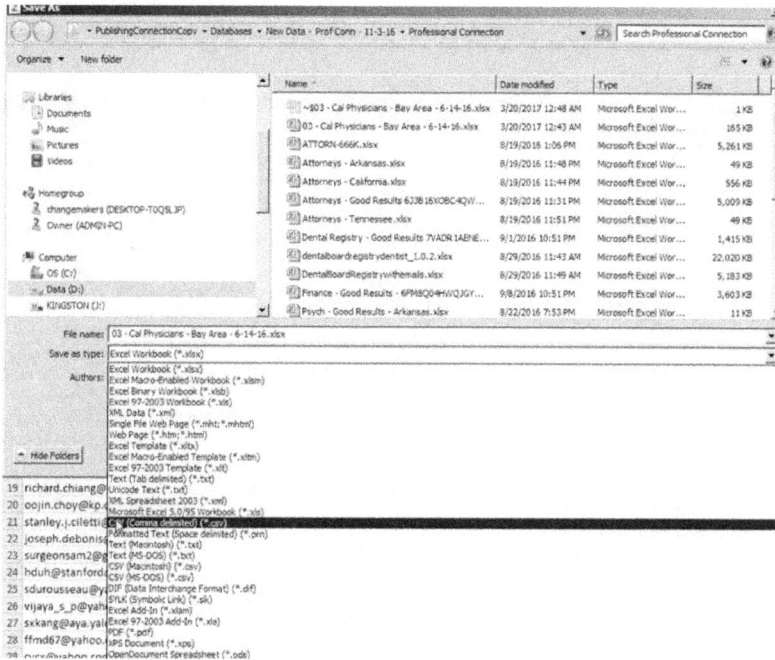

328

And here it is as a .csv file, which looks almost exactly the same as an Excel file. But now it's ready to be imported into whatever software you use, such as GroupMail 6, to be explained.

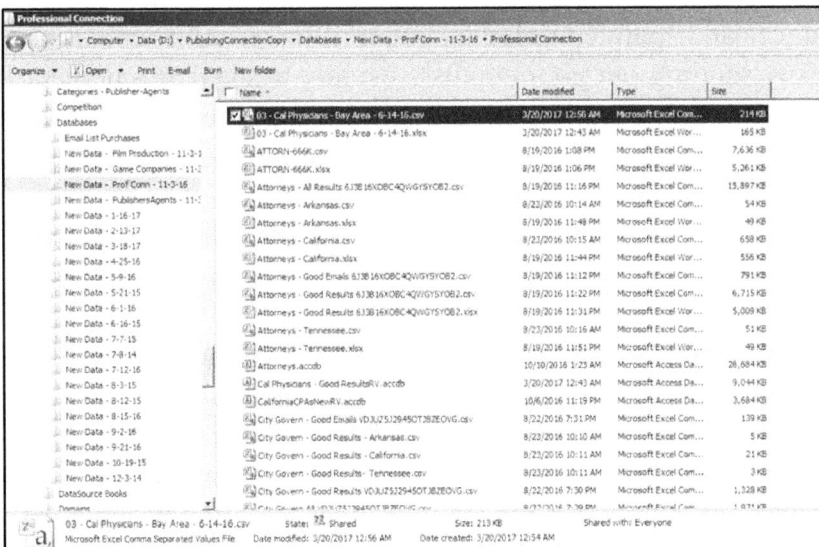

Updating Your Database with Changes

In working with a database, you should use certain codings to make changes in the database as a result of a mailing, such as if an email bounces, is rejected by the recipient as "spam," or if someone has left the company, changed their email, is no longer interested in what you offer, or if the company has gone out of business. You can use any codings you want, along with any explanation to let you know why you are using that coding. You can place that coding in a separate column for changes, or preferably in the email column, so you will exclude any emails with that coding when you do a query on the database.

For example, the codings I have used are these, followed by the date of that mailing which led to excluding that email.

RETX (DATE) (REASON, such as "Spam" or "no such domain."

XXX (DATE) (REASON, such as "retired," "deceased," "charges money," or "no longer interested,"

ZZZ (DATE) (duplicate email)

In the event a new person has taken over that position, I either replace the old information with the new information or indicate the date of the change in the "Comments" column. Or I use the XXX coding and the reason; then I add in a new record for the new person.

It's important to keep your databases updated, so any list you use is as current as possible. Otherwise, if you send out an email that results in a lot of bounces and spam complaints, you will lower your reputation with the company sending out your emails – usually tracked as a percent from 0-100%. Should your reputation drop below a certain level due to repeated bad mailings, an email service is likely to suspend your account, because they want to be sure their clients are not sending out spam or mailing to outdated emails, reflected in a high percentage of bounces and spam complaints. Ideally, you want your percent to be at last 90%, though occasional dips are okay.

For example, my reputation has typically averaged about 92-95%, and in a few cases, went as high as 100%, though I had a few drops to 79-83%, after I sent out a mailing to about 1500 finance professionals after I hadn't mailed to this group for about 6 months without cleaning up the list, so about 20% of the emails bounced. Fortunately, I had been a long time customer, so I was able to bring my reputation up again through several subsequent mailings to lists I used regularly. But when an associate who had just signed up for the same service experienced a 15% bounce rate in a mailing to 2000 professionals, her account was suspended, and she had to find another service to send out her emails.

CHAPTER 3: USING SPECIAL SOFTWARE TO SEND YOUR EMAILS

Once you have your targeted email list in a .csv file, you can use special software to mail to that group, personalize the email, and include any email you choose in the send and reply fields. Then, depending on what SMTP server you choose, you may have to additionally verify the send email by sending a test email to that selected email, so you can respond back to indicate that you received this email. After that you can use this email until you want to change it. But with other SMTP companies, it is not necessary to use this additional verification; as long as you are a client with an account in good standing, you can put any email you want into the send and reply fields.

Selecting a Send and Reply Email

Generally, it makes sense to use the same email for sending your email and getting replies. Commonly, people will simply reply to an email, unless you have set up a clear "click here to reply," message, so recipients are likely to click that, though others may continue to respond directly. Then, too, when your reply email matches the email in your signature or in the contact listed for a release or announcement, that contributes to your legitimacy. It shows that the query has gone out from the same individual or company that is offering the product or service.

Yet, if you have a good reason, you can always set up the mailing so you use one email for sending the query -- the email your query appears to come from when the recipient sees the email, and another email for the reply field. This reply field is where the responses will come if a recipient directly responds to that letter. You can also put any email you choose in the letter, announcement, or release you send out, along with instructions to respond to that email. And when an email goes out with a no-reply email, recipients have to reply to the specified email. In any case, this no-reply option can be a good approach when you want to send an official query from your company, but want any responses to go to you or a designated person in the company who is ready to reply to any responses.

However, one caveat in selecting what email to use. You can use any of your emails or your clients' emails with their permission. And with some providers, you have to respond to a test email from your send and reply email, so you need an email you and the client can reply to in a short time to validate the email. Otherwise, you can't use that email.

In any case, even if you can use any email address without having to do a validation test, don't do so without permission. If you do, once the person with the email finds out, you can be in serious trouble for impersonating someone else, misrepresentation, and any other problems that result due to sending a mailing seemingly from someone else. Plus, imagine what could happen if you use the email of a public official, even the U.S. President. You could soon find the FBI or Secret Service at your door thinking you had some nefarious purpose. So don't use someone else's email in a mailing without permission, even as a joke.

Using Special Software to Set Up and Personalize Your Message

While there may be other software programs you can use to send out a bulk email and personalize your mailing with the recipient's name, I will focus here on a program I have used for over 13 years. It is now called GroupMail 6, after going through a series of iterations. It started as Group Mail 3, and then Group Mail Plus, before its current revision. I began using it in late 2003, when I first started sending out emails.

Should you opt to use another software program for your own mailings, you can apply the basic principles of how to do this to another program. I'll briefly mention some alternatives after I describe how to obtain and use GroupMail 6.

Obtaining the GroupMail 6 Software

You can obtain the software from the company website at www.group-mail.com.

There are a series of packages, but when you are just getting started, I recommend using their basic package, the GroupMail 6 Business Edition, which I have used since they developed this from their earlier versions. It's $149.95, and you get a one-time license which you can use on your computers in one location, which includes your laptop. You can get yearly updates for about $90 a year.

Should your company grow, there is a faster version with more features and you don't need to use an external SMTP mail server. But for now, the basic GroupMail 6 version is ideal.

If you want to try out the program with a small number of mailings, such as if you are sending a newsletter to your subscribers, you can use a free version of the software to get started.

Using GroupMail6 to Send Out Your Query

The basic way that GroupMail6 works is with the following steps:
- Set up your email account for sending your email, which includes indicating the proper settings and sending a test email;
- Create the group to send the email to and import the .csv file you have created into that group.
- Write or copy your message into the message box and put your subject line in the "Subject Line" box;
- Preview your message;
- Double check that you are sending the right message from the right account to the right group;
- Click a button to send your email, and indicate any exclusions, such as mailing to a subset of the full list (i.e.: sending 2000 emails at a time from a mailing to 10,000 retail store buyers);
- Finally, click a button to confirm you want to send the email; it will go out to about 1000 contacts in a few minutes, depending on the speed of the SMTP service you are using to send out your emails.

Following are a series of images that shows how this works.

Getting Started

Once you open the software and put in your account name and registration number, the software indicates three basic areas for sending a message: Accounts, Messages, and Groups.

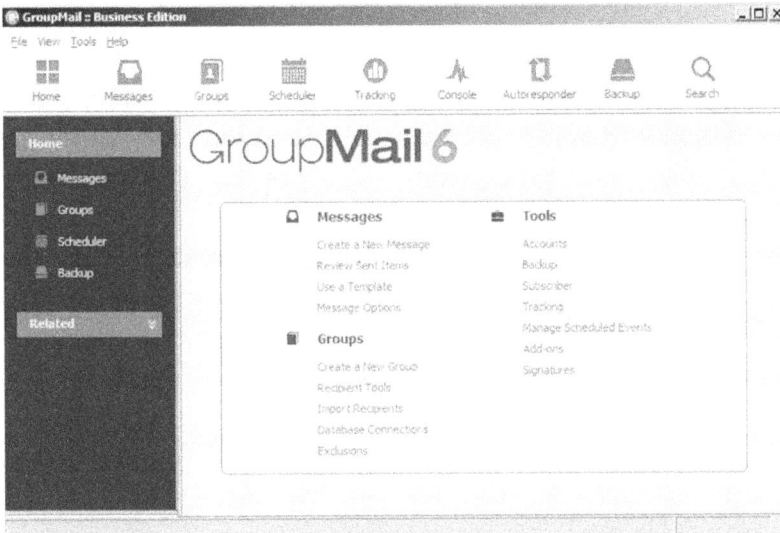

You have to already have the account with the email you want to use to send from before you set up your message, but otherwise, you can create your account, group, or message in any order. Preferably though, I find it works well to create your account, then set up your group, and finally insert a prewritten message and subject line.

Setting Up Your Account

Once you click on the Account button, the Account Manager will pop up and will indicate all the accounts you have already created.

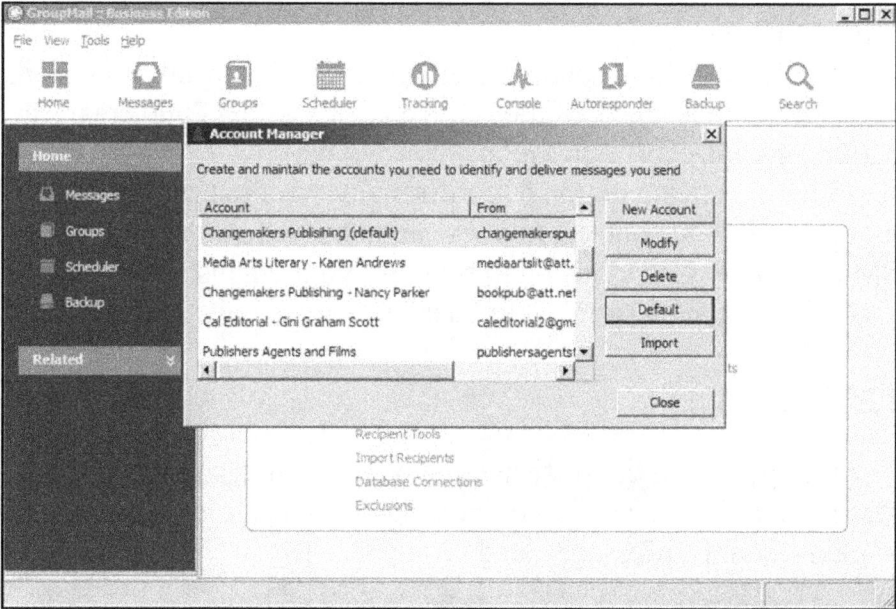

Later, you can always modify these accounts. You can change the User name which will appear in the send line to indicate who is sending the email. Or you can change the "from" (send) or "to" (reply) email. I usually use the same email in the send and reply fields.

For example, here's an account for Changemakers Publishing I have already created. As you can see, I have listed the name for the account and have put the emails associated with this name – changemakerspub@att.net -- in the "from" and the "reply to" fields.

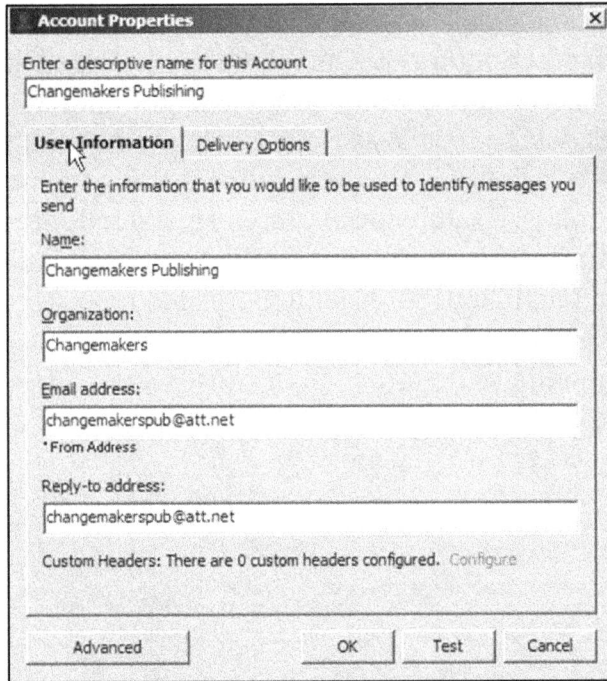

Account Properties

Enter a descriptive name for this Account

Changemakers Publishing

User Information | Delivery Options

Enter the information that you would like to be used to identify messages you send

Name:

Changemakers Publishing

Organization:

Changemakers

Email address:

changemakerspub@att.net

* From Address

Reply-to address:

changemakerspub@att.net

Custom Headers: There are 0 custom headers configured. Configure

Advanced | OK | Test | Cancel

Then, I have to set the "Delivery Options" and the "Advanced" options. One of these choices is the SMTP port settings, which you get from the SMTP service you use for the mailing. In this case, the port setting is "587." Another service I used for some emails uses the "2525" port. Just enter whatever number your service tells you to use.

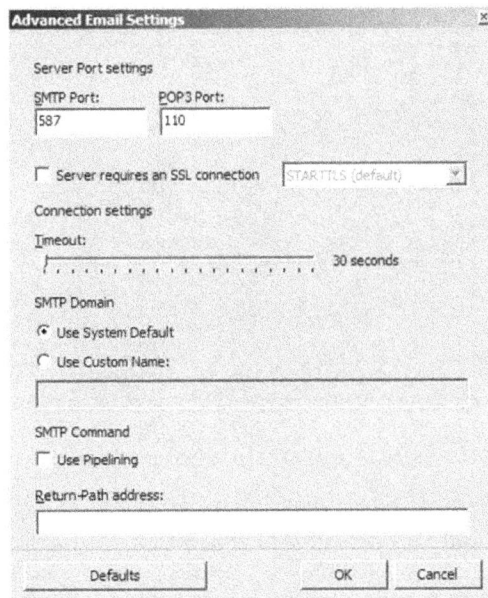

Advanced Email Settings

Server Port settings

SMTP Port: 587   POP3 Port: 110

☐ Server requires an SSL connection   STARTTLS (default)

Connection settings

Timeout:

30 seconds

SMTP Domain

⦿ Use System Default

○ Use Custom Name:

SMTP Command

☐ Use Pipelining

Return-Path address:

Defaults | OK | Cancel

Next, set up the delivery options.   In this case, I use the Standard delivery, though other options are direct, Outlook, and pickup, which you can research to decide if you would prefer another option.   There are some standard options, which I leave as is for Connections (2), the length of any Pauses (such as withhold for 5 seconds after sending 25 messages before sending the next 25).   Usually these pauses are a good idea, since this helps to prevent the mail server from thinking this is a spam mailing, which usually goes out continuously.   Additionally, and most importantly, I list the SMTP mail server, which is the service you subscribe to, so you get so many emails a month, as described in the next section.   Each SMTP company has its own policies and protocols.   Here I have entered "sendgrid," the server I use the most.

```
┌─────────────────────────────────────────────────────────────────┐
│ Account Properties                                          [X]   │
├─────────────────────────────────────────────────────────────────┤
│ Enter a descriptive name for this Account                         │
│ ┌─────────────────────────────────────────────────────────────┐  │
│ │ Changemakers Publisihing                                     │  │
│ └─────────────────────────────────────────────────────────────┘  │
│                                                                   │
│   User Information   │ Delivery Options │                         │
│                                                                   │
│ Select how you would like GroupMail to deliver your messages:     │
│                                                                   │
│ Delivery Options:                                                 │
│ ┌──────────────────────────────────────────────────────────┬──┐ │
│ │ Standard                                                   │▼ │ │
│ └──────────────────────────────────────────────────────────┴──┘ │
│ Send via dedicated SMTP Server (Standard)                         │
│                                                                   │
│ SMTP Server:                                                      │
│ ┌─────────────────────────────────────────────────────────────┐ │
│ │ smtp.sendgrid.net                                           │  │
│ └─────────────────────────────────────────────────────────────┘ │
│ ☑ Requires Authentication              ┌──────────────┐          │
│                                        │    Setup     │          │
│                                        └──────────────┘          │
│ Connections:                                                      │
│ ┌────────┬─┐                                                      │
│ │ 2      │▲│                                                      │
│ └────────┴─┘                                                      │
│ Pause every              messages for                             │
│ ┌──────────────┬─┐       ┌──────────────┬─┐                      │
│ │ 25           │▼│       │ 5 seconds    │▼│                      │
│ └──────────────┴─┘       └──────────────┴─┘                      │
├─────────────────────────────────────────────────────────────────┤
│ ┌──────────┐          ┌──────┐ ┌──────┐ ┌──────┐                │
│ │ Advanced │          │  OK  │ │ Test │ │Cancel│                │
│ └──────────┘          └──────┘ └──────┘ └──────┘                │
└─────────────────────────────────────────────────────────────────┘
```

Typically, you associate a particular email account with a particular server.   For instance, here are names of other emails accounts associated with the other servers I currently use -- SMTP.Com and Turbo-SMTP.com.

I have indicated the name of the server in the SMTP Server box. This name is assigned to me when I sign up for a subscription to that service.

For the last step in setting up the account, I set up the user name I have with the SMTP server and my password. For example, the first one shows my user name and password with SendGrid; the second one my user name and password with Turbo-SMTP.

Finally, test the account settings by clicking "Test." If you have set up the account properly, you will see "Success!" If not, you will see that the test has failed, and you have to check what you entered incorrectly; then test again. To begin the test, click the "Test" button, and click "Test" again.

The test email will go to the email address you have selected. If the test is successful, you'll see the announcement by the "Status" bar as "Success!"

Then, if I go to that email address, I'll see the results of the test. And here it is.

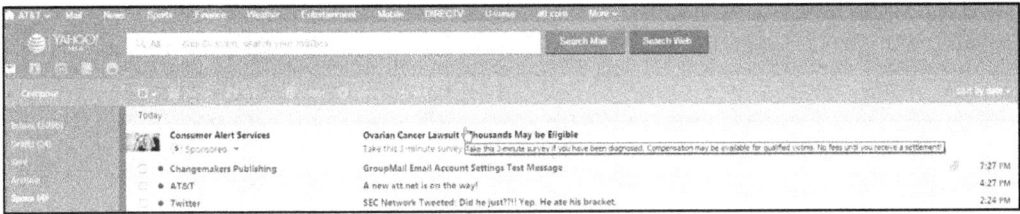

The email lets me know this is a GroupMail Email Account test message. If I see it, it shows me that the account was configured correctly.

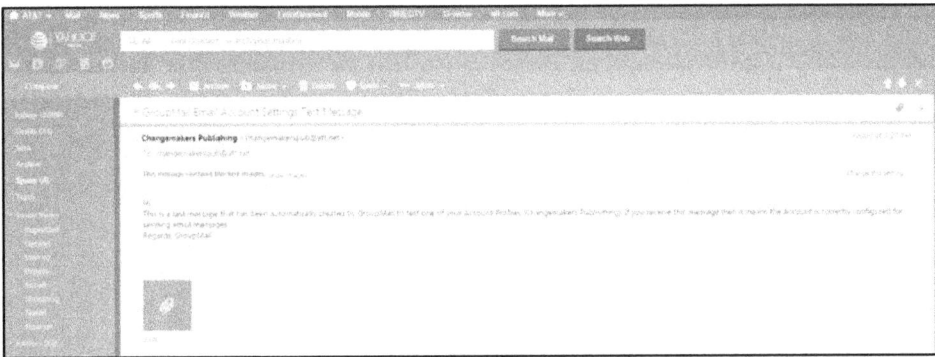

Creating a New Group

The next step is creating a new group. While there are three options, the default is storing the groups in GroupMail, and that's what I've used.

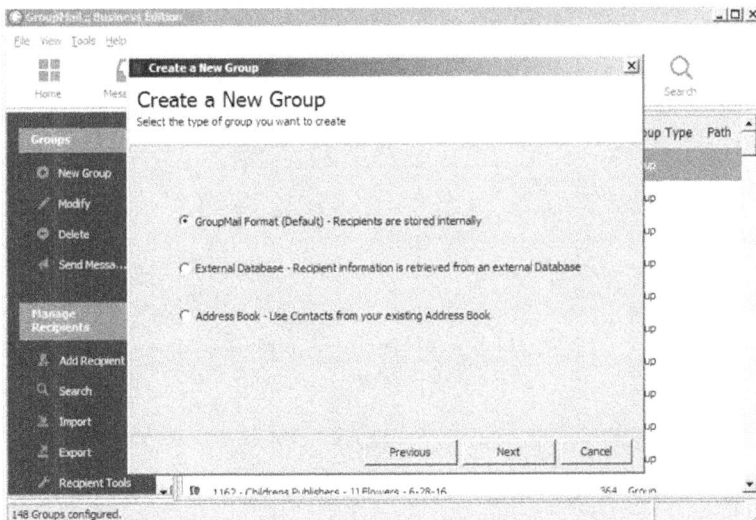

After that, there are a series of prompts with default settings for creating a new group whch you can skip by clicking "next," "next," and "next." These prompts ask you if you are storing the group locally (the default) or if you want to specify another location and indicate the different field names to be used. First up is the email field, and then the most relevant fields are the "First Name" and "Last Name" fields. If the full name is in one field, whatever you call it, such as "Contact" or "Name," you only use the "First Name" field. If the first name and last name are in separate fields, use both the "First" and "Last" name fields.

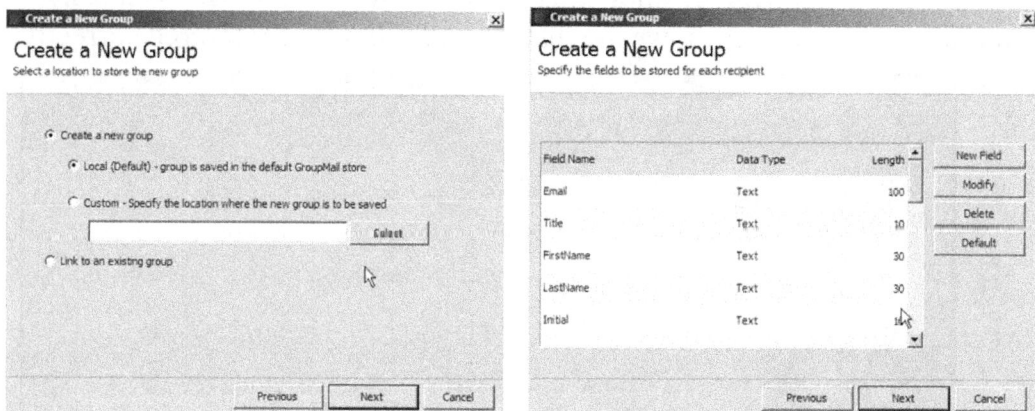

Next, when asked about selecting the fields with the recipient's email address, you can skip that, too. Be sure to leave unchecked the box about allowing duplicate email addresses to be stored in the group, since you don't want to send your email to duplicate email addresses.

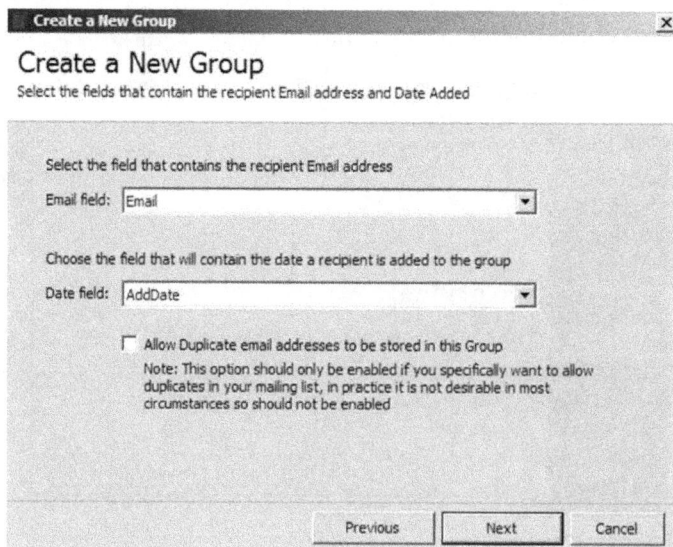

Now you get to name the group. If you are using a chronological system for a series of mailings, it helps to begin with a number in the series, followed by a brief title to indicate what the group is for and the date of sending the mailing. For example, you might write something like: 1201 – Letters about Real Estate Sale – 3-20-17 or 1202 – PR Release – Top Seller Award for 2016 – 3-20-17.

After you hit "Create," your group is created and goes to the bottom of all of the groups you have created.

After this, you can open the group to add your email address to get a copy of what you sent out and any other email addresses you want to add to the email list of targeted contacts you have already created. For instance, if you want a copy of your email to go to a publicist or social media consultant, you are working with, add them here. Just click the Add button.

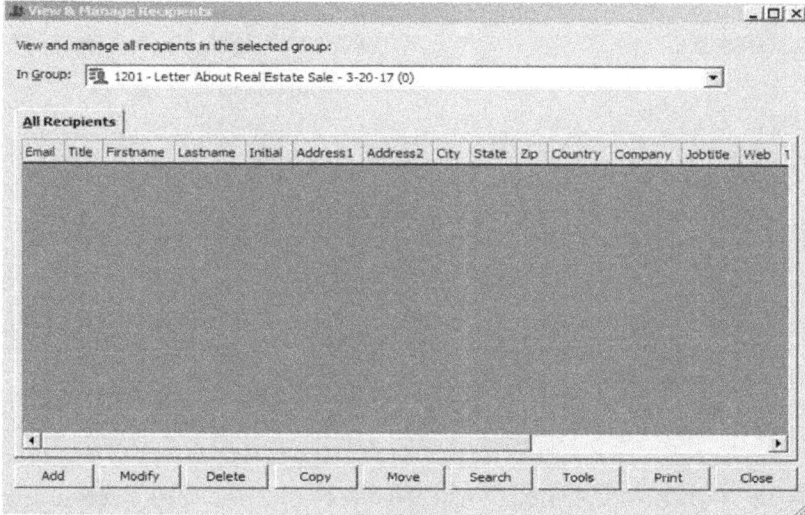

Then, add the person's email address and the first name and last name in the Firstname box or in the Firstname and Lastname boxes, based on whether these names are in a single column or in two columns in your database.

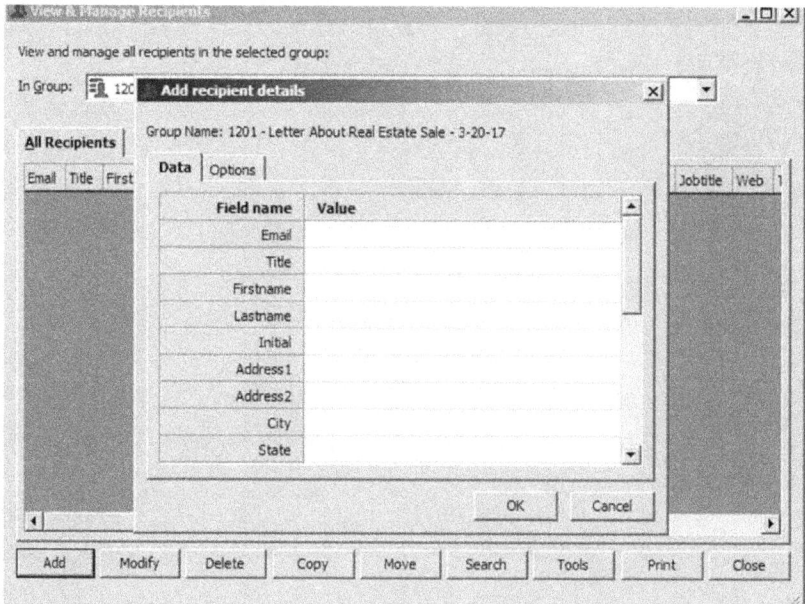

For example, here I have added my name and email, clicked okay, and I can see where my name has been added on the View & Manage Recipients screen.

After adding any additional names – though you can do this later, the next step is importing all the targeted contacts in the .csv file you have created.   To do so, first close the View & Manage Recipients screen, where you can see the selected group highlighted – or highlight it yourself.

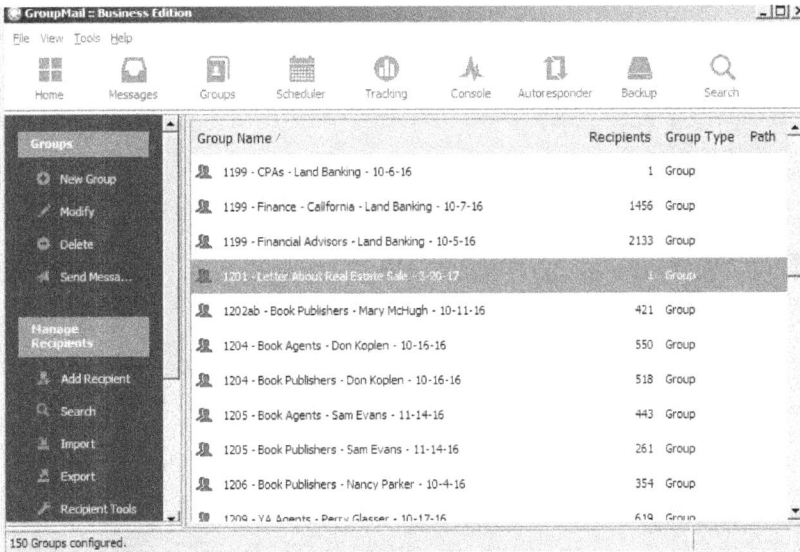

Then, import in the .csv file you created by clicking "Import" under the Manage Recipients section.

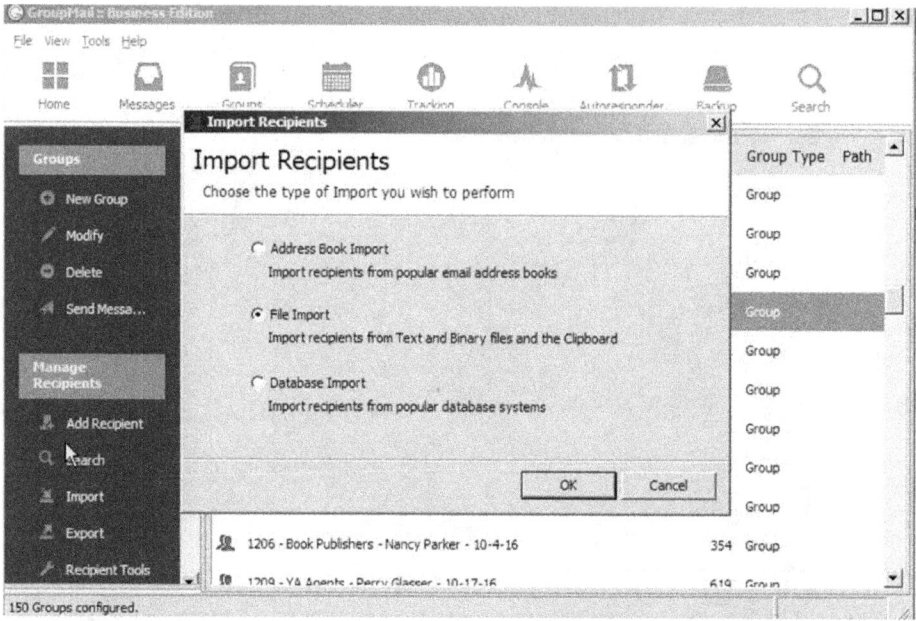

Since you'll be importing the .csv file, select "File Import," and click OK. Then, locate the file you want to import by clicking the "Select" button. If you previously searched for a file, that will show up in the "Import Recipient Data from a File" box.

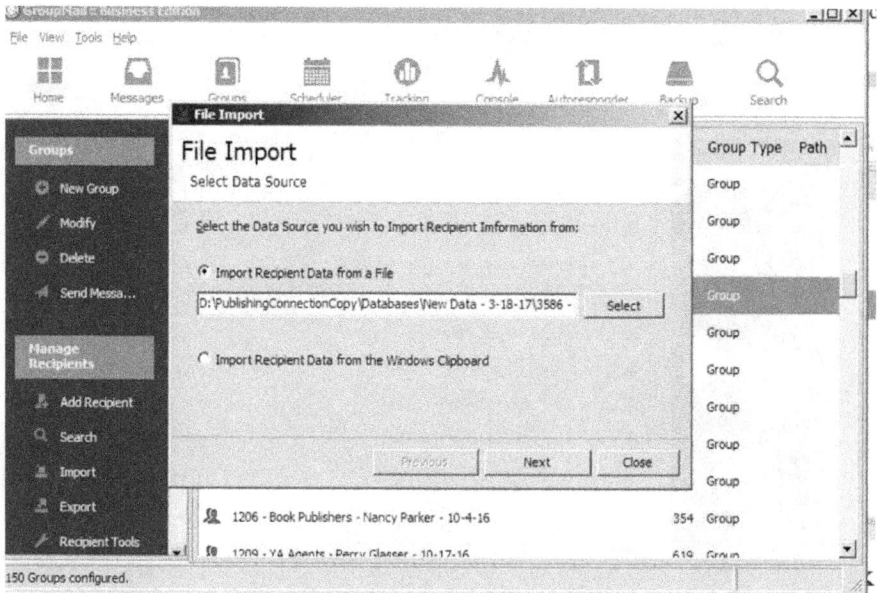

Next, pick a file to import, such as here, where I have selected California Physicians in the Bay Area.

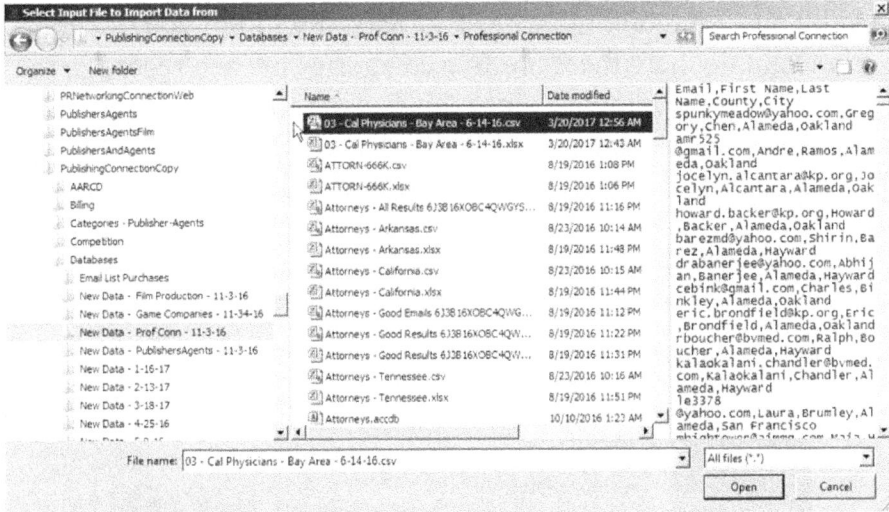

Once you click "Open," the file you have selected shows up on the File Import screen, with its location on your computer listed first.

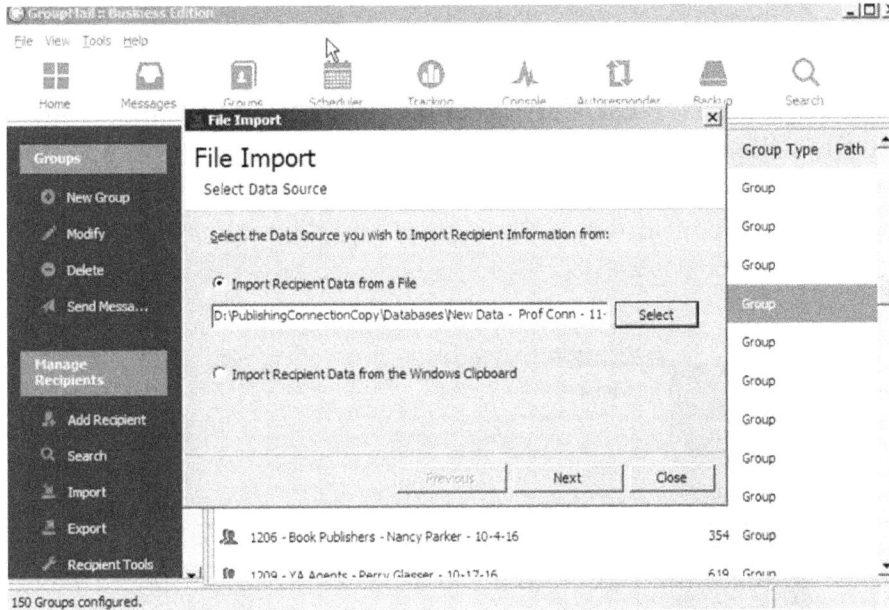

After that, you get some input on the data you will be importing. As long as it's a .csv file, which is a delimited text format, you will be advised how many fields are in each line of data. (Or if you have a text file delimited by tabs, semicolons, spaces, or bars, it will tell you that too).

For example, here there are five categories in each record in the file, which is delimited by commas, since this is a .csv (comma separated values) file. If you mistakenly open the Excel file or if you want to import data from another type of file, such as all the emails in a Word document or PDF, the "All other File/Data formats" category will be selected.

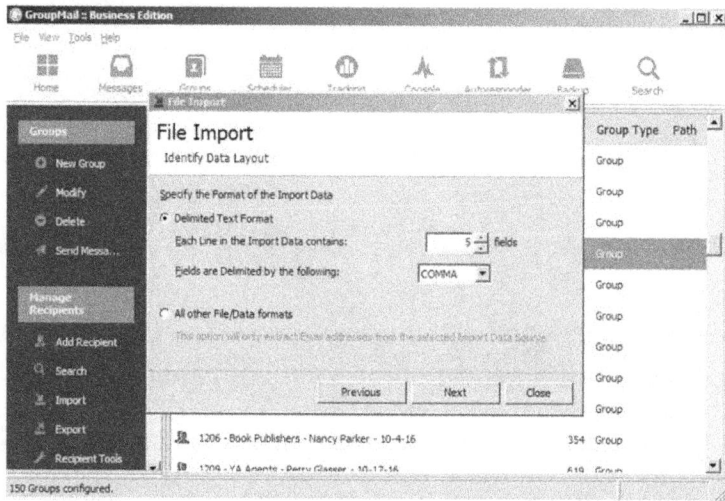

Once you click Next, you select the group where the information on the .csv file will go. Check the "Check for Duplicates" box, so you don't end up sending to duplicate emails. For instance, here I have chosen to import the Bay Area California Physicians into the real estate sale file.

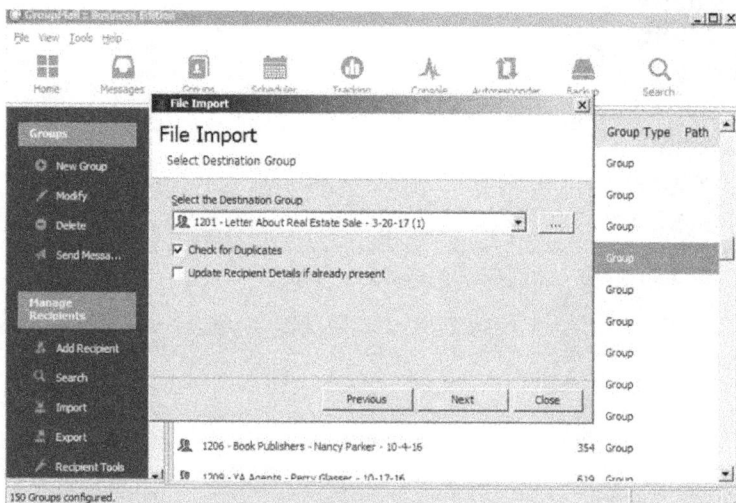

Once you start the file import process, you tell the program which categories of data to import for your query. The key ones to import are the email addresses and first names (or first names and last names if listed in separate columns). Plus you can include other information, such as if you want to indicate a person's sales area and have a column for that category. You would then create a field for that category of information in your letter, so the information from each record will go there in your messages,

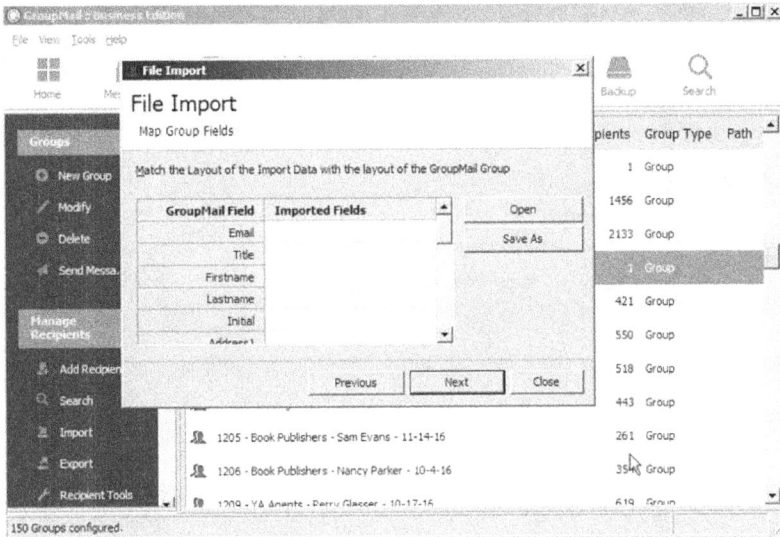

For example, to only include the email address and first name in your query letter, you just designate those categories, as I have, by selecting Email and FirstName as the categories to include in importing the data.

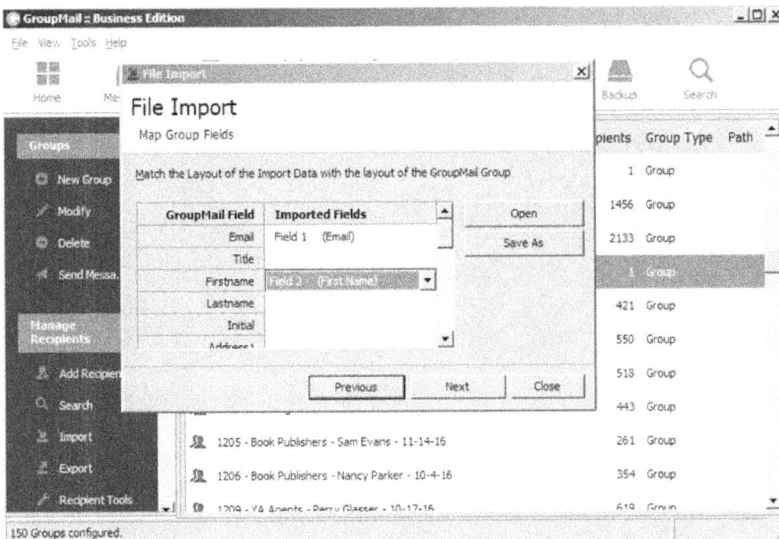

The next step is to press "Start" to start the upload process.

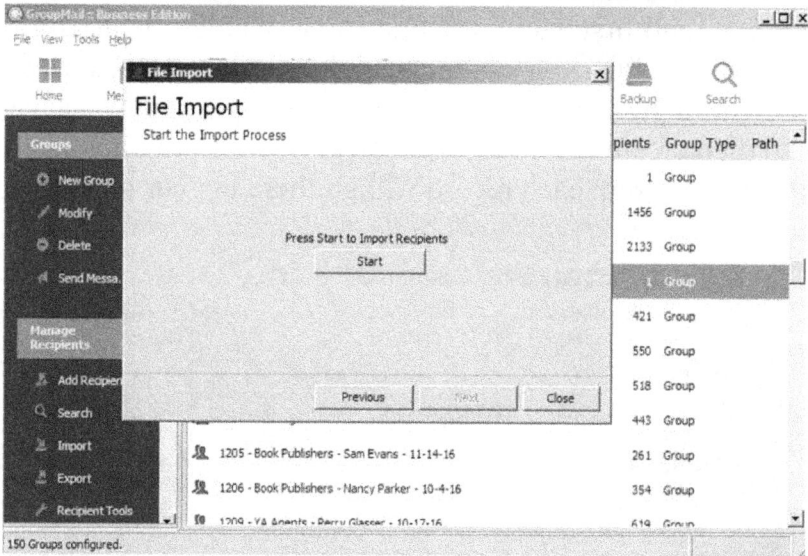

The file begins to upload.

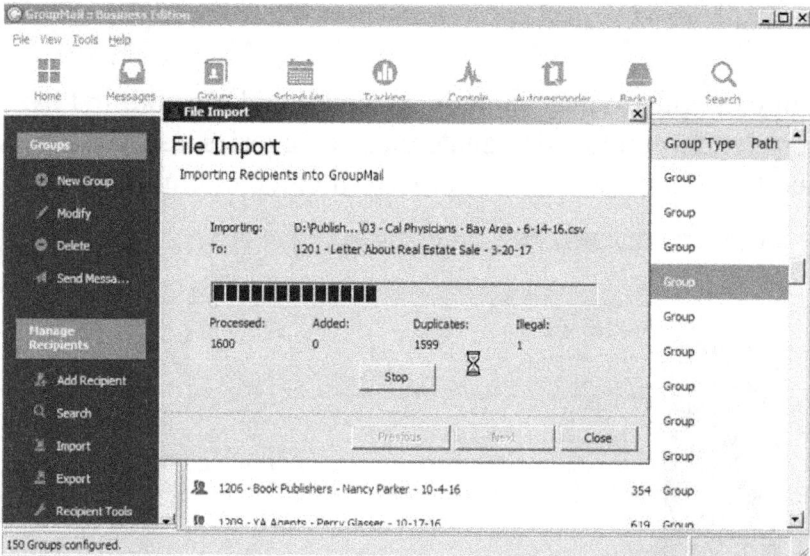

After all the files are imported, you get an indication of the number of files included, along with the number of duplicate emails, if any, and any illegal emails – usually due to a mistake in the entry, such as including a website rather than an email address, have an extra space or dot, or are missing a ".com" at the end of the email address. If you want to see what was imported or skipped, you can see the log file by clicking that link.

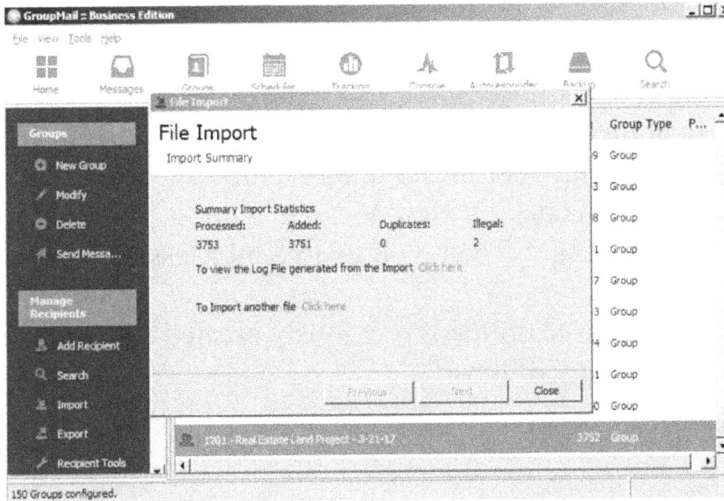

Finally, it's done! Now you can open up the group to see all of the records you have imported. These will feature categories you have included, such as the email and first name. Your message will go to these recipients, and you can personalize your message by including the person's first or first and last name, so it looks like you are only sending this message to that person.

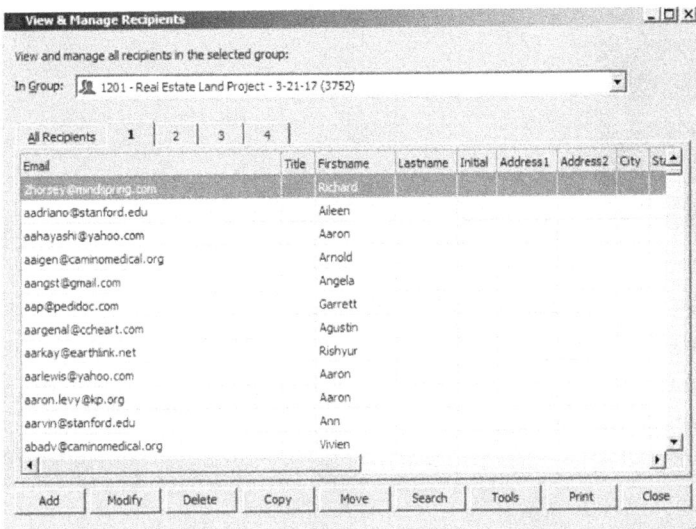

You can also add other names and emails by clicking "Add" or modify any of the names or emails that are listed. You can delete selected records to exclude a particular person or company for some reason. Plus, you can search the imported records to determine if someone is there or not, and if missing, you can add that person. Or if you don't want someone to get a mailing, simply hit "delete."

Creating Your Message

The final piece of sending a targeted message to your list is writing or copying and pasting your message into a message form. To do so, go to the Message tab, and click on New Message, unless you want to use a previously sent message. Then, you go to Sent Messages and select one of those.

You can also see drafts of previously created but unsent messages if you want to revive any of those.

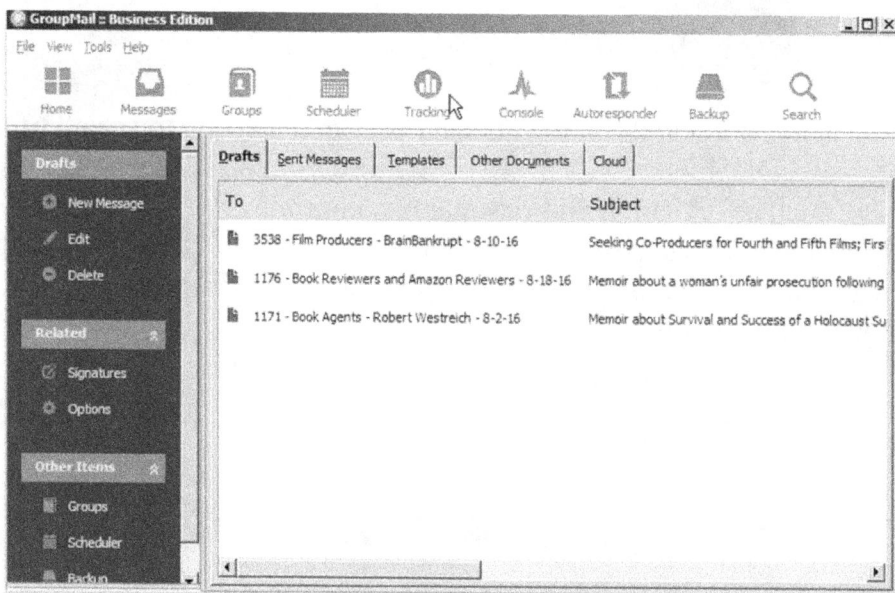

Once you click the New Message button, the New Message form pops up and you can paste your message and subject line there. You'll also see your last mailing with the account name, email you used, and the group you previously mailed to.

For example, in the form below, I previously sent a mailing to 453 children's publishers from one of my companies – Changemakers Publishing. I have to change those to put in whatever account email and targeted group I want for my mailing.

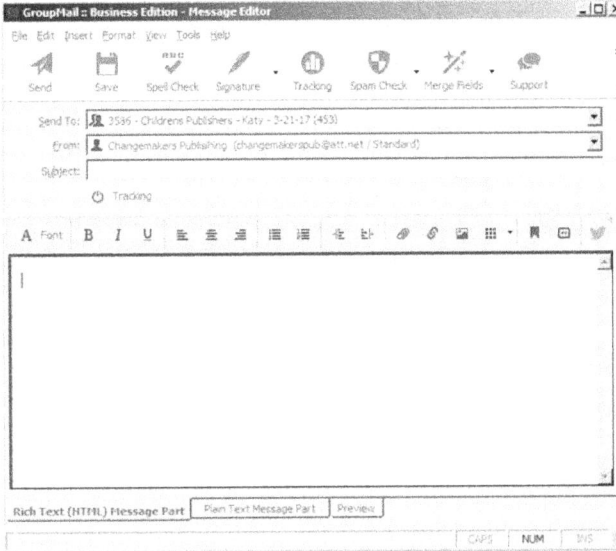

To illustrate, here's a mailing I did to film investors. I changed the Send To and From fields to list the new target market (Film Investors), the account name, and the sending email (Changemakers Productions – Gini Graham Scott (changemakersprod@att.net). Then, I copied and pasted in the letter, which is indicated beflow.

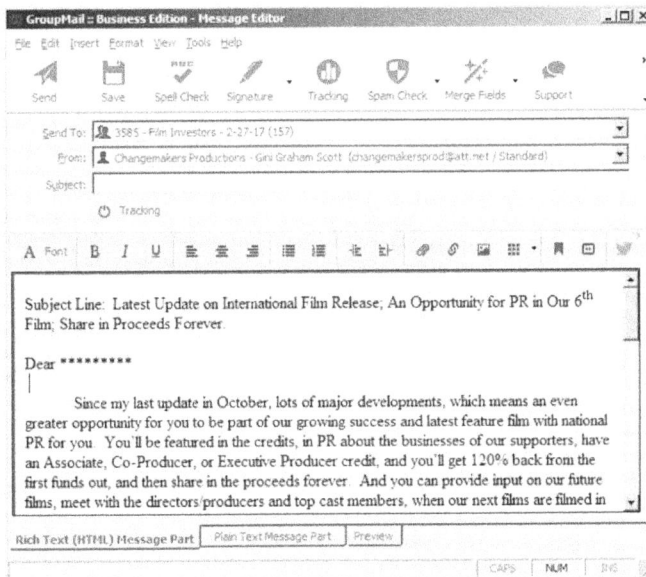

Then, you move your subject line into the Subject field and insert the category of the records to insert, such as the Firstname field as the salutation, as indicated below. To insert this, go to the Insert tab, select Merge Fields, and indicate the named field you want from the drop down menu.

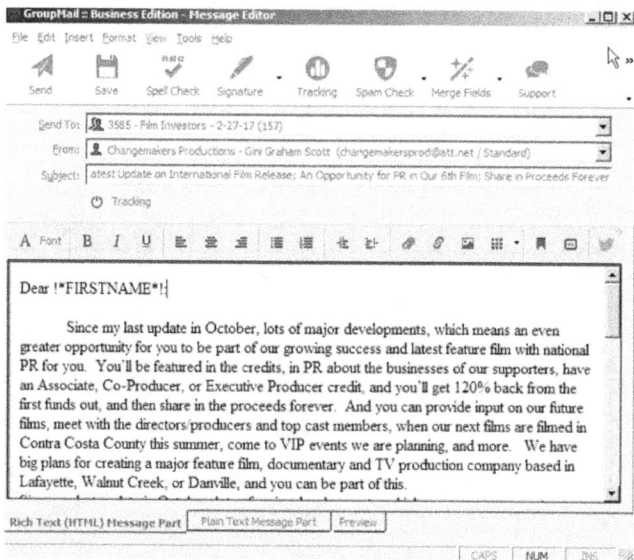

To insert an image, just indicate where it goes in your copy, press the image icon, and find the image to insert on your computer or from a remote image on a website. Here to illustrate, I'm sending a query letter to potential investors about one of my films *Infidelity,* and I selected an image of the poster to insert.

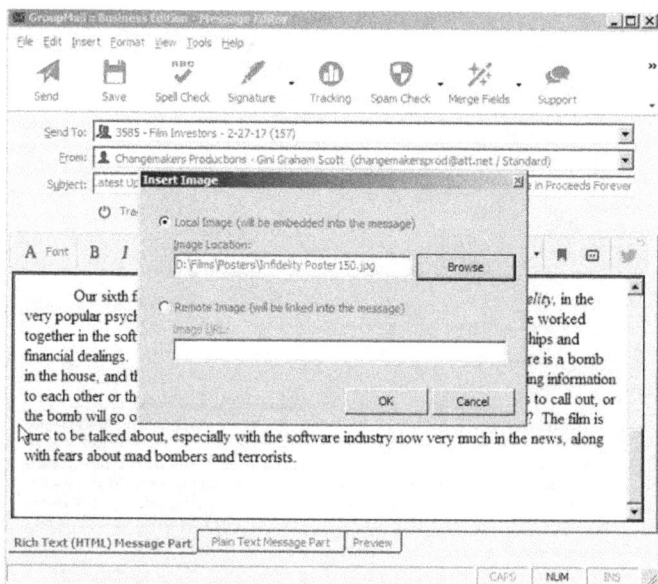

The image goes into the query where I have indicated, as illustrated below.

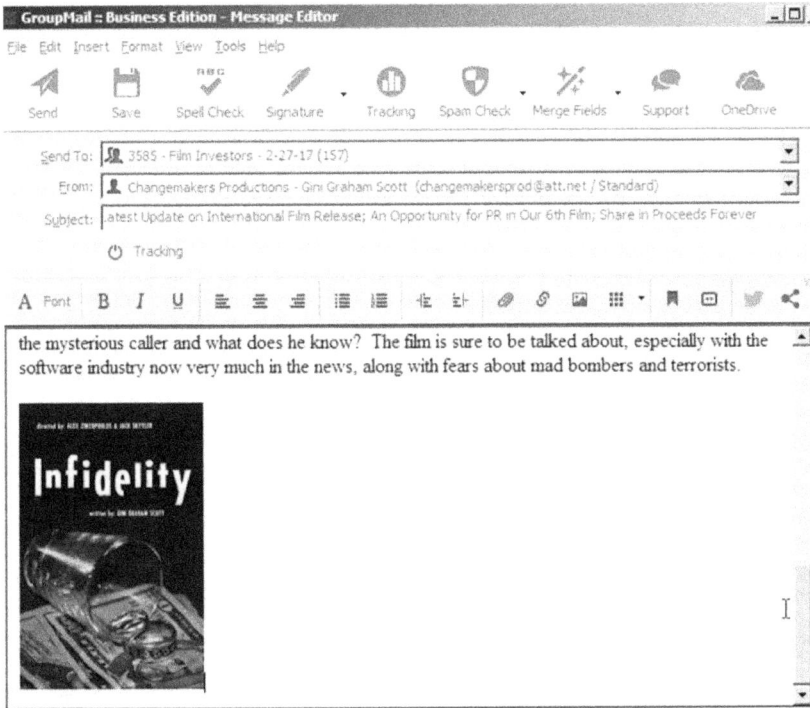

You can similarly add in other images throughout the email letter. You can place them next to the image that's already there or sprinkle a few more illustrations through the letter.

Once you finish the letter, check that it is going to the correct group with the right target audience (such as Film Investors) and from the correct account (such as Changemakers Productions – changemakersprod@att.net). Once everything is set, with a click of a button, your email is ready to go.

Now there is one last optional step, unless you skip it, which I don't recommend. You get to preview your email to make sure it's correct. To view it, click the Preview tab, which will open the Preview menu, where you can send out a test message to whatever email you want, as well as preview what the message will look like in a browser – usually Chrome.

For example, as indicated below, the message will go to publishersagentsfilms@gmail.com.

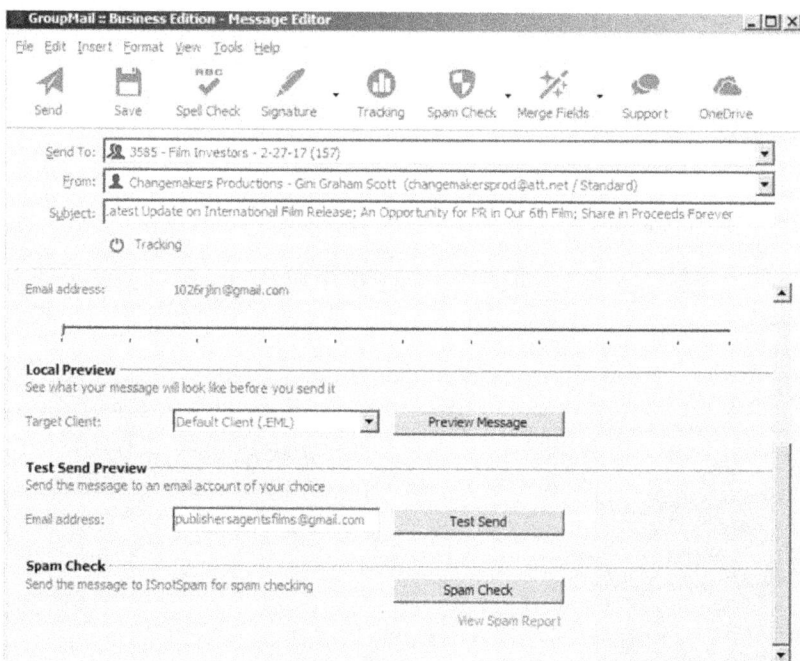

And here's how it will look in the recipients' email. The salutation for the person with each email record will show that person's name from the "Firstname" field, and the rest of the email will show the rest of the copy and images in that letter.

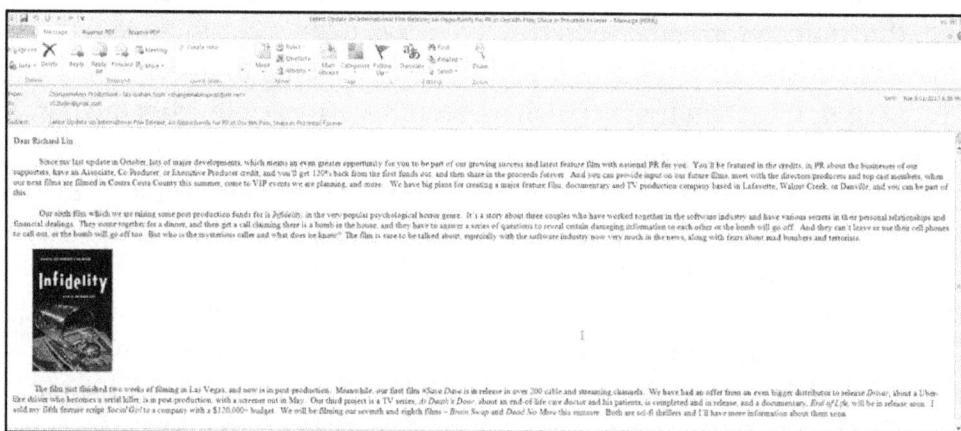

Because each email is personalized for the recipient, if you use the "Firstname" or "Firstname Lastname" fields, it will look like you have individually sent a letter to that person from whatever email you have selected. While many recipients are aware that many personalized letters are generated in this way, they at least may think this could be a personal letter from you. Plus, this software makes it much faster and easier to send out these personalized letters to a very large group.

Potentially, you can send this personalized email to many thousands of recipients, though with more than 10,000 contacts, consider hiring a special service to do these emails, especially if you could have a lot of bounces for a very large number of emails. But for a mailing to a few hundred to up to 5000 or 10,000 recipients, using GroupMail 6 or other personalized mailing software or services is ideal.

CHAPTER 4: USING AN SMTP SERVER FOR BULK EMAILS

While GroupMail 6 and other email formatting programs enable you to configure your email to go from a selected email to targeted recipients, you need an email server to send it out. At one time, emailers commonly used their own dedicated email servers to do this. That's what I did in the early years of Publishers, Agents, and Films until the mid-2000s, though these servers were quite expensive – I paid about $375 a month for a fairly small server. But now the way to go is to use an SMTP server, a mass-mailing service, or a special mailing service, like Mail Chimp or Constant Contact.

How an SMTP Server Works

The SMTP name may be unfamiliar, since it is used so commonly by that name, but it actually stands for "Simple Mail Transfer Protocol," and it is a TCP/IP protocol for sending and receiving e-mail. The way it works is that it sends out the emails it receives from another service, and generally it is used with POP3 or IMAP protocols, so the user can save messages in a mailbox on a server and periodically download them from there. In this way, the SMTP procedure is used for sending e-mail and either POP3 or IMAP protocols are used to receive mail.

Today, the SMTP protocol has become the most common one used by most email systems to send emails from one server to another. Then, the recipient uses either a POP or IMAP server to retrieve the mail.

However, if you are not tech savvy, don't worry. As an end user you are unlikely to encounter these under the hood processes. In fact, although I have been using SMTP servers for about ten years for Publishers Agents and Films, I never knew any of these details. I just knew enough to put in the name of the company's STMP log-in (such as "smtp.sendgrid.net" or "mail.smtp.com") and enter my user name and password in the designated boxes, so the email platform I used – GroupMail 6 – could send out my email through this server.

Though you don't need to know the details of how this all works as a user, you normally have to select an SMTP provider to use with your platform to send out the bulk emails for you, unless your platform already has its own platform.

Selecting an SMTP Server

There are many SMTP servers you can use. Sometimes there is a close relationship between certain platforms and a particular SMTP program, such as GroupMail 6's tie-in with SMTP2Go. But you can generally use any SMTP program with any platform. And you can use multiple SMTP programs with the same platform. You just have to indicate which SMTP server is being used for a mailing with a particular account.

For example, I primarily use SendGrid for most of my mailings through GroupMail 6, but at times I use SMTP.com or Turbo-Smtp.com for mailings from other email accounts. I like SendGrid because it seems faster and has easy to review information about what emails go delivered or didn't for various reasons. It also allows me to put in an emails I want for sending and replying without my having to validate them when I first use them. And it doesn't send the returns to my reply email. But I like using the other email servers as backups when I first test out new emails. When I change from using one email to another, I simply change the SMTP link and the different user name and passwords for that account. After that, I test out the system to show it is working, and the mailer is ready to go.

While selecting a single SMTP server is fine, it is helpful to have one or two additional servers as backups in case one goes down or to help in cleaning up new databases or ones you haven't used in some time. For example, if your main SMTP server is more critical about bounces, drops, and spam reports, so your reputation goes down, you might use a backup server to do a mailing of your new or rarely used lists to check on what emails are still valid. This way, you use your most recently cleaned up lists on the server you like the most so your reputation stays high, and you do any list or database cleanup on another SMTP server.

These servers commonly provide you with an activity report of the number of emails you send out, along with a report on the number of opens, clicks, bounces, drops, and spam reports, so you can clean up your list. Some offer to clean up your list as well. However, you don't want to use these SMTP services as a clean-up service, when you expect a high percentage of returns, since that will lower your reputation, expressed as a percentage. If your reputation level gets too low, your account is likely to be suspended. But if your returns are under 3% to 7%, that shouldn't be a problem. Your reputation may be lowered slightly if you get a small number of returns, but as long as your returns remain at no more than 7% or approach zero, that's considered part of normal turnover, so you should be fine.

You can also use an email delivery service to assess how well your email campaign is connecting with others. If you find one of the emails you are using isn't reaching many of the recipients because of a high percentage of blocks or drops, you can use another email in the future. This high level of blocks or drops could happen if you do a series of emails to a contact after getting a business card or a person opts in through an email form on your website offering a free gift, such as an industry, in exchange for an email address. But then that person no longer wants to get your emails, so they put a block on your email.

To give you an idea of how these SMTP services work, I'll describe the companies I have worked with in more detail and then list some of the other SMTP services.

SendGrid (www.sendgrid.com)

SendGrid is the main service I have used for over a year. Here's a brief introduction to their service, which describes itself as an "email delivery engine." You can use it to send emails through other platforms or set up an email campaign through SendGrid directly.

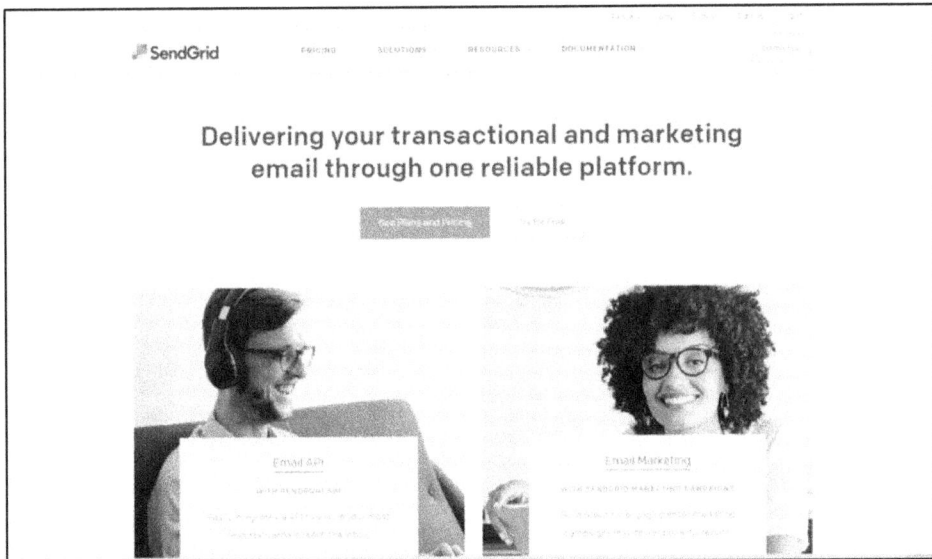

The service can work as an email relay through a third party service, such as a GroupMail 6. You can also use it as a web API, where you send the emails through your own website application, commonly for password resets or order confirmations. Or you can use it to upload and manage recipient lists, build or upload your HTML email templates, or schedule and send out bulk mail or newsletters.

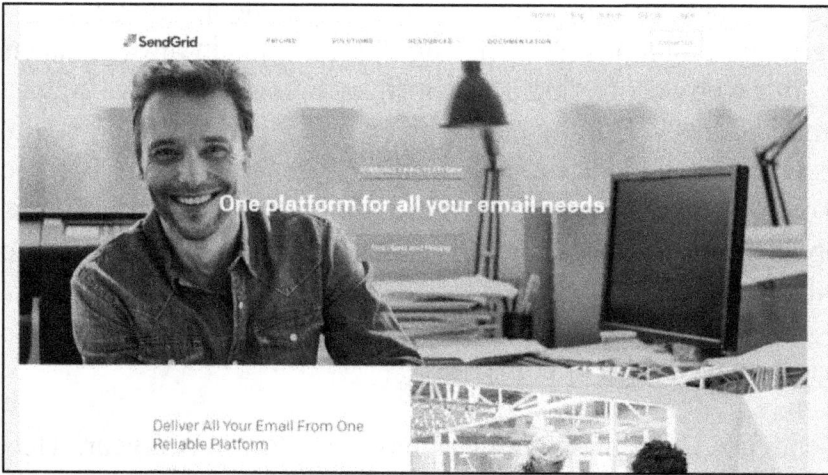

I used SendGrid as an email relay, and here's how that works.

Once you sign in, your dashboard shows your activity for the past week, which includes the number of emails sent, the number opened and clicked, and any bounces or spam reports. In my case, I sent about 450 emails, which were delivered to 79% of the recipients, and nearly all (94%) opened it. Though only a small percentage (22%) clicked, there was only one bounce and no spam reports.

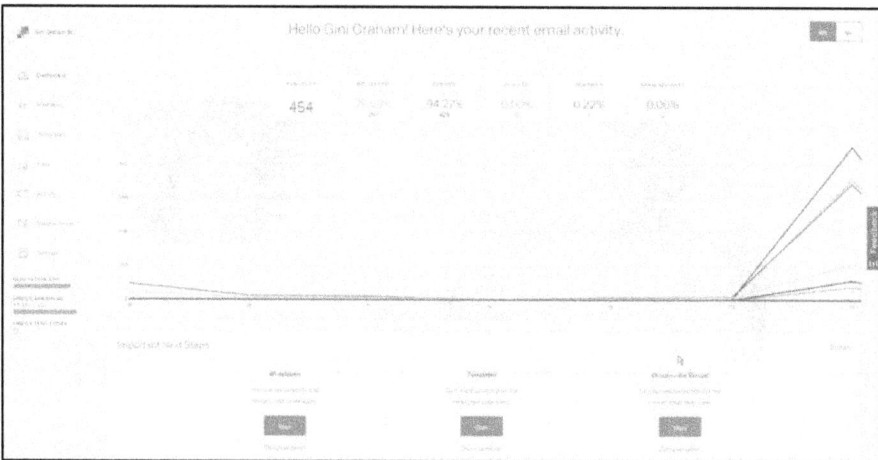

The dashboard also shows your current reputation – here mine is 89%, which was reduced from 100% due to a single mailing with a 15% bounce rate. But over time, my mailings have had fewer bounces and no spam reports, so that percentage has been going up – now at 99%.

You can additionally see a detailed listing of all opens, clicks, delivered, bounces, and other activity for each email. You can see the number of blocks and drops, if any, by turning off the other filters.

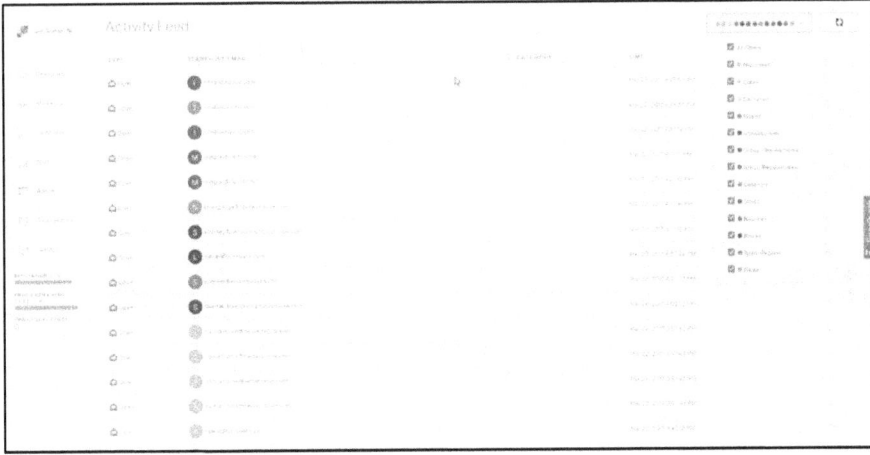

It costs about $10 a month to start with up to 40,000 emails, with increased costs for sending out any number of emails – even 2 ½ million or more. Like most SMTP companies, SendGrid offers a free trial – in this case, up to 40,000 emails for the first month.

SMTP.Com (www.smtp.com)

The second SMTP service I use from time to time is SMTP.Com, which similarly offers both a relay service and a marketing campaign, as described on its website.

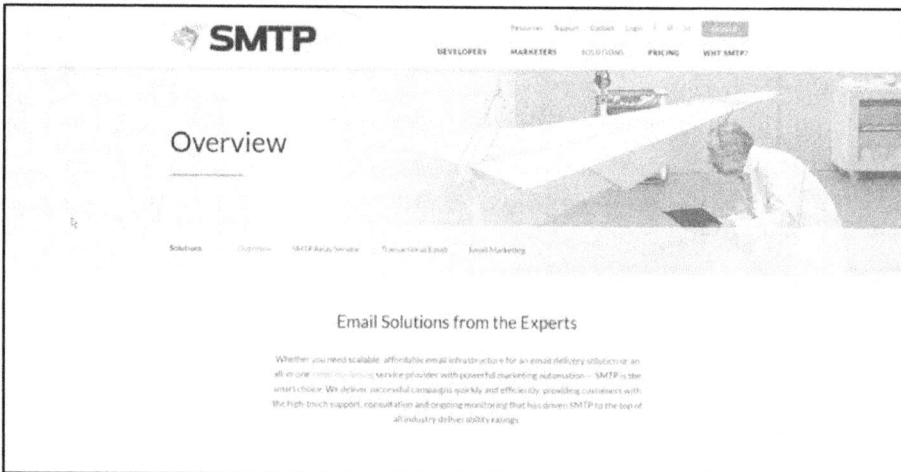

Here's the dashboard which has the same basic sending statistics as SendGrid -- emails sent, delivered, opens, clicks, bounces, complaints (or spam reports). Also, it lists the name of each account from which you can send emails, after you individually enroll them. Unlike SendGrid, where you can put any email into your third party platform plus your account password, in SMPT.com you have to separately set up an email account for each person with its own password. However, you can use the same password for each one, which makes it easier to remember.

To add a new account, click on "Manage Senders."

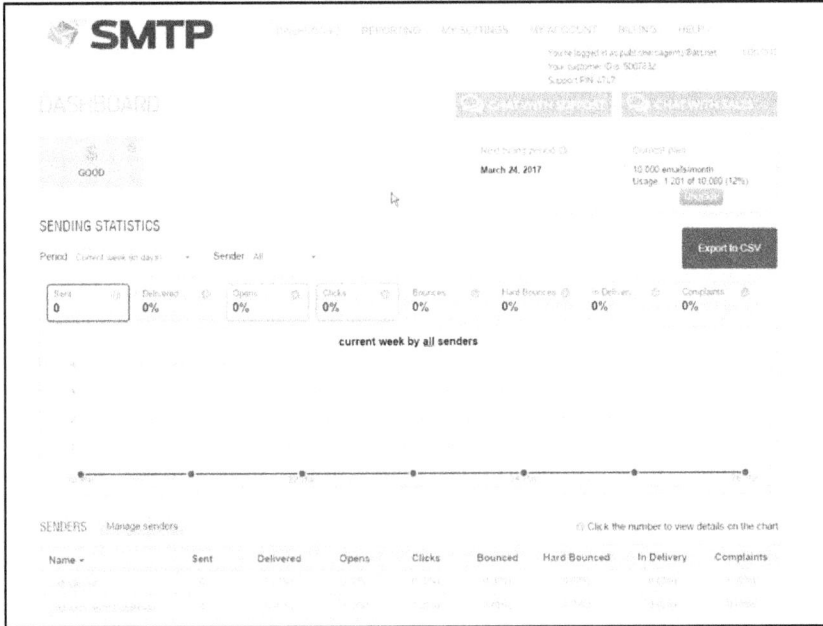

Then, go to "Add Sender."

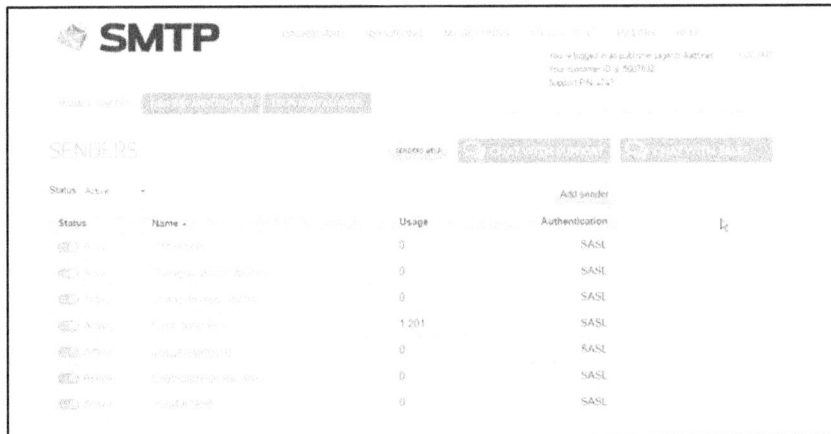

Finally, add in the identifying information for the "New Sender".

Thus it's a more involved process to use SMTP.com, though it has an added level of security. The other big difference from SendGrid is that if emails bounce, are dropped, or are returned as spam, they come to your sending email. If there are many of these returns, they can clog up your email until you review them, so you can take them out of your database and delete them from your email. On the plus side, this can be a quick way to see what to remove from your database, as an alternative to seeing the returns online.

The pricing is a little more expensive, since it's $15 for only 10,000 emails a month, though at 100,000 or more emails, you can have your own dedicated IP. But despite the higher price, I find SMTP.com makes a good a back-up, when using another SMTP service.

Turbo-SMTP

Turbo-SMTP is the third SMTP system I use. I find it a little slower than SendGrid, though its starter package is less expensive than that of many other SMTP providers.

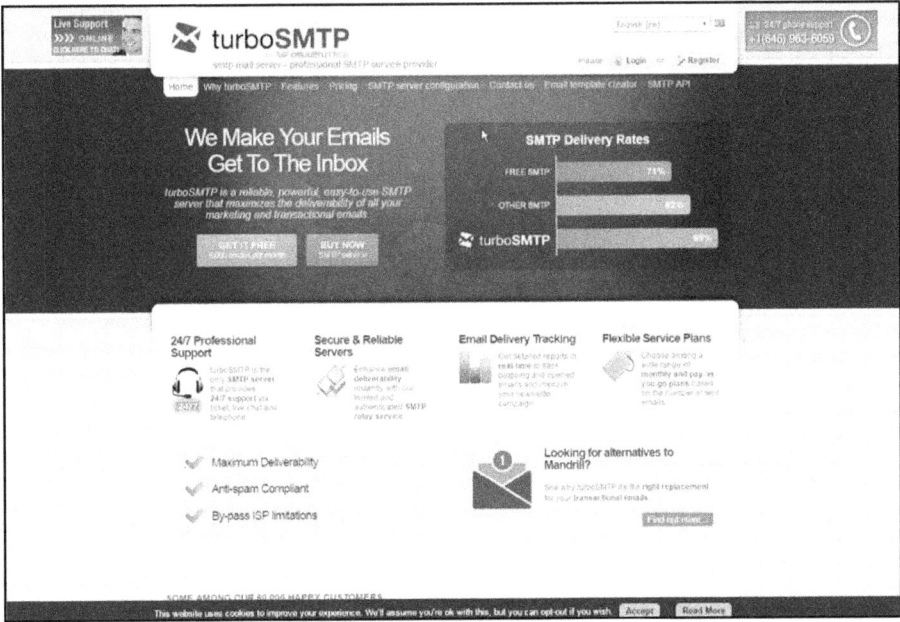

In this case, you have a master dashboard for your main account.

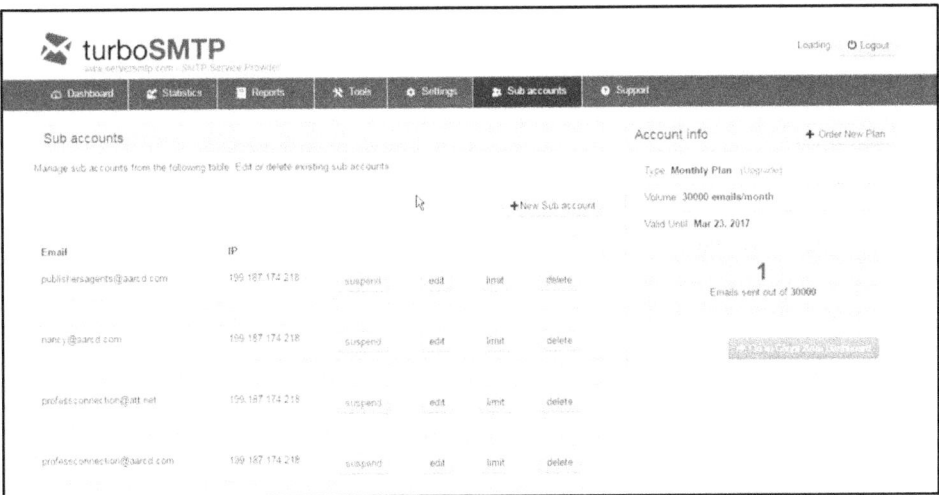

You have to set up separate accounts for each email which has its own dashboard . Each dashboard lists the emails sent out for each account, with the usual filters for delivered, opened, clicked, and returned emails, as in this example, where I haven't sent out anything recently.

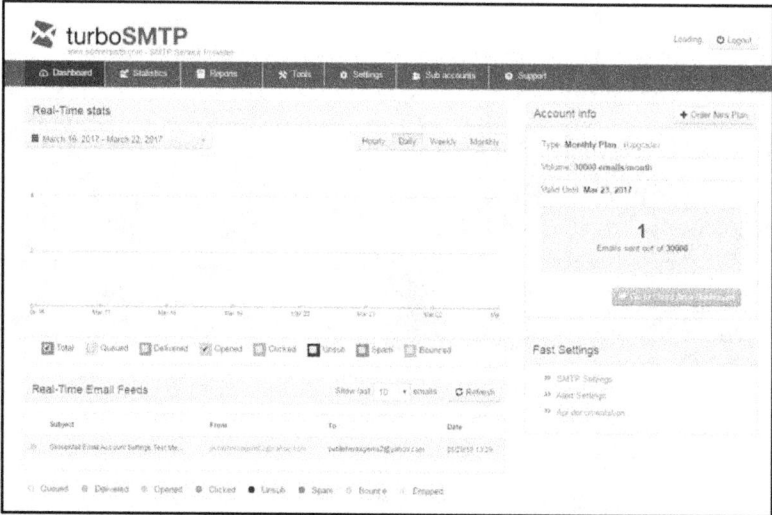

You can see your overall stats on an hourly, daily, weekly, and monthly basis. Any returns are listed online, as in SendGrid.

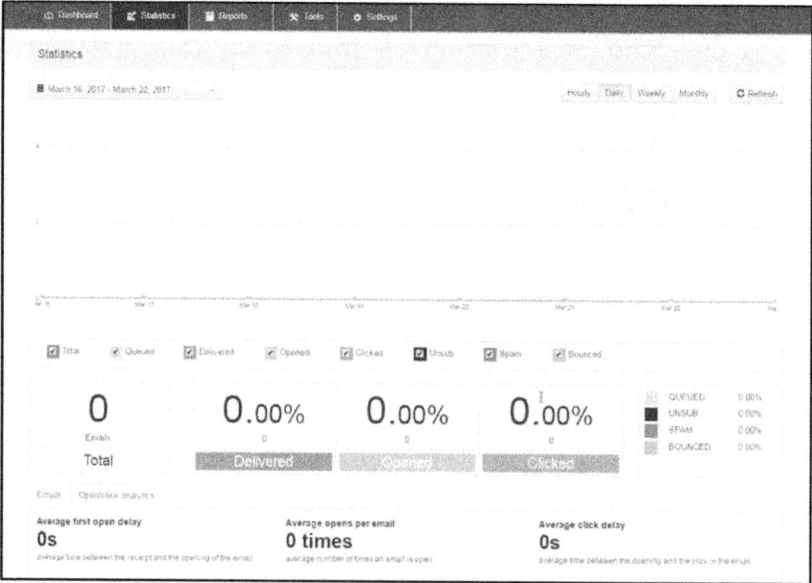

To add a new account, you click the New Sub account button and add some details about that account, including the email and password. Then, you can use the new account for sending out emails.

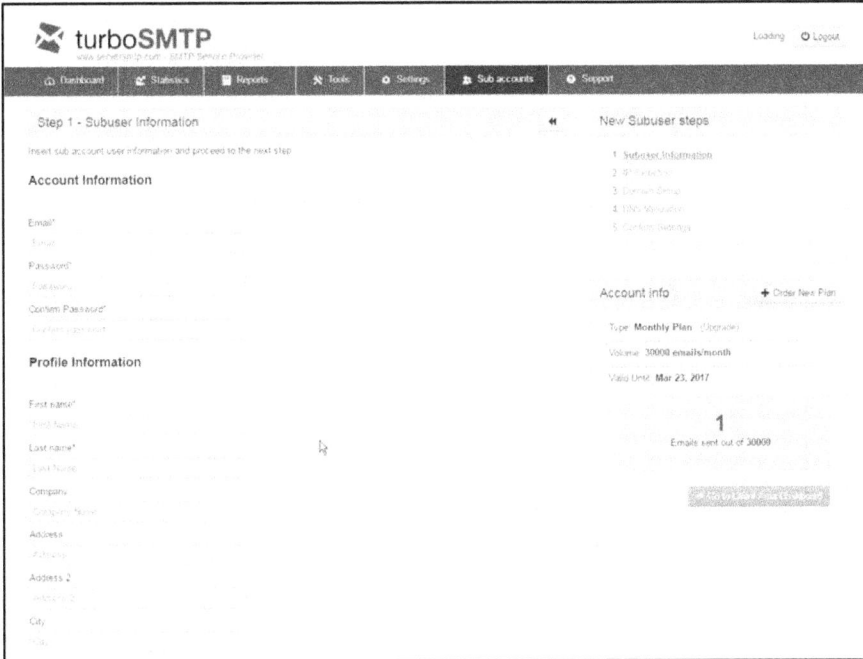

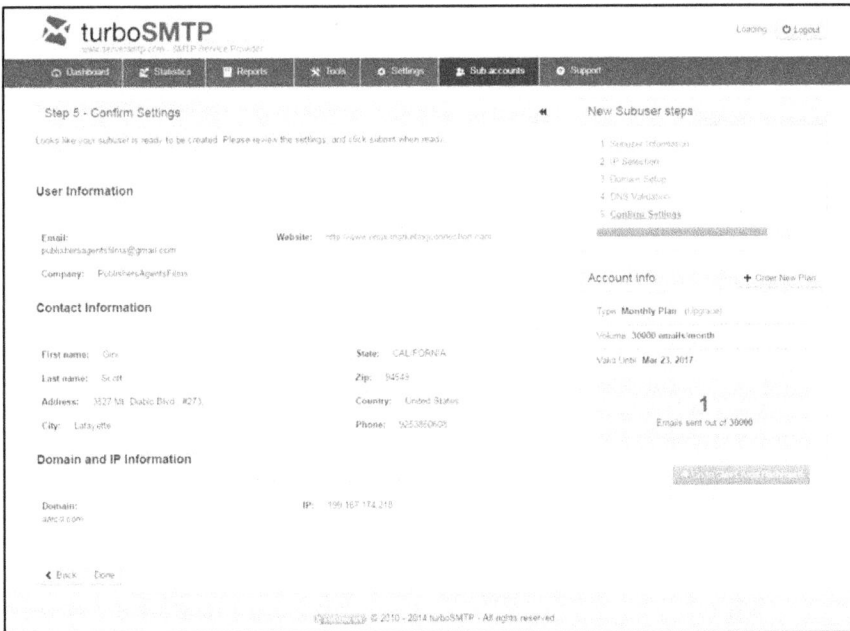

To get started, you can sign up for free for up to 6000 emails a month, or 200 a day. Or for up to 30,000 emails a month, it's only $9. Other plans go up to 1 million emails a month.

Other SMTP Services

There are dozens of these SMTP services if you search for them on Google. I'll feature a few more that I have worked with in the past and then list some other popular services.

SMTP2Go (www.smtp2go.com)

SMTP2Go is one of the older services, in business since 2006. However, SMTP2Go has a number of restrictions, including not using the service to send out mass emails or emails involving multi-level marketing, affiliate marketing, nutritional marketing, or even sending out your CV. It also insists that any emails be 100% opt-in, that you have sent emails to those on the list within 3 months, and that you include an unsubscribe link.

But if you meet their criteria, it can be a great service, and it is integrated into the GroupMail 6 service which I use.

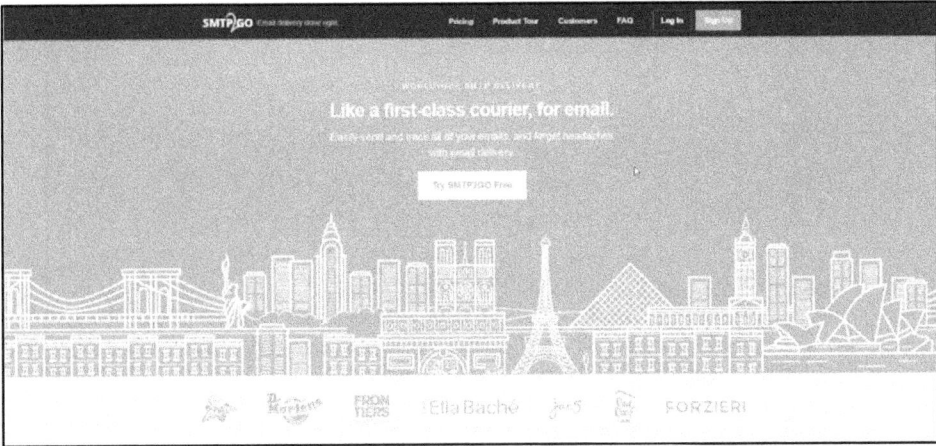

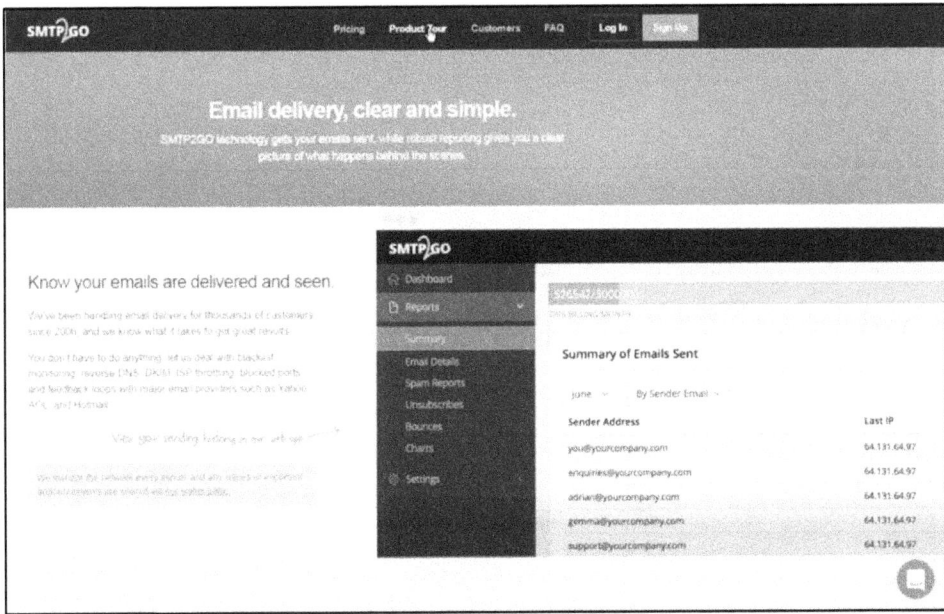

Like other services, you can try out SMTP2Go for free, and you can continue to use it for free with up to 1000 email a month, and it sends out 25 an hour. Or you can choose plans starting at $14 a month for 20,000 emails, with plans for 100,000 to a million or more emails a month.

AuthSMTP (www.authsmtp.com)

This is another service which I used when I began my email connection service back in 2001.

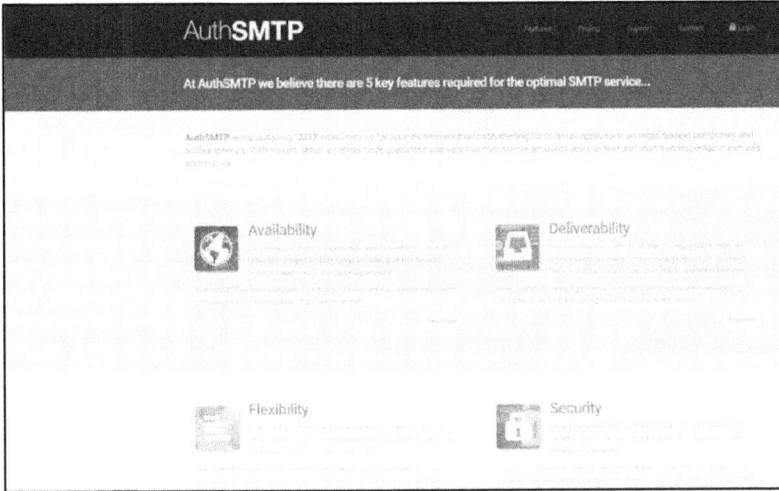

AuthSMTP is one of the few services with a yearly fee based on how many emails you want to send each month. The fee starts at $32 a year – less than $3 a month -- for 1000 emails a month up to 2 million. For comparison with the other services, it's about $15 a month for 10,000 emails -- the service level that I subscribed to.

Still Other Services

Besides the services I'm familiar with, here's a list of other services which are listed among the top 10 SMTP service providers based on a Google search.

MailGet Bolt (https://www.formget.com/mailget-bolt)

AuthoMailer (http://www.authmailer.com)

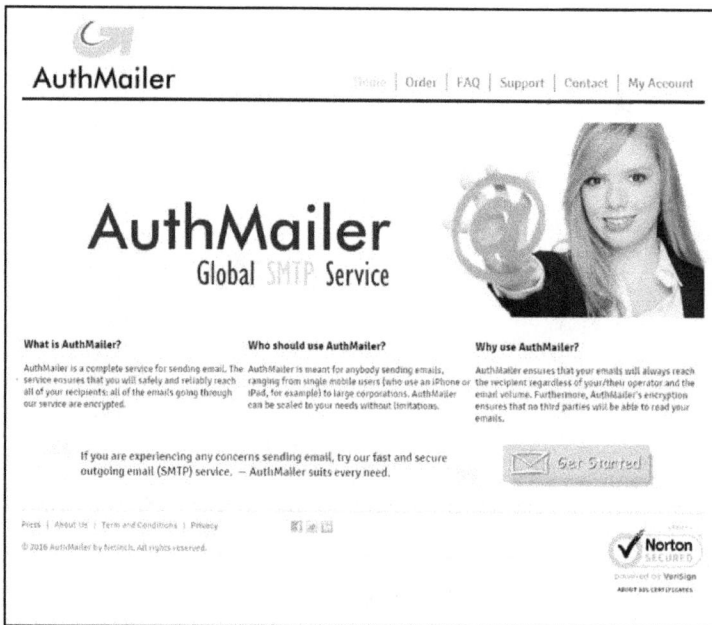

Elastic Email (https://elasticemail.com)

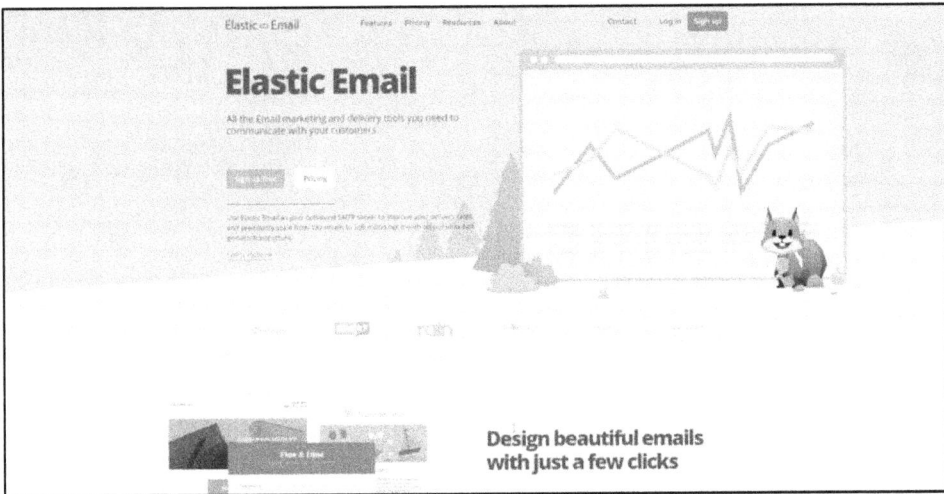

SocketLabs (https://www.socketlabs.com)

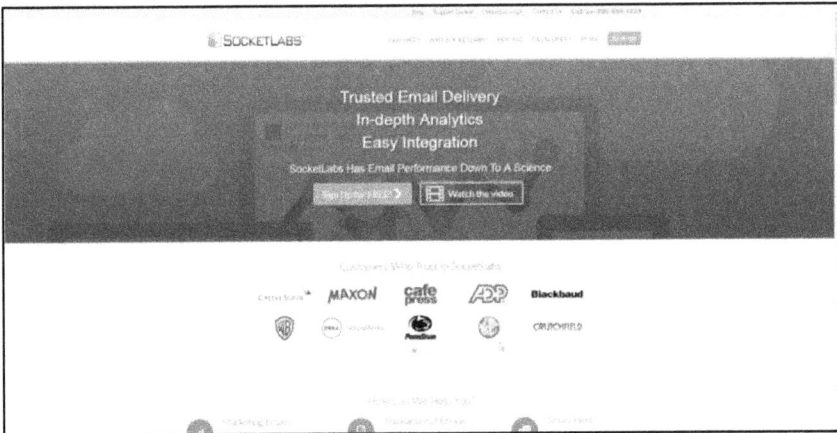

CHAPTER 5: USING SPECIALITY MAILING SERVICES

There are some email services that provide a complete package. They include a mailing template along with a mailing to your mailing list, so these are much like using a dedicated email server or an SMTP service to send your email. However, they are much stricter in making sure that you use opt-in email lists collected through your business, rather than from obtaining and cleaning up lists or gathering business cards at meetings and adding them to your list.

Such comprehensive mailing services are especially good for regular mailings to a list you have already put together, such as if you are producing and sending out newsletters. They are generally more expensive than using an SMTP service with your own platform. But they have been very successful with companies who want to send recurring mailings to the same group on a regular basis.

The most well-known companies in this category are Constant Contact and Mail Chimp. I'll describe them next in some detail.

Constant Contact

Constant Contact is one of the first email marketing companies, going back to 1995, when it began in a small attic in Brookline, Massachusetts. At the time, people mainly used email to communicate with friends online. But the company's founders saw email as a valuable marketing tool to help small businesses better compete against big businesses.

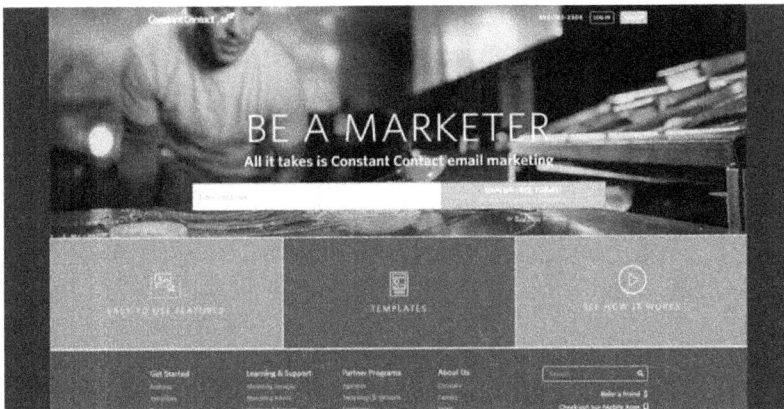

The model soon proved successful, and in a little over 5 years, in 2005, the company had over 50,000 customers, and two years later, they doubled that number to 100,000 customers. By 2009, they had over 250,000 customers. The company also began adding other products, including Event Marketing; expanded to other offices in Loveland, Colorado, San Francisco, and the UK; and added various coaching and support operations, including online chat. It also created an interface to be an "all-in-one marketing solution." In 2016, it was acquired by the Endurance International Group, which owns several webhost companies, including Bluehost and Hostgator, and now Constant Contact has over 5 million small business customers.

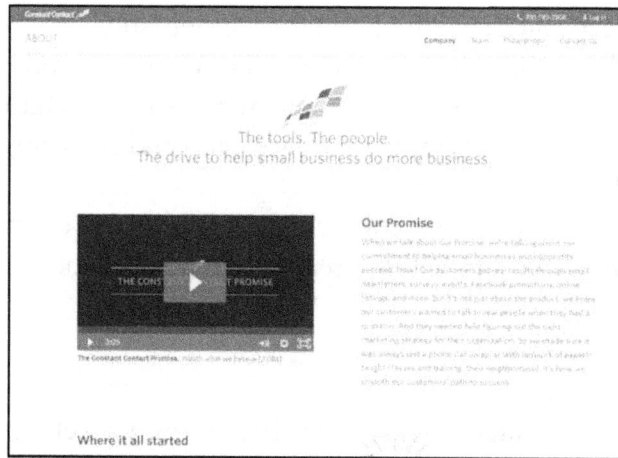

How It Works

The company begins with the premise of making powerful email marketing simple.

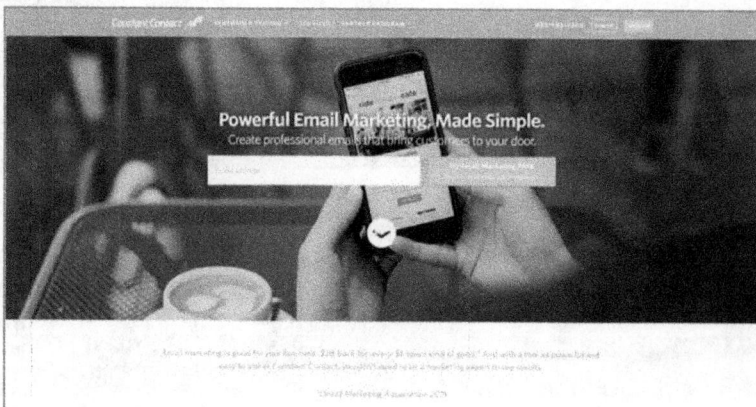

To this end, the company provides a series of templates you can customize. This approach is ideal for sending newsletters and ads, in contrast to the GroupMail 6 approach of creating largely text emails that look like personal letters directed towards a particular individual.

Here's an example of how Constant Contact offers these easy to customize templates, which are also mobile responsive.

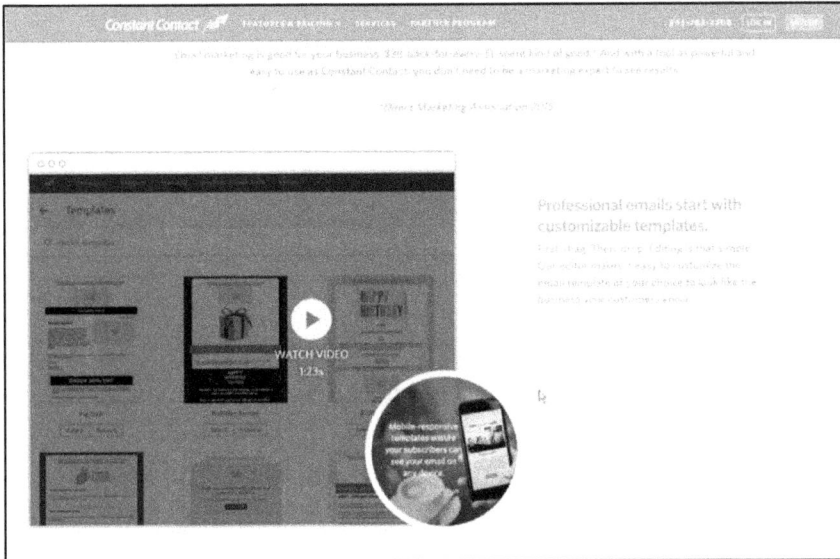

Here are some examples of templates from its introductory video about the benefits it offers.

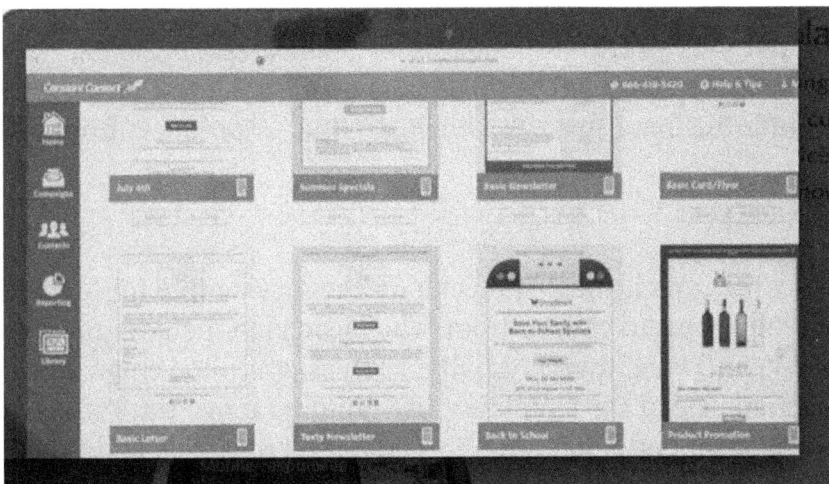

Essentially, the way Constant Contact works is you pick a template and can readily adjust it to include your logo, copy, and other features.

Then, you upload your existing contacts, and Constant Contact sends your email to them. Additionally, your email will include a sign-up form to connect you with new people. To recruit even more signups, the company has social media tools, so with a few clicks you can transform your emails into social media posts.

After you send out your emails, you can get a report on who is opening, clicking, or sharing them. This information also helps you know which messages work the best, so you can get better results in the future.

Additionally, Constant Contact has tools to promote events, offers coupons, and uses an autoresponder to respond to prospects. A typical appeal is offering a free gift to those who express interest in something; then you offer the opportunity to buy a product or products from you.

What It Costs

So what does it cost? You can try the service free for 60 days, and then have two plans to choose from. The basic plan includes most of the features you will want to use initially, such as unlimited emails for a set cost per email, use of the templates, list-building tools, tracking and reporting, and support and training. The e-mail plus plan additionally enables you to have up to 3 users and provides additional storage, email automation, event marketing, surveys and polls, and coupons.

Here's a more detailed description of these plans.

And here's what it costs.

It can get quite expensive if you are mailing to a large list or series of lists. For example, if you have up to 500 contacts on your list, it's $20 or

$45 a month after your free trial, depending on whether you choose the basic or the plus plan. If your mailing shoots up to 5000-10,000 on your list, the cost is $95 or $125 a month, making this approach much more expensive than using an SMTP mailing with a third party software like GroupMail 6, where a mailing to this size group is $9 to $15 a month.

This approach might work well when you have a dedicated email list you mail to regularly. But as you create a large list of emails, particularly when first building your email relationship with contacts, such as if you collect 100s of business cards at a trade show or gather 1000s of opt-in emails from online list building, the cost can be too much for a big email campaign. On the other hand, if you have a high end product or service with a high percentage of conversions, the high cost might be worth it.

Mail Chimp

Another very popular comprehensive email marketing service is Mail Chimp. It describes itself as the "world's leading email marketing platform" with over 15 million customers, from small e-commerce companies to online retailers.

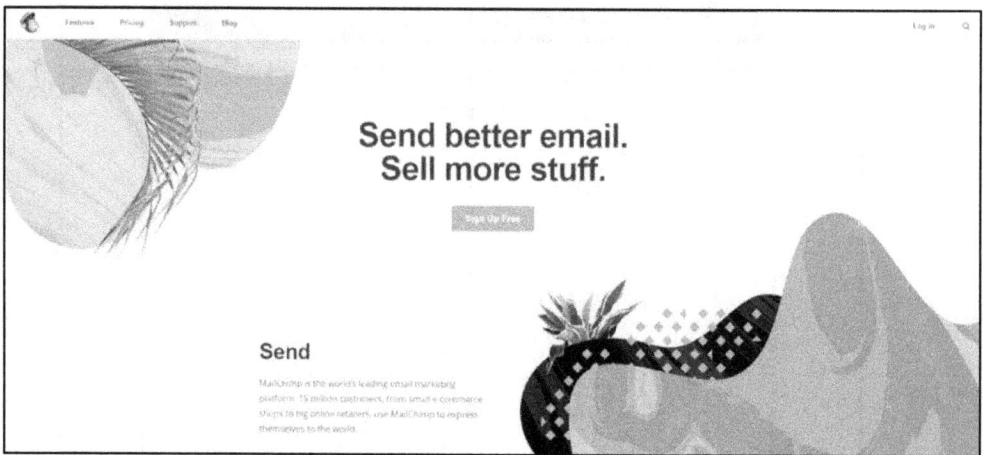

With Mail Chimp, which also has a free sign up, you start by connecting your store using Shopify, Magento, WooCommerce, or BigCommerce. Then, you create targeted campaigns, set up product follow-ups, and recommend products to your current and prospective customers.

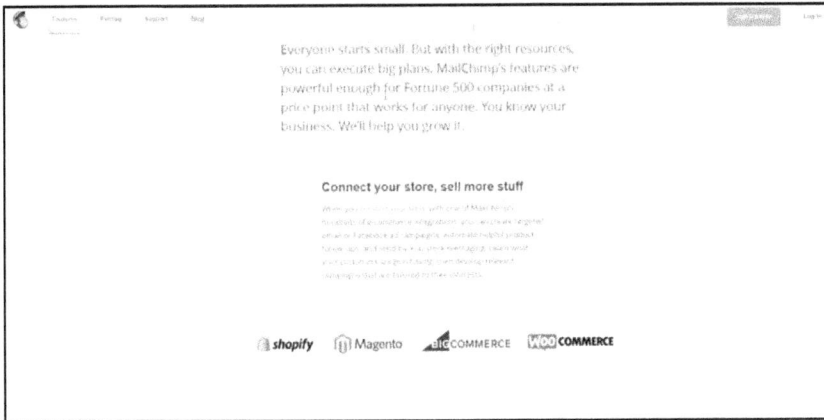

You can use Mail Chimp's templates to create your email campaigns, and the company provides guidelines for creating your own HTML emails, if you are a front-end web designer with basic knowledge of HTML. Otherwise, just use the drag and drop templates

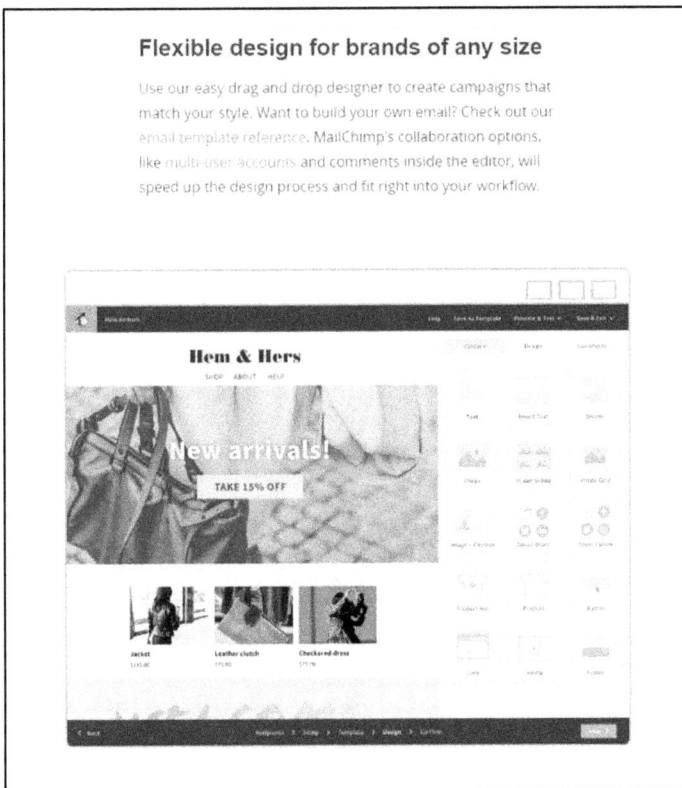

For example, in using a template, you can drag and drop different content blocks and image where you want them.

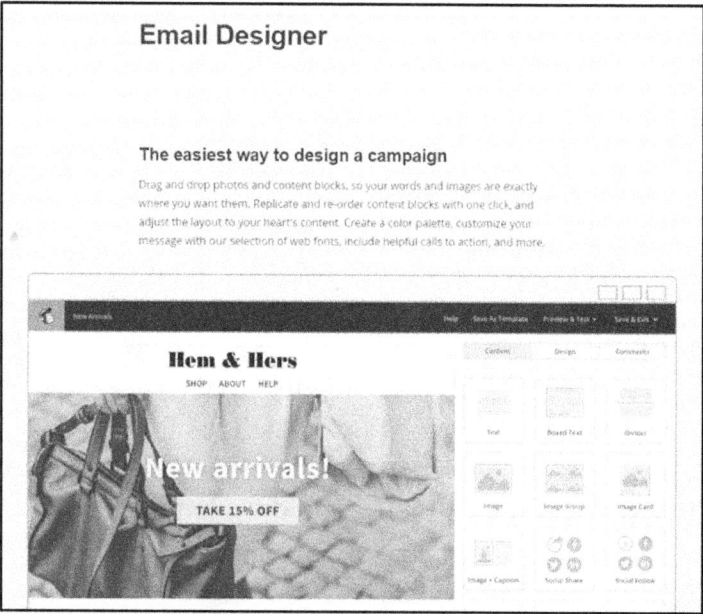

Mail Chimp also has templates designed for sending different types of emails, such as to showcase your products, share big news, tell your story, send a follow-up email, or explain how to use your product .

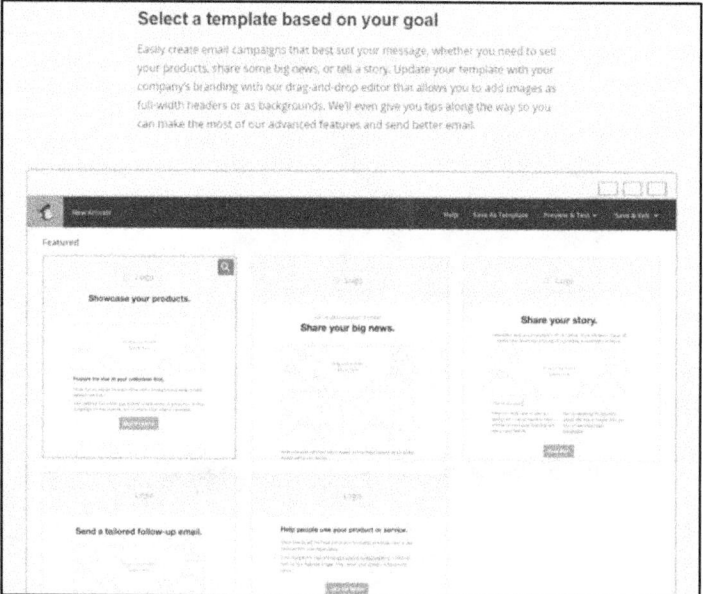

The company additionally helps you automate your email campaign, so you can target customers and prospects based on their behavior, preferences, and previous sales. You can offer a free gift to get more customer response and trigger more sales.

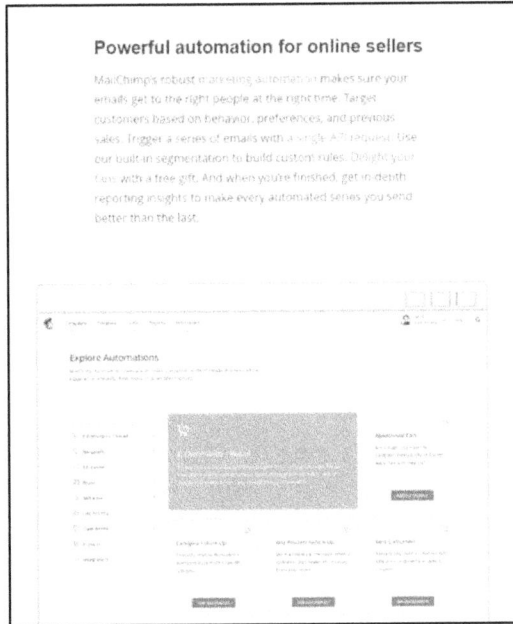

Mail Chimp also offers various analytic tools, so you can see who is buying what and adapt your email campaign accordingly.

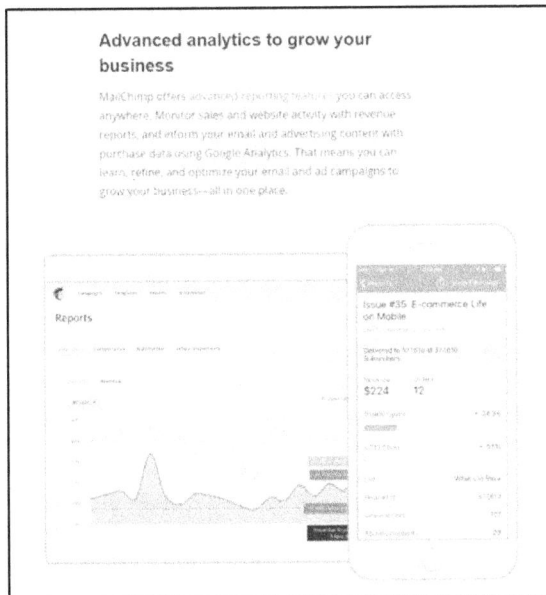

The company can also help you create an effective Facebook ad campaign, using its design and targeting options. Its tracking reports can tell you the number of customers you gained and how much they spent.

The service is integrated with many popular apps, too.

Mail Chimp even has a Forever Free program, if you are getting started and want to send up to 2000 people up to 12,000 emails a month.

So if you still have a small email list, Mail Chimp can be a great way to get started and use its templates for sending emails or creating Facebook ads to reach out to new customers.

As you expand, you can send unlimited emails to your 2000 or under list for $20-25, and $30-35 a month for 2001 to 2600 emails.

Then, for even more -- $199 a month – you can sign up for Mail Chimp's Pro package which offers targeted sending, more comprehensive tracking, and more sophisticated reporting.

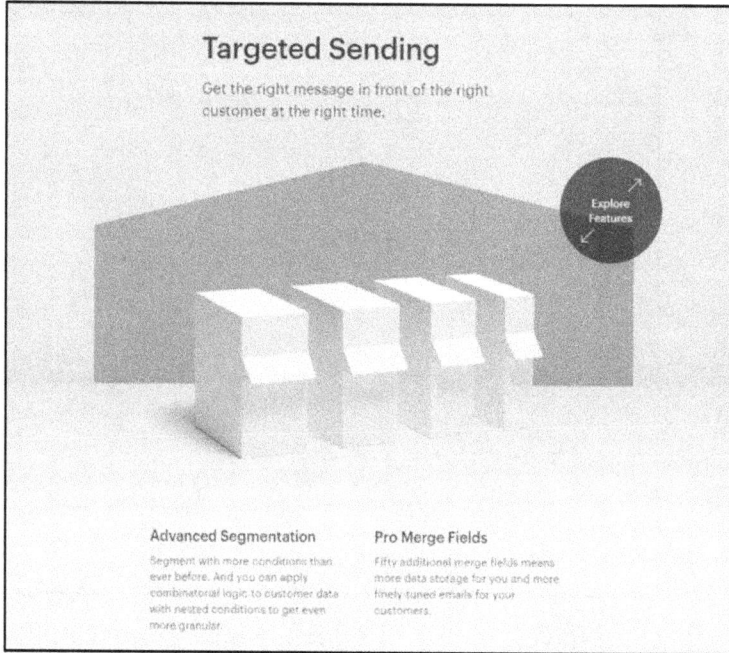

As with Constant Contact, this approach is good when you have a limited number of customers you contact on a regular basis, such as for newsletters and surveys. But for the big email campaigns, especially if you obtain large lists and validate them, the SMTP or bulk email approach is the way to go.

Other Email Marketing Services

Besides Constant Contact and Mail Chimp, there are some other email marketing services that combine tools for creating your email with sending it out to your own lists. These services are not supposed to be used for sending marketing or promotional emails to get new customers. I have listed the ones that are most widely recommended by a number of email marketing rating services, and I have included their pricing. Of these, iContact is especially highly recommended, while Mad Mimi is the least expensive.

iContact (www.icontact.com)

Benchmark

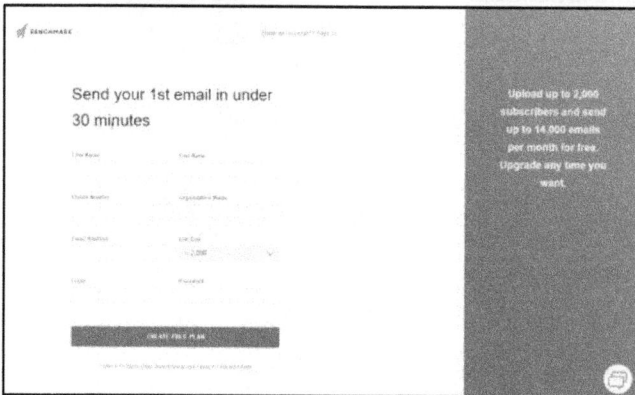

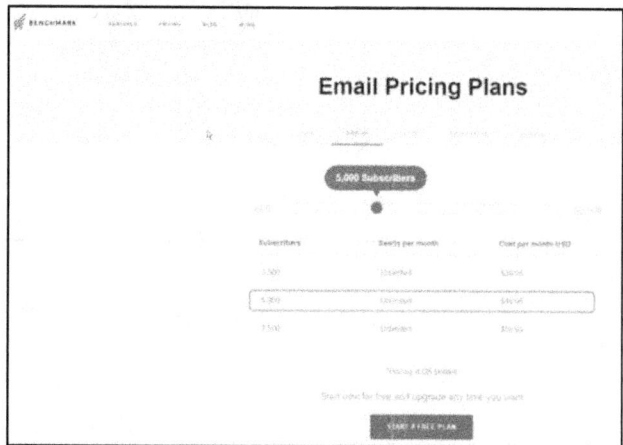

Campaigner: (www.campaigner.com)

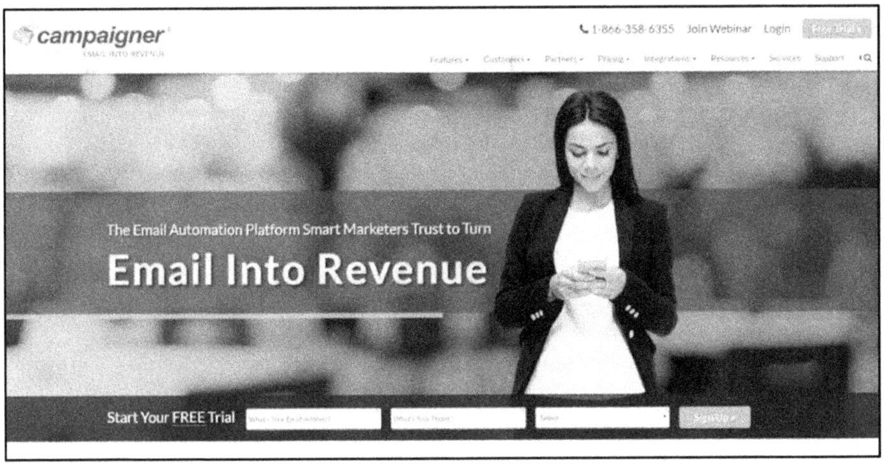

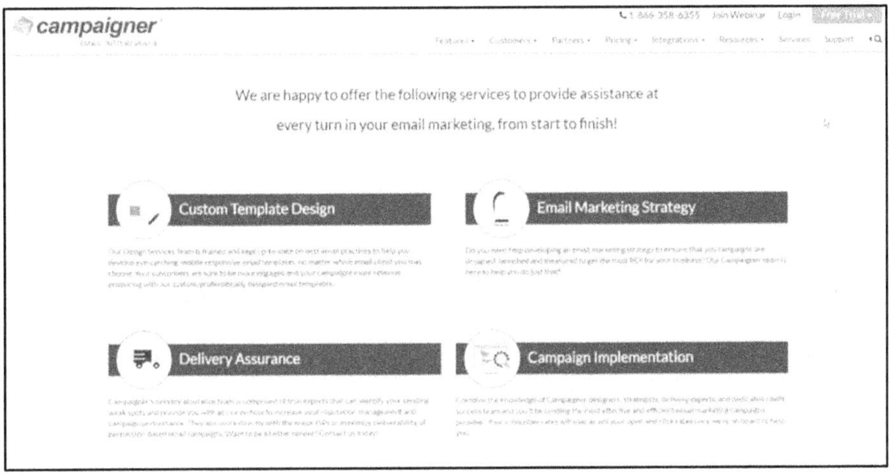

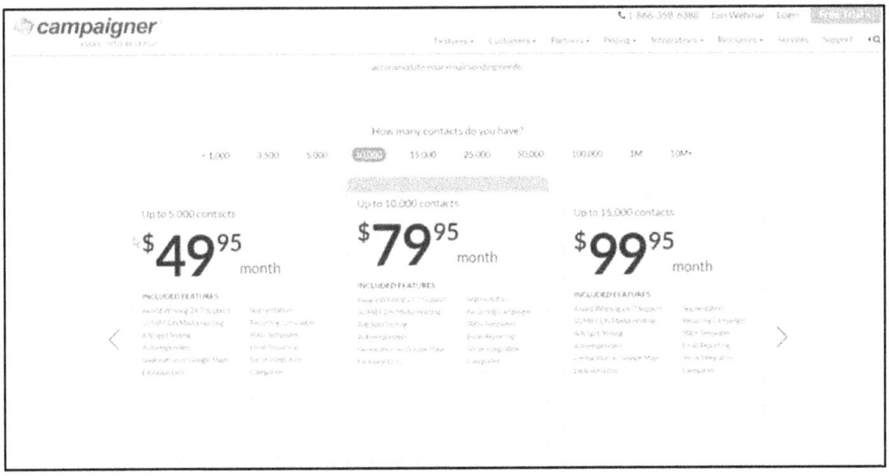

Pinpointe (www.pinpointe.com)

OUTGROWN YOUR CURRENT EMAIL SERVICE PROVIDER?

Get advanced email marketing features that fit your needs.

Here's What Pinpointe Can Do For You Today

Go Mobile: Over 1,000 Email Templates

1-800-920-7227 sales@pinpointe.com

Pinpointe
Target. Deliver. Measure.

HOME PRODUCTS PRICING RESOURCES CUSTOMERS & PARTNERS ABOUT CONTACT

Pricing – Which Plan is Right For You?

Pinpointe is the most feature-rich email service provider for businesses sending **permission-based, opt-in email campaigns**. Select from our flexible email marketing price options. Our top-rated support is available via chat, knowledgebase and email. Phone support available for Enterprise customers.

Need more credits or contacts that the options listed below? Call us to discuss your specific requirements.

PRICING BASED ON THE NUMBER OF CONTACTS IN PINPOINTE

Select the number of **active contacts** you will upload to and store in your Pinpointe email contact lists. This subscription plan is ideal for customers who send regularly. Pre-pay for 6 months for an additional 10% discount. If you need to send to your full list more than 6 times / month - please call for high frequency discount prices - US 408-834-7577, Option #2.

Total # Contacts in Pinpointe	5,000 Contacts	10,000 Contacts	25,000 Contacts	50,000 Contacts	75,000 Contacts	100,000 Contacts	200,000 Contacts	>200,000 Subscribers
Monthly # Emails Send Limit (*)	40,000	80,000	200,000	300,000	450,000	600,000	Call	
Monthly Cost	$49 per mo.	$74 per mo.	$150 per mo.	$245 per mo.	$365 per mo.	$480 per mo.	$898 per mo.	$Call
	SIGN UP	SIGN UP	SIGN UP	SIGN UP	SIGN UP	SIGN UP	SIGN UP	
Pay 6 Mo. 10% Off	$42 $252 total	$66 $399 total	$135 $810 total	$220 $1,325 total	$330 $1,984 total	$432 $2,592 total	$808 $4,849 total	$Call
	SIGN UP	SIGN UP	SIGN UP	SIGN UP	SIGN UP	SIGN UP	SIGN UP	

SendinBlue (www.sendinblue.com)

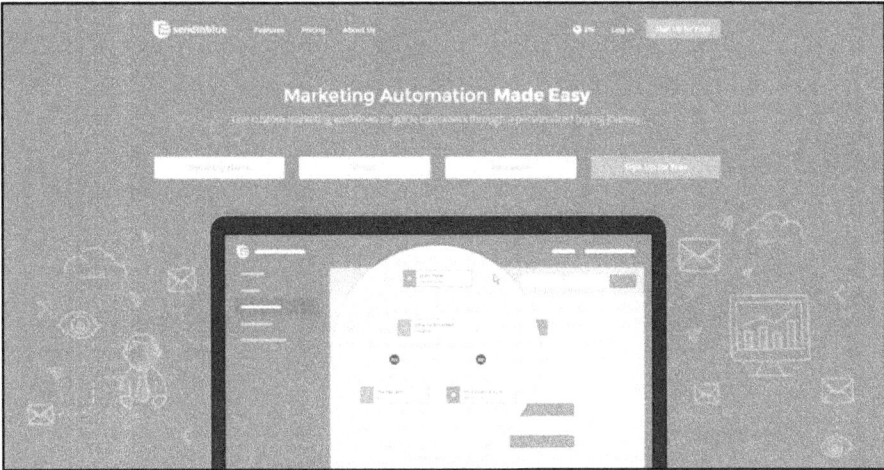

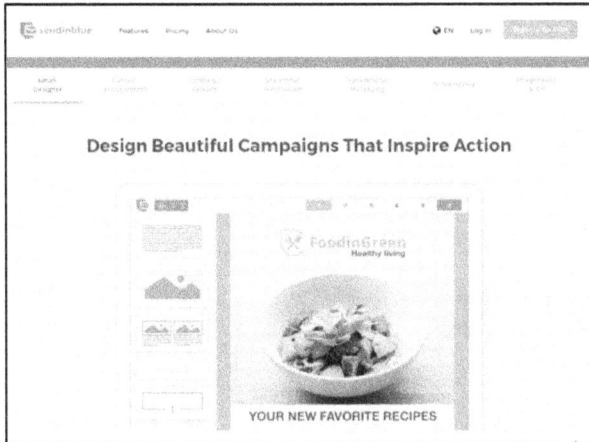

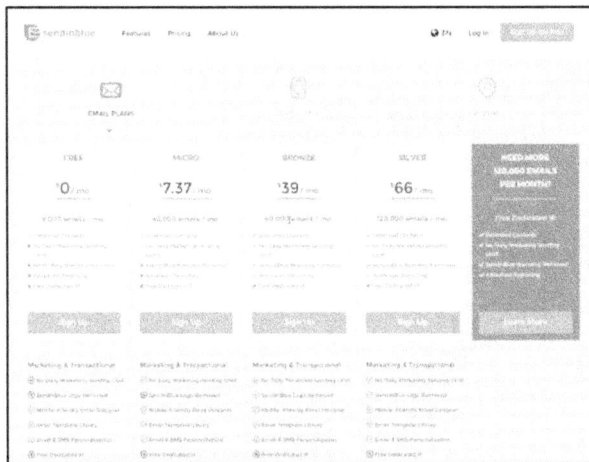

Campaign Monitor (www.campaignmonitor.com)

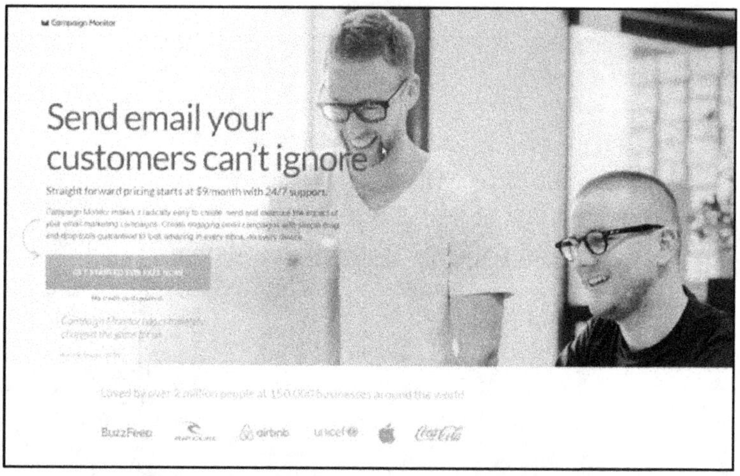

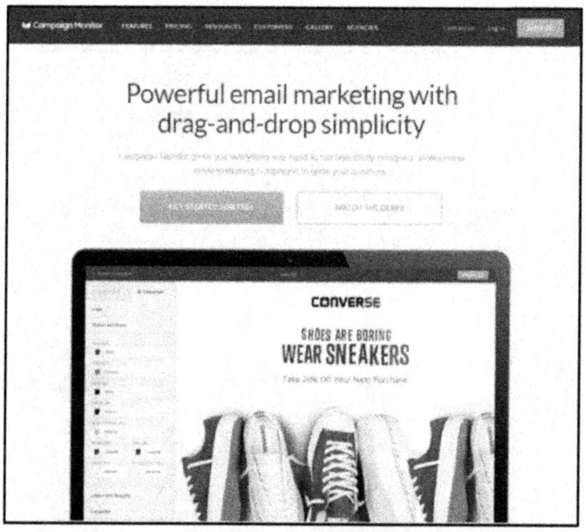

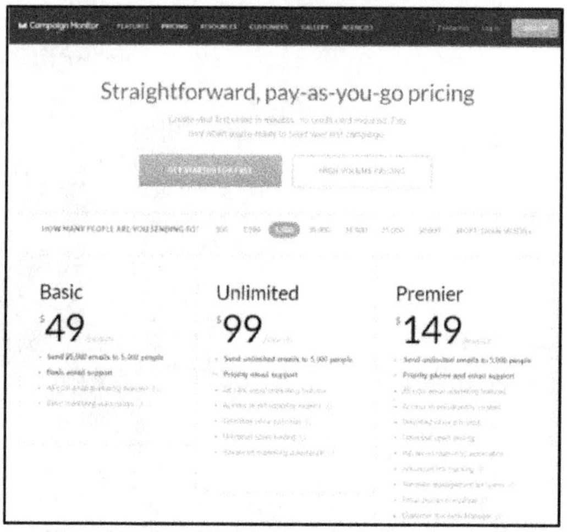

Mad Mimi (www.madmimi.com)

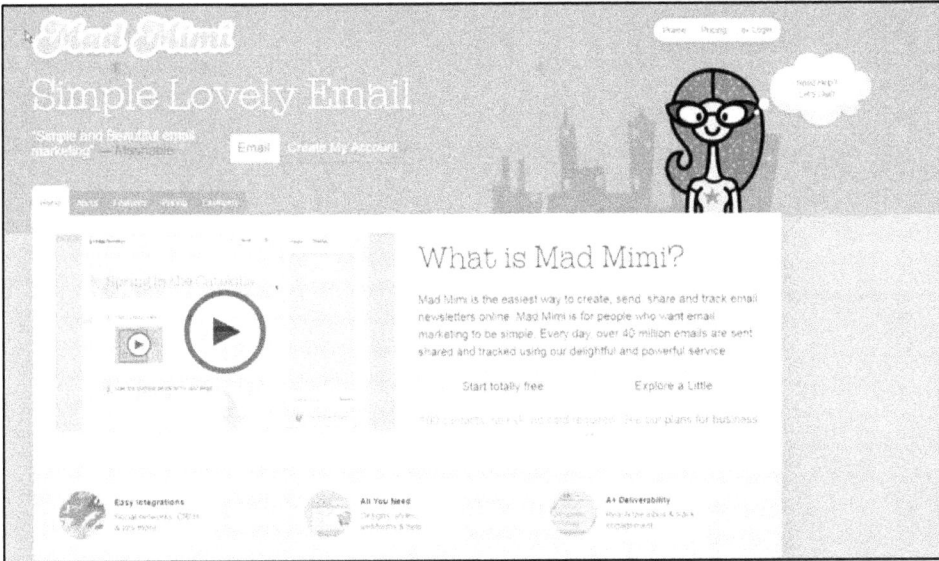

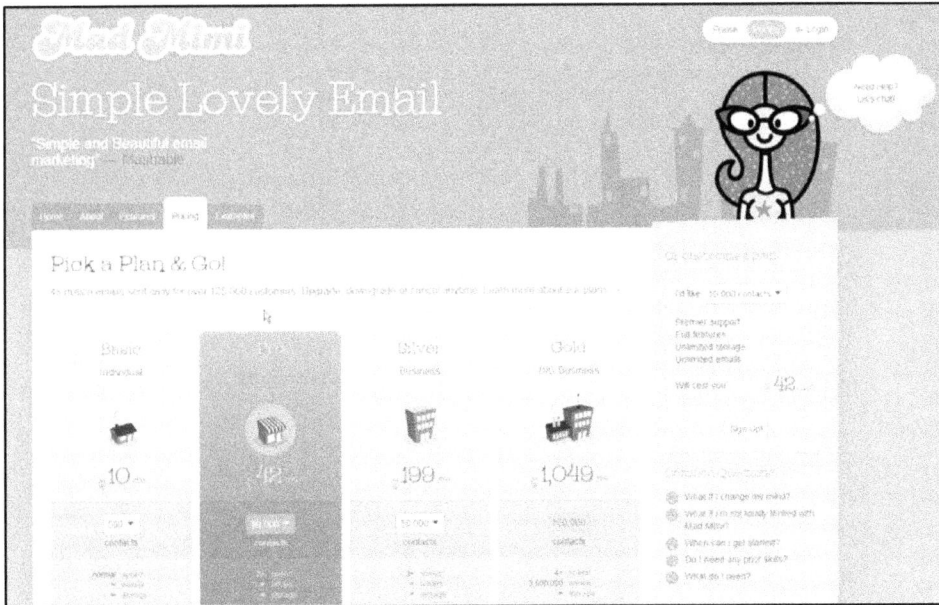

CHAPTER 6: USING BULK MAILING SERVICES

For very large mailings, especially to find new customers or clients, you can use bulk mail services. This is a good way to go if you are sending emails to 10,000 or more individuals in a single mailing. Using a bulk mail platform is different from sending transactional emails, which require a transaction with a customer. This occurs when a customer does something, such as places an order, fills in an email form to request information, or joins a group, and you send an email.

Why Use a Bulk Email Service

While you can send out emails with an SMTP service or use one of the specialty or transactional platforms, it's better to use a bulk email service for these large mailings. This is especially important if you are using a list you haven't mailed to for a while, or mailing to a relatively new list that you have purchased, even if you recently validated it. That's because you might get a high number of bounces, drops, or spam reports with such large mailings. And that can hurt your reputation and lead the SMTP provider or marketing service to suspend your account. That's when it might be better to use a bulk mailing service to do the mailing for you under its own name.

Another good reason for using a bulk mailing service is that you have found that building a list by getting traffic to your website or landing page or placing ads through the social media is slow and expensive. You are not getting a large enough conversion rate to justify the cost of your ads or the time you are spending on traffic and list building strategies.

When you send out bulk mails, such emails are supposed to include an unsubscribe link, according to the CAN-SPAM act, whereas transactional emails, to be further described in the next chapter, aren't required to do this.

Bulk Mailing Requirements

Many bulk mailing services are associated with companies selling lists, and those are the ones I've used, after buying and validating a list. I'll describe those first and then list some of the other bulk mailing services.

Emarketing Solutions

Emarketing Solutions is one of the sources for buying lists I previously discussed in *Book V: Buying and Validating Email Lists for Large Mailings.* The company is well established, in business since 1997.

Aside from selling lists, which you can buy from the company or use your own, Emarketing Solutions has several different programs for sending out large numbers of emails.

1) Sending a mailing to the company's consumer and interest databases,

2) Using their web based marketing system to send email campaigns through your web browser,

3) Obtaining the company's email broadcasting software for your email campaigns,

4) Purchasing your own semi-dedicated or dedicated email server.

I'll describe each one in turn.

Sending a Mailing to Up to 100,000 or More Contacts

Emarketing Solutions is the bulk mail service I am most familiar with, since I used it to send out a mailing to 100,000 consumers interested in buying books for one of my clients. In this case, I purchased the database through the company, though I could have purchased that database elsewhere.

The company sends out the query through its own system as a no-reply email, so you have to include a reply email in your letter for an interested prospect to click on. You provide the company with the database to use or indicate which of their databases you have purchased. Then, you send them a copy of your query letter with a subject line to send out. They do the rest. After the mailing is completed, you get a report of the emails sent and delivered, which includes the start and completion times of your campaign, the number of emails delivered, the number of opens and how many prospects read your email, and the number of click-throughs to your site.

One advantage of using a database purchased from the company is it regularly cleans and maintains its databases to verify each email record for accuracy and deliverability. The company also adds new email data to the databases, and it employs a filtration process before using the database in and email marketing campaign. In doing so, it eliminates any contacts who have asked to "unsubscribe." Then, too, all of the company's mailings are sent out in accordance with the U.S. Anti-Spam Act, so all of their data comes from opt-ins. You also get a file with all of the contacts included in the mailing, which you can later use for more detailed mailings, such as by breaking out the database on state or regional information.

The cost of these mailings are included below -- $99 for a mailing to 100,000 contacts; $199 for 250,000 contacts, and $399 for 2 million.

You can find pricing for other breakdowns and even larger mailings to even 50 million people, if you're really thinking big. These campaigns are ideal for a general interest audience, though you can target your campaign based on various categories, including interest, hobby, gender, age, occupation, industry, state, city, or county for an additional $249.00. The big cost break comes if you want to pitch your campaign to 2 million or more contacts – only $0.09 or less per email after that.

The way to send out your campaign is simple. Create your message in a Word. text, or html file, along with a short subject line, preferably up to 4 to 5 words, and use an appealing subject line to get prospects to open your email. For instance, mention something about benefits in your email. After you click the "Add to Cart" button and make your payment, you receive an order form that indicates what to put where, and your campaign goes out within one to two business days.

Using a Web-Based Marketing System

With this web based email marketing system, you can send campaigns directly through your web browser, so you bypass your ISP and use the company's much faster servers and bandwidth.

You create your campaign using text or HTML in the company's easy-to use Ad Builder. You upload your ad into the Ad Builder and can adapt it with your own creative touches. You can use the mail-merge features to use the name, address, or other data about the recipient to give your email a personal feel, just as in GroupMail 6. Plus you can send your email from a "from" address, so recipients can reply back directly to you.

Once your email letter is ready to go, you can send your campaign at a high rate of speed – up to 200,000 emails per hour. After that, at any time, you can easily manage your email lists to quickly add, delete, remove duplicates, and otherwise clean your lists. Plus you can use the usual monitoring analytics which indicate how many emails have been sent, how many were read, the number of clicks, and the number of unsubscribes. The software automatically handles unsubscribes and unsubscribe equests, as well as verifies and cleans your email list of undeliverables, as it sends out your email. You can schedule the timing of when your campaign goes out, and you can easily log in from any computer to work on your campaign.

Should you want to run multiple campaigns simultaneously, you can do that. The pricing, based on the number of emails sent per month, ranges from 100,000 emails for $125 to over 100 million or more for $1125. For sending to a small numbers of recipients, the pricing is about the same as sending out email marketing campaigns through the company's servers. But the pricing is substantially less when you start sending out 10 million or more emails. And an advantage of using a web based system is personalizing your emails and having your own "from" address.

Reliant Email Broadcast Email System Pricing

Emails Sent p/ Month	Pricing	
100,000	$125.00	Add to Cart
500,000	$250.00	Add to Cart
1,000,000	$375.00	Add to Cart
5,000,000	$500.00	Add to Cart
10,000,000	$625.00	Add to Cart
30,000,000	$750.00	Add to Cart
50,000,000	$875.00	Add to Cart
75,000,000	$1000.00	Add to Cart
100,000,000	$1125.00	Add to Cart
Unlimited	$1250.00	Add to Cart
Larger Packages	Inquire	

Reliant Accounts:

- 1) Each Reliant Email account allows you to upload and use your own email lists.
- 2) If you do not have your own data, you may purchase lists based on your needs here: (General Email Lists or Targeted Email Lists)

404

Using Email Broadcasting Software

The third bulk sending approach involves getting your own email broadcast software, which is ideal for high speed large scale campaigns. You also get the major features of the company's web based service, which includes bypassing your ISP's mail server, sending emails through the company's fast servers and bandwidth, fully tracking of each campaign, and monitoring by the number of opens, clicks, and unsubscribes. You can similarly personalize your emails with the contact's first and last name, send out HTML newsletters and ads, which have a better response rate than newsletters and ads created in plain-text, though you can send in both formats. You can easily import your email list from any sources, including Access, Excel, and Microsoft Outlook.

The company also has a Corporate Mailer software that allows you to use targeted email lists directly from your computer. The program enables you to create opt-in newsletters and email marketing campaigns in minutes to send to your subscribers, and you can send personalized messages, account statements, reports, and bills to customers, too.

The advantage of the Platinum Corporate Mailer, which costs an additional $189, is you can create targeted email campaigns directly from your computer, and it includes a bulk email engine, so you don't need an SMTP relay server. Instead, you can deliver your message from your computer directly to the recipient's email inbox, so you bypass your Internet Service Provider's (ISP) SMTP server. This enables you to send out your emails at much faster speeds, although the system can work directly with your ISP's current mail server if your ISP isn't compatible with bypassing your ISP.

The software includes an Address Book, where you can load and store your email lists and other details. The software makes sorting, filtering and organizing your contact records simple. You can break down your lists into separate groups, so you can send emails to the whole group or to specific individuals in the group, as well as exclude recipients you don't want to contact. Then, too, you don't need to export your data from a database into an Excel or .csv file, since the software can extract email records directly from the database, and it updates any changes in the database, such as bounces and dropped emails. Additionally, the software creates a plain text version, so recipients who can't see the HTML version can see your message in plain text. You can schedule when the email goes out, too.

Purchasing a Semi-Dedicted or Dedicated Bulk Email Server

If you conduct major email campaigns, you can purchase your own bulk email server – either a semi-dedicated server you share with others or a dedicated one of your own. One advantage of having your own server is that these are designed for the large scale delivery of promotional and advertising emails, whereas many ISPs have strict terms of service (TOS) or acceptable use policies (AUP) that prohibit the large scale delivery of such emails. Should an ISP receive complaints or discover that you are using your account to send out large volumes of email messages, they are likely to shut down your account.

But with a bulk email server, you can send out large volumes of emails without being shut down.

The dedicated server is a computer devoted to a single user, and since it isn't shared, you can more quickly upload lists, have more processing power, and a faster sending speed. With a dedicated server, you can send out about 200,000 messages a day or more, and the server has its own SMTP server, reverse DNS, and dedicated IP address for the best deliverability. With a dedicated bulk server, you can send out unlimited, unmetered email delivery.

To do a mailing, you simply upload your lists, create your messages, and send. And there's no need to worry about complaints, because the company promises not to shut down your server if you get any.

The basic cost is high -- $1298 per month, plus a $99 set-up fee, but if your large-scale email campaigns are very successful, this should make these high costs worthwhile.

For a slightly lower amount - $935 a month, plus a $50 set-up fee, you can get a semi-dedicated server, where you share the server with multiple users. However, each user has a login to manage email campaigns from his or her computer. With this shared system, you can send about 100,000 emails a day or more, but otherwise, all the arrangements with the company are the same. For example, you have unlimited bulk sending and unmetered bandwidth; you upload your lists, create your message, and send; and the company agrees not to shut you down due to any complaints.

EmailListUS

Another service which combines an email sending service with selling email lists is EmailListUS. I have bought several lists from them, though I haven't used them for mailings.

While they sell all kinds of business and consumer lists, they only offer to send emails to staff members at elementary and junior high schools.

Other Email Sending Services

You can find many other email sending services through a Google search. I've listed one of the services that offers very high volume email marketing - think up to 10 million or more emails. Their monthly charge of around $950 for sending out emails or $1500 for a mailing package may seem like a very expensive recurring monthly fee. But if you are sending 10 million or more emails, the cost per email is relatively low.

Ongage (www.ongage.com)

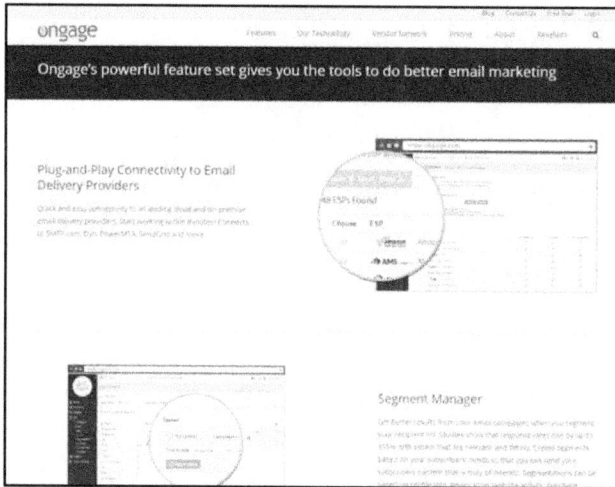

CHAPTER 7: USING TRANSACTIONAL EMAIL SERVICES

While some transactional email services also offer a bulk mail service, many permit transactional emails only. The difference is that a transactional email occurs when a user takes some action, such as when you send a welcome email, order confirmation, respond to a comment, and provide a password reset. The basic requirement is that the recipient has first responded to you, such as by filling in a form on your site and providing an email. By contrast, a bulk email is used for marketing, promotions, announcements, and newsletters. It does not require an action from the recipient.

Many of these transactional services include templates as well as sending out emails. They all offer free trials – usually30 days – to check them out, and they typically provide a way for you to start small and build up to a much higher number of contacts. Some are designed for recurring emails to your subscribers each month, though you can usually set up a single mailing to see how it goes.

Since I haven't used transactional email services, I'm listing the ones that are most highly recommended by the sites rating these services. I've included the home page and pricing to illustrate.

Email Servers for End Users

The following servers provide easy to follow procedures and guidelines so end users can use these servers without any major tech background.

Mail Jet (www.mailjet.com)

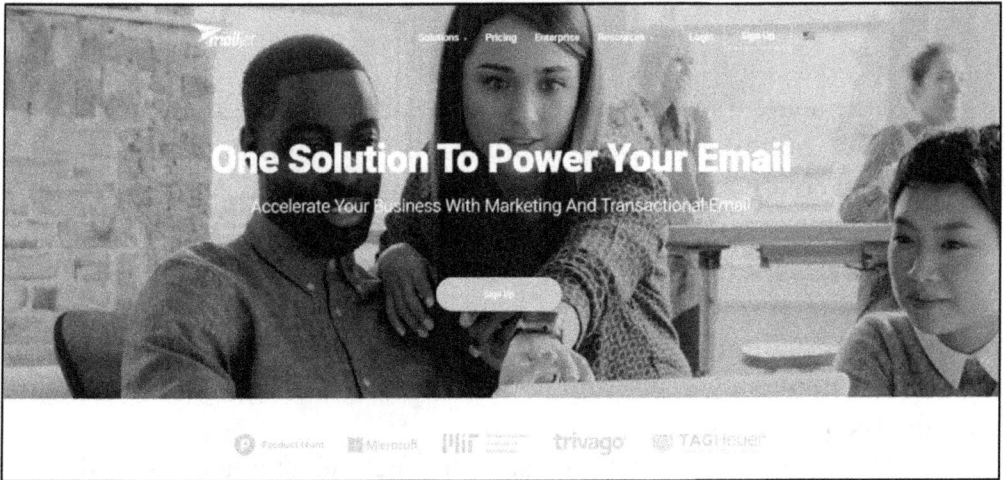

Postmark (www.postmark.com)

Postmark   Why Postmark?   Pricing   Customers   Resources ⌄   Support   Log in   Start Free Trial

A fast & reliable transactional-only email platform for web applications

INBOUND PROCESSING AND PARSING

FAST AND RELIABLE TO THE INBOX

45 days of full content and message history

Opens, delivery and open tracking for all messages and recipients

Trusted by industry leaders around the world

When you can't afford to lose an email.

As low as **$0.25** per **1,000** credits.

1 Credit = 1 Email sent or processed

Credits never expire. Use them as you need them.

Money back guarantee on unused credits.

Your first 25,000 credits are free. Really!

Save money with volume pricing
Let us know how many emails your application sends or receives monthly, and we'll find the sweet spot for your volume.

Emails sent or received per month

Example: 4,000   Calculate

Credits	Price/1,000	Min. Cost
1,000+	$1.50	$1.50
200,000+	$1.25 Save 17%	$250
500,000+	$1.00 Save 33%	$500
1,000,000+	$0.75 Save 50%	$750
2,000,000+	$0.50 Save 66%	$1,000
5,000,000+	$0.25 Save 83%	$1,250

$

What's the best tier for you?

Let us know how many emails your application sends or receives monthly, and we'll find the sweet spot for your volume

413

Green Arrow (www.drh.net)

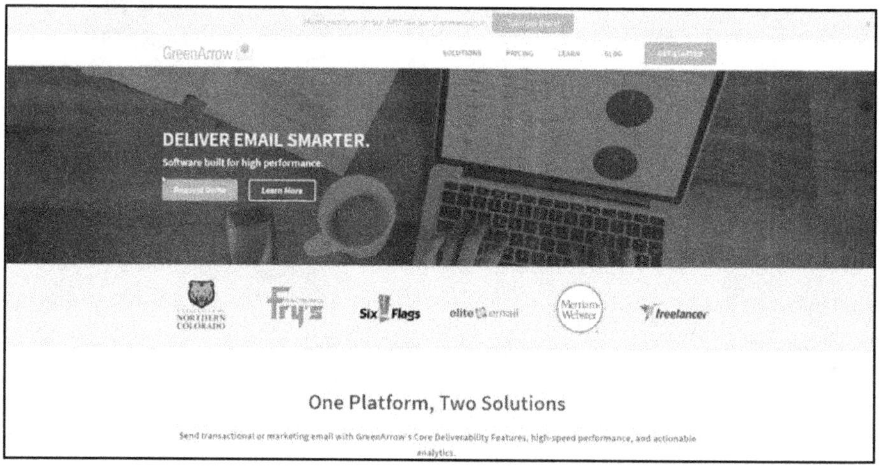

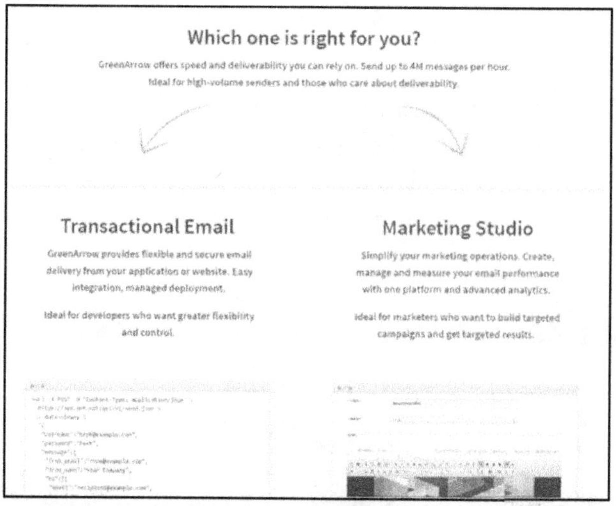

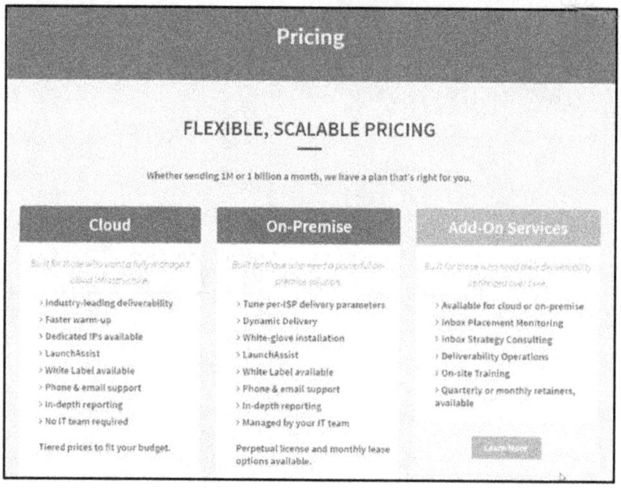

Email Sending Services for Developers

While the previously described transactional services can be used by end users with limited tech skills, some email services are designed for developers of webs or apps, and you need some tech know-how to use them. If you do have this knowledge or can learn the necessary tech skills, these services offer high-volume emails at a relatively low cost per email. Here are three of the more highly recommended services.

SparkPost (www.sparkpost.com)

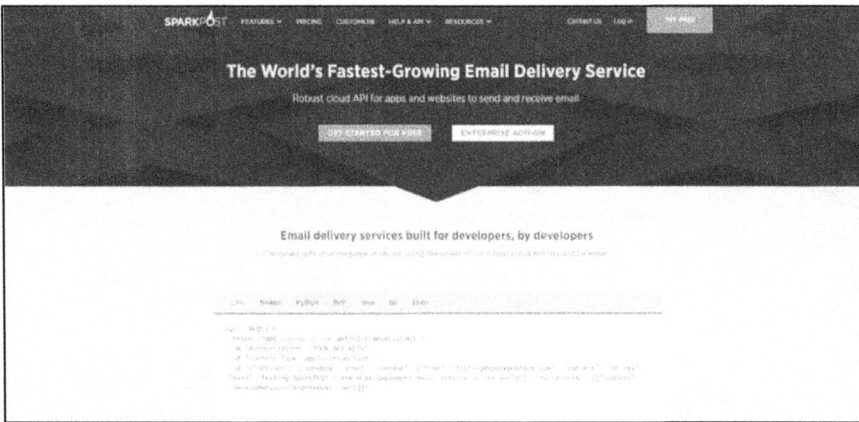

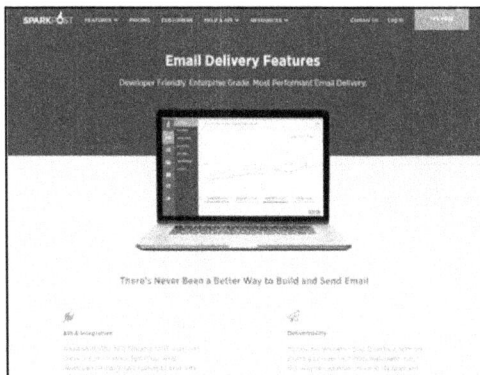

Mailgun (www.mailgun.com)

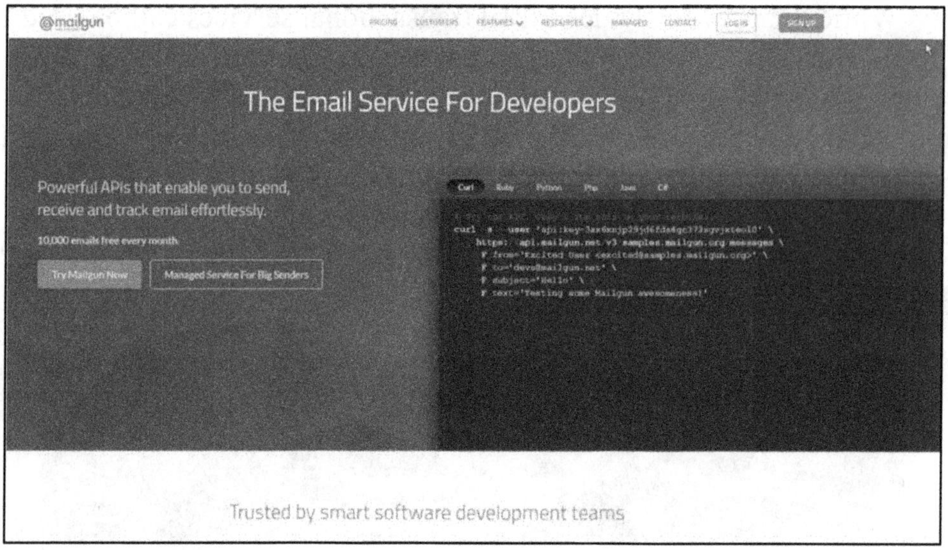

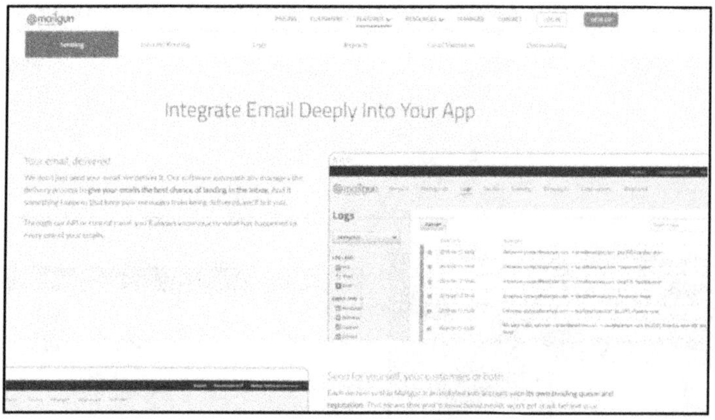

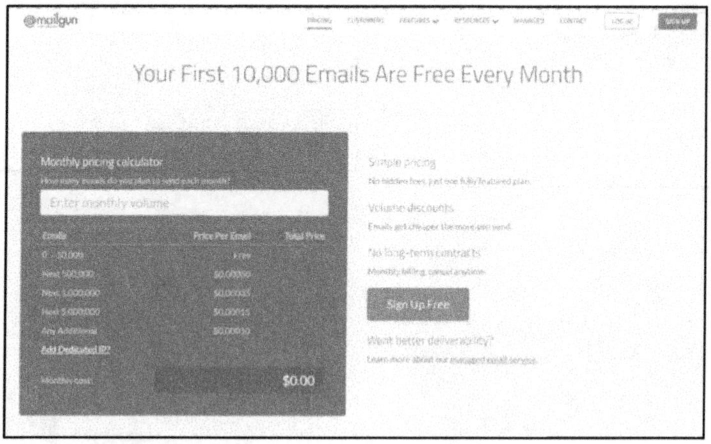

Knowtify (www.knowtify.io)

It's ALL about user engagement.

We build tools that enable companies to understand and drive scalable user engagement.

ENGAGEMENT TOOLS FOR YOUR TEAM

Elegant all-in-one email solution

Get Started   Request Demo

Smart AND beautiful made easy

Plans built for every team

All accounts come with Knowtify's **Whatever-It-Takes** support

Startup	Growth	Pro	All-Star
$59	$149	$449	$999
Per Month	Per Month	Per Month	Per Month
2,500 Contacts	20,000 Contacts	100,000 Contacts	200,000 Contacts
5,000 emails/mo	50,000 emails/mo	400,000 emails/mo	1,000,000 emails/mo
		A/B Testing'	A/B Testing'
			Extended Event Storage

Get Started Today: 14 Day Free Trial

Start Free trial now   Request Demo

CHAPTER 8: SELECTING THE BEST EMAIL SERVICE FOR YOU

In the previous chapters, I described various ways to send out emails to multiple contacts to market or promote your products or services or to respond to an online ecommerce transaction.

An initial step is to prepare your email list files for email sending programs. Depending on which program you are using, this list is commonly converted into a .csv file, although sometimes you might extract this data from an Excel file or database. If you are sending the email without trying to personalize it, you can use almost any text format, such as Word or a PDF.

I also discussed the importance of keeping email lists up-to-date to reduce the number of returns, which can ruin your reputation if you repeatedly have a high number of bounces, drops, or spam complaints. But many email sending services do their own clean-ups when you use them, and some bulk mail senders won't cancel your account because of complaints.

Then, the next chapters focused on the different ways to send out an email. These are like having a repertoire of possibilities, and you can choose from them the best approach to use, depending on who you want to contact for what purpose. For example, you might use one approach for sending an email with a regular newsletter to subscribers; another approach to respond to people who have expressed interest in your product or service or placed an order; another to create a marketing and promotional campaign to a small targeted group of prospects; and still another approach for a large-scale mailing to 50,000 or more contacts.

Your email approach will also vary depending on whether you have developed the list from your personal contacts at local events, created the list from opt-in subscribers on your website, or bought a list of contacts in a certain target market.

To summarize, the main types of approaches are the following, which are covered in individual chapters. You also choose among the profiled or listed companies in each category, or do further research to find still more services. These approaches covered are these:

- Using special software along with an SMTP server to send out personalized emails to a list of contacts;

- Using an email marketing service to design your email as well as send it out to an opt-in list;

- Using a bulk mailing service to mail to lists you have bought and validated;

- Using a transaction email service to send emails in response to an opt-in request for information, an order, or other type of request;

Often you may combine replying to transactional emails with an autoresponder, such as AWeber or GetResponse, which will respond to a request from a prospect or customer by directing that person to a "thank you" or order fulfillment page. These autoresponders are also used in conjunction with list building and traffic increase programs, so when prospects opt-in to get more information from you or reply to an to go to your website, the autoresponder program will direct them to the appropriate page, so they can get the requested information, product, or service. But using autoresponders is a topic for another series of books, which I will cover there, along with the techniques for building your list and attracting more traffic to your website.

Also, you need to track and monitor your results to see what works best and modify your email marketing efforts accordingly. I've described a few strategies in Chapter 9.

CHAPTER 9: TRACKING THE RESULTS OF YOUR CAMPAIGN

Whatever email approach you use, track your results to determine which approach is most effective. A CRM or Customer Relations Management system, as discussed in Book IV on doing a local email campaign, is one type of tracking approach.

When you are using an email campaign to a larger group of prospects, you need a system adapted for assessing such a campaign, since you are not just sending emails to contact and follow-up with individual customers or clients. The following chapter provides a broad overview of these different approaches.

Keeping Your Emails Updated

Most basically, you want to keep your email databases updated, using the information you get from any returns to your mailings that come to you directly or are provided by the email servers and systems you use. Some services not only report the returns, but when you do another mailing through them, they will not send your emails to any returned addresses or to any recipient requests to be removed or unsubscribed. You ideally want to start out with as clean an email list as possible.

Assessing Your Results

The other major type of tracking is assessing the responses you get from your mailings to valid emails. The key tests are the following:
- using the split-test method, where you vary one or two conditions in your email – such as the subject line, image, message, time of mailing, and other factors, while you hold the target market for the mailing constant. This test is designed to assess your content and how you are framing your message.
- testing out how your approach plays with different demographic and interest groups. The goal here is to assess your market appeal to different audiences.

Through this testing, you can try out different subject lines, tag lines, images, copy messages, and the responsiveness of different demographic groups to different approaches. Such testing works particularly well when you are doing a mailing to a large number of recipients, such as when you have collected a great many business cards from networking events and trade shows; when you have gotten a large number of opt-in emails from people visiting your website and requesting more information or your free gift; or when you have purchased and cleaned up a list for a bulk mail campaign.

Then, you can use the results to step up your campaign based on what works with a targeted audience; or you can modify your message or your audience, and test again to look for a better approach.

Testing Your Content

This test for content is often used to try out different subject lines and determine which results in more email opens. It can be used to compare different messages, offers, closes, images, and other elements in your copy to see which approach result in more click-throughs and requests for free gifts or more information. This testing can also be used to determine which approach results in more or larger sales, commonly referred to as conversions, in that you are rating what percentage of emails convert to purchases, subscriptions, or other types of sales.

Commonly, this type of comparison test is referred to as a split-testing, A/B testing, or multivariate testing, which is more formally characterized as a method of conducting a controlled experiment in order to improve a website, email, or other metric, based on an indicator of success, such as clicking a link, completing a form, or making a purchase. Marketers use this type of testing in numerous situations to discover what is working best in a campaign.

Generally, in any test, you want to limit the number of variables you change, so you can better assess what works best, though you can use several categories in that variable. A variable is a type of factor, such as age or education, while a category refers to the different forms or states of that factor, such as different age groups or different educational levels.

For example, if you are assessing which copy works best, you might test out two, three, or four different subject lines to see which results in the most views, clicks, and orders.

A test becomes more complex when you test out two or more variables, such as if you not only test out different subject lines, but also include different age groups. In that case, you have to multiply the number of conditions for each variable. For instance, if you are testing out three subject lines and two different age groups, that becomes six conditions in your test. If you then want to compare the results based on gender, which is divided into males and females, you have 12 conditions.

If you want to look at the results for several variables, it is best to do a series of separate tests, so you don't have more than two to six comparisons to make in each test. Otherwise, your testing can become so complex with so many variables that it becomes hard to tell what is working or not.

Testing Your Market

The other major type of test is of your audience. In this case, you want to look at the differences in the response of different demographic groups, such as based on age, sex, education level, ethnicity, religion, occupation type (i.e.: professional or trades), or region of the country, and groups based on interest or attitudes, such as comparing individuals who like different types of sports or have different personality types (such as extroverts and introverts).

In doing such a test, begin with what you think are likely target markets for your product or service. Then, break a particular category into two, three or four subcategories (such as active and non-active churchgoers; individuals who pursue a more sedentary or active lifestyle).

Again, keep the number of variables down, though you can combine a test for your market with a test for an element in your content, such as testing the response to different subject lines by different demographic groups.

Assessing Your Results

In doing these tests, you should have at least 50 email contacts – and preferably 100 or more, so you have a large enough number of responses to compare the results for different groups.

In making this comparison, you want to compare the results according to some criteria, such as the number of opens, click-throughs, requests for information, orders, or the size of any orders.

Then, convert those numbers into percentages by dividing the responses into the number of emails sent to that category. In doing this, exclude any emails that were returned from your calculations – and later take them out of your database. You only want to take into consideration the responses from those individuals who actually received your email.

For example, if you send out 100 emails with one subject line and 100 with another, you would first eliminate the returns to determine the number of valid emails, say 80 with one subject line, 88 with the other. Then, if you are comparing the number of clicks for the two subject lines, you would divide the number of clicks received by the 80 valid emails in the first case and 88 in the other. Say there were 20 clicks in the mailing with 80 valid emails, that would be a 25% response rate. Then, would do the same with the other group. Say there were 44 clicks in the mailing would 88 valid emails, that would be a 50% response rate, so obviously the second subject line has better results.

You might also turn this testing into an analysis of several levels of responses, such as:
- the percentage of opens
- the percentage of click-throughs from those opening your email
- the percentage of those requesting more information from those who click through
- the percentage of those placing an order
- the size of the order from those placing an order.

By doing this comparison testing, you can assess the effectiveness of different sections of your sales funnel in getting a recipient to open your email, click to learn more, place an order, and for how much. You can also assess where the drop-off occurs, which might suggest what to do better next time. For instance, if you are getting a lot of opens which lead to click-throughs, but you don't get a high percentage of orders from these, consider what might be wrong. Maybe it's the message, the cost of the product, or something else. Take some time to assess the likely possibilities, make changes, test again, and see if the results are better.

In short, consider these tests a chance to get more information about the response of prospective customers or clients to your product or service, and as needed, modify your message or your target market. In effect, you are applying the principles of good market research for any kind of product or service to email marketing.

ABOUT THE AUTHOR

GINI GRAHAM SCOTT, Ph.D., J.D., is a nationally known writer, consultant, speaker, and seminar leader, specializing in business and work relationships, professional and personal development, social trends, and popular culture. She has published over 50 books with major publishers. She has worked with dozens of clients on memoirs, self-help, popular business books, and film scripts. Writing samples are at www.ginigrahamscott.com and www.changemakerspublishingandwriting.com. She is a Huffington Post regular columnist, commenting on social trends, business, and everyday life at www.huffingtonpost.com/gini-graham-scott.

She is the founder of Changemakers Publishing, featuring books on work, business, psychology, social trends, and self-help. It has published over 50 print, e-books, and audiobooks. She has licensed several dozen books for foreign sales, including the UK, Russia, Korea, Spain, and Japan.

She has received national media exposure for her books, including appearances on *Good Morning America, Oprah,* and *CNN*. She has been the producer and host of a talk show series, *Changemakers*, featuring interviews on social trends.

Her books on business relationships and professional development include:

Turn Your Dreams into Reality (Llewellyn)
Resolving Conflict (Changemakers Publishing)
A Survival Guide for Working with Bad Bosses (AMACOM)
A Survival Guide for Working with Humans (AMACOM)
Credit Card Fraud with Jen Grondahl Lee (Rowman)
Lies and Liars: How and Why Sociopaths Lie (Skyhorse Publishing)

Scott is also active in a number of community and business groups, including the Lafayette, Pleasant Hill, and Danville Chambers of Commerce. She is a graduate of the prestigious Leadership Contra Costa program, is a7 member of two B2B groups in Danville and Walnut Creek, and a BNI member. She is the organizer of six Meetup groups in the film and publishing industries with over 5000 members in Los Angeles and the San Francisco Bay Area. She does workshops and seminars on the topics of her books.

She received her Ph.D. from the University of California, Berkeley, and her J.D. from the University of San Francisco Law School. She has received several MAs at Cal State University, East Bay.

CHANGEMAKERS PUBLISHING
3527 Mt. Diablo Blvd., #273
Lafayette, CA 94549
changemakers@pacbell.net . (925) 385-0608
www.changemakerspublishingandwriting.com

www.ingramcontent.com/pod-product-compliance
Lightning Source LLC
Chambersburg PA
CBHW081800200326
41597CB00023B/4093